READING and UNDERSTANDING RESEARCH

SECOND EDITION

Lawrence F. Locke
University of Massachusetts, Amherst

Stephen J. Silverman
Teachers College, Columbia University

Waneen Wyrick Spirduso
University of Texas, Austin

SAGE Publications
International Educational and Professional Publisher
Thousand Oaks ▪ London ▪ New Delhi

For information:

Sage Publications, Inc.
2455 Teller Road
Thousand Oaks, California 91320
E-mail: order@sagepub.com

Sage Publications Ltd.
1 Oliver's Yard
55 City Road
London EC1Y 1SP
United Kingdom

Sage Publications India Pvt. Ltd.
B-42, Panchsheel Enclave
Post Box 4109
New Delhi 110 017 India

Printed in the United States of America

Library of Congress Cataloging-in-Publication Data

Locke, Lawrence F.
Reading and understanding research / Lawrence F. Locke,
Stephen J. Silverman, Waneen Wyrick Spirduso — 2nd ed.
        p. cm.
Includes bibliographical references and index.
ISBN 0-7619-2768-9 (Paper)
    1. Research. 2. Research—Methodology. 3. Reading. 4. Information retrieval.
I. Silverman, Stephen J. II. Spirduso, Waneen Wyrick. III. Title.
Q180.A1L63 2004
001.4'2—dc22

2003022544

This book is printed on acid-free paper.

06   07   10   9   8   7   6   5   4

Acquisitions Editor:	Lisa Cuevas Shaw
Editorial Assistant:	Margo Crouppen
Production Editor:	Diane S. Foster
Copy Editor:	Meredith L. Brittain
Typesetter:	C&M Digitals (P) Ltd.
Proofreader:	Mary Meagher
Cover Designer:	Michelle Lee

Contents

Preface to the
Second Edition

This book is about how to read research reports. It was written to serve people who have a wide variety of backgrounds and interests. We had in mind all of those who, in attempting to read reports, have been discouraged by the formidable nature of what they found. Also considered were people who have never tried to access the ideas and information found in reports but who now believe that it might be useful or interesting to do so. Finally, we were very much mindful of the beginners, whom we know best. Undergraduate and graduate students at colleges and universities across the nation are a large captive audience that must learn how to navigate through the mysteries of reports—whether or not doing so seems useful and interesting!

Given such diversity among our potential readers, the book was designed to be used either as a stand-alone tutorial, resembling a self-help guide for individuals, or as a supplement to instruction and practice within the format of a traditional university or college research course. For the former, we have provided lists of other resources that will help replace the supports ordinarily provided by an instructor and fellow students. For the latter, we have suggested activities that take maximum advantage of the opportunity to learn and to practice in a group setting. Finally, for both kinds of users, we have shared a number of tools (recording forms, exercises, checklists, and so on) that our own students have found helpful.

That final point signals something that is characteristic of the way this book has been written. This is a distinctly personal product. It reflects the beliefs and experiences of three authors whose careers have engaged them in performing, teaching, writing, directing, and reading research—to this very day. It is our work, sometimes our play, and always our passion. We intend to be fully present in the pages of this book, both as advisors to your efforts and as commentators on what you are learning. In consequence, the words *we* and *you* appear without apology on almost every page.

At the outset, it is reasonable for you to wonder how much we have presumed our readers will bring to the book—and the many tasks it requires. About that we can give a quick and simple answer. Nothing is required in terms of technical vocabulary, general scientific and mathematical knowledge, or particular background in the tools of research (most notably, statistics) that would not be possessed by a typical high-school graduate.

It is true that college-level experiences in any or all of these areas would allow you to move faster (and more easily) through the chapters—and probably push more quickly beyond the introductory-level skills that are the objective here. Nevertheless, this is a book for beginners. Nothing more than fundamental literacy and a willingness to study and practice are required to make it work.

The only accessory that you really must have (beyond a good supply of pencils) is some way to obtain copies of research reports. That means you will need access to academic journals that serve as the primary publication outlet for such material. If you are using this book in a college course, obtaining reports probably will not be a concern. If you are on your own, a college library (and many of the larger public libraries), a copy machine, and several rolls of coins will serve to get you started. Of course, if the reports are available electronically, you need only your computer and a printer.

All of this introductory information is intended to inspire confidence in your ability to use this text; our experience has been that your confidence will be well-founded. We have watched all sorts of people learn how to read research with sufficient comprehension to extract whatever they are seeking. There are several limits to what can be accomplished, however, and we would be remiss if those were not made clear.

First, some areas of inquiry employ such highly specialized languages that their reports simply cannot be read by outsiders. Nothing you read here will make much of a dent in that limitation. Second, being able to understand what an author is explaining in a report is one thing, but knowing whether the study met all of the standards for correct research procedure is quite a different thing. We can offer you the means to recognize a wide range of the problems that sometimes occur in research, but critical expertise is not a reasonable expectation—if only because it is not the purpose of this book.

Our objectives here are based on modest ambitions for our readers and our own commonsense view of research as an enterprise. Most of the ideas about research that you will encounter here are well within the mainstream of what most scholars believe. Certainly, we have made no effort to take radical positions, nor do we have a desire to equip you with anything other than a sound understanding of how traditional scholarship works.

Nevertheless, the idea that nonspecialists can profitably access documents that were written as contributions to an "insider's conversation" (more about that in Chapters 1, 2, and 3) will be surprising to some in the academic community and perhaps unsettling to others. We will not press our beliefs about that subject here, but we do ask you to remember that the proof of the pudding is in the eating. Either this book helps you to do what you want (or have) to do, or it does not. Whatever small heresy we might have committed, we rest our case entirely in your judgment.

❖ SUGGESTIONS FOR USING THIS BOOK

The eight chapters that make up the main portion of the book are organized around five functions—and thereby can be clustered into the same number of sections (of unequal size, but equal importance). The first section consists of this Preface and Chapter 1, which, together, serve both to introduce the book (and the authors) and to frame the task of learning to read research reports within a wider social context. The opening chapter provides an unblinking examination of why many people, perhaps including yourself, would not voluntarily elect to read research. The chapter concludes, however, with an introduction to our main argument—one that is woven into all of the following chapters—which asserts a much more optimistic view. Research reports contain information and ideas that you will find valuable, and, with our assistance, you can learn how to access those treasures by reading reports.

The second section consists of two chapters that are designed both to encourage you to believe that there are conditions under which it makes good sense to seek out research and to recognize signals that help to identify what is to be trusted when you find it. In Chapter 2, we undertake to (a) explain when it is (and is not) cost-effective to read actual reports, (b) describe the truly surprising variety of interesting and useful things you can find in reports, (c) briefly outline the major content sections of the typical report, and (d) define for the purpose of this book what is (and is not) to be considered a genuine research report. Chapter 3 then offers an explanation of (a) where and how research reports are created and by whom, (b) how they are processed for publication, and (c) what hallmarks to look for when deciding how much to trust the veracity of what you read.

The third section consists of two chapters that constitute the heart of our effort to teach you the specific skills needed to read several kinds of research reports as well as research reviews. Chapter 4 deals with the obvious housekeeping chore of locating and selecting reports that are appropriate for a beginner as well as the initial mental adjustments of expectation and attitude that are essential if your reading is to be fruitful. Finally, Chapter 5 leads you step by step through the reading of reports from both quantitative and qualitative studies, and then through a typical research review. Each of the three sets of instructions is built around an instrument designed to provide an organizing framework for the reading process, one that will help you avoid feeling overwhelmed by technical detail or becoming lost in the initially unfamiliar format conventions that are employed in reports.

For those readers who have the advantage of studying in a group setting (whether in a formal college class or in an informal study group), the last part of Chapter 5 suggests a series of exercises that we have used to accelerate the progress of beginners. Based on the familiar premise that the best way to learn is to teach, the exercises involve the task of "explaining" reports, and they can be used with as few as two people or with groups of progressively larger size for more complex forms of practice.

The fourth section contains the final three chapters. These constitute a user-friendly introduction to the different types of research that the beginner might encounter (Chapter 6) and an effort to help readers begin to examine quantitative and qualitative reports with a critical eye (Chapters 7 and 8). All three chapters are based on the premise that people do not require a great fund of specialized and highly technical knowledge to recognize what kind of research is at hand in a report, understand in broad terms how that sort of design should function, anticipate where errors of commission and omission are most likely to occur, and learn how to maintain a wary attitude while reading. Accordingly, the entire section has been given a strong practical tone. In Chapter 6, summaries of actual reports are used to illustrate the discussion of types of research, and, in Chapters 7 and 8, we identify specific key points that you can look for when evaluating the quality of a report.

The fifth and final section consists of the appendixes (A through C). Several of these simply contain material that is supplementary to particular chapters. Two, however, have special significance in themselves. In Appendix A, we provide abstracts for a variety of research texts that can be used in conjunction with this book. Because you will encounter (from the outset) a number of topics that are given only cursory treatment in the text, it is important that you know where to find additional information and explanations. We suggest that you review those abstracts at an early point in the process of using this book. You certainly should do so before starting Chapter 3. Whether or not you elect to seek out and use any of those references is an individual matter, but, in any case, you should know what is available.

In Appendix B, we provide examples of completed reading guides for two studies and a research review. Finally, in Appendix C, we confront the most common anxiety found among beginners—the specter of statistical analysis. In our beginner's guide, we offer a tour through some of the most ubiquitous statistical operations. In doing so, we demonstrate that neither advanced knowledge of mathematics nor unusual skills of intellect are required to grasp a functional understanding of how statistics are used in research.

It has been our experience that most beginners will find it easiest to progress through the chapters in their present serial order. Chapter boundaries, however, always represent arbitrary divisions, and virtually everyone will encounter at least some points at which it makes sense for them to skip over a particular portion of the text or jump ahead to find the answer to a particular question—and then return. Some readers, for example, might find that reading Chapters 6, 7, and 8 much earlier in the sequence yields a more comfortable sense of linear development. There is absolutely no reason to do anything other than suit your own needs. We intended this guide to be used as a workbook, in conjunction with both a variety of actual research reports and, when appropriate, other resource texts. Our only injunction is that, whatever strategies you use for study, you will obtain the best results if you finish the entire book. We have tried to avoid detours into topics that are not essential to the development of a sound foundation for reading research. Accordingly, we believe that what is here really matters.

For the purpose of full disclosure, we note that some of the examples used, notably in Chapters 6 and 7, were devised by us for the purpose of maximizing effective explanation and were not drawn from actual reports (all of which are identified by standard citations). In all such cases, the fictional data or research procedures are similar to what might be found in typical reports.

Finally, readers who bring more than a beginner's background in research might be tempted to conclude that we have oversimplified some issues and omitted attention to the myriad special circumstances that can invalidate our rudimentary explanations. That is a problem to which we have given a good deal of thought. We have four responses that reflect our position on the limitations of what has been attempted in this book.

First, readers cannot complete this book and believe that they know how to do research or that they have an in-depth understanding of any aspect of method or data analysis. Second, we make a special point to provide frequent referrals to some of the best introductory research texts that are generally available. Third, what is presented has clearly been designed to serve as a foundation for further study. Fourth, and finally, we were confronted by the simple fact that in urging people to believe that they actually can—and should—learn how to read research reports, it was absolutely essential that we make it seem fully possible to do so. Beginners need only the most basic skills, and to impose more than those rudiments is to put the enthusiasm and confidence of the novice at risk. For us, having students read this book and then never again read a report would constitute failure. In sum, we believe that there is more to gain by inviting our readers into a world that seems understandable than there is to lose by picturing that world with less than complete and perfect detail.

❖ ABOUT THE SECOND EDITION

Over the five years subsequent to publication of the first edition of *Reading and Understanding Research*, we have been collecting feedback from both our readers and our academic colleagues. That information has been used here as the basis for improvements in both the clarity of our explanations and the breadth of topics covered. Those who previously adopted the text for use in college courses will note, in particular, the considerable streamlining in Chapter 7 ("Reading Quantitative

Research Reports—Critically"), the provision of a new chapter (Chapter 8) on critical reading for qualitative research, improvements in all of the 12-step guides for reading research reports, and new attention given to understanding reports that involve multiple methodologies.

In addition to these changes, because the research enterprise always is an ongoing process, the references, specimen examples, and annotated resources have required considerable updating for the second edition. Not only have new books and journals appeared in print, but new retrieval and archival systems are now available as well. Accordingly, the list of annotated references in Appendix A has lengthened, and fresh, more contemporary examples are used in Appendix B.

Acknowledgments

M any people have contributed to this project whose names do not appear on the cover. First among them are our students at the University of Massachusetts at Amherst; Teachers College, Columbia University; and The University of Texas at Austin. In addition, the graduate students in Professor Lorraine Goyette's research courses at the Elms College in Massachusetts have generously allowed us to observe this text in action and, over seven recent semesters, have provided critical commentary that was both vigorous and thoughtful. All of these user groups have provided a lively human context for development of our ideas about learning to read research, as well as invaluable feedback concerning the various instruments contained in this guide. As with most teaching endeavors, we have learned from them as they have learned from us.

We wish also to acknowledge the contributions of Professors Judy Placek, Patt Dodds, and Linda Griffin, who reviewed significant portions of the manuscripts for the first edition of this book, and who, over the course of many years, have contributed directly to the evolution of the various teaching strategies described here.

As with several incarnations of our other textbook published by Sage Publications, *Proposals That Work*, Professor Joseph A. Maxwell has shared extensive notes concerning the use of *Reading and Understanding Research* in his graduate courses on research methods at George Mason University. His scrupulous attention to detail and keen insights into how students learn to understand research have been enormously valuable.

For the present text, as well as for the four editions of our other book, *Proposals That Work*, the people at Sage Publications have been both helpful and endlessly patient with us. Our former editor, C. Deborah Laughton, encouraged us to undertake this revision and got us started. Lisa Cuevas Shaw, our present editor, has provided steady support throughout the writing and editing process. Finally, the deepest appreciation and thanks must go to Lorraine, Pat, and Craig for once again extending their understanding and patient tolerance through the long hours of effort that were subtracted from our time with them. In this undertaking, as with so much else in our lives, it is their support that sustains us every day.

1

Introduction

❖ WHY THIS BOOK?

Why is it, exactly, that most people do not read research reports, either
with or without the experience of having received some relevant education? It is not difficult to invent hypotheses that sound at least plau-
sible. Is the neglect a consequence of the fact that it is impossible to
read research without specialized training? Could it be that people just
never encounter reports, or material drawn from reports, in their
everyday lives? Is research perhaps not sufficiently valued within the
context of our culture?

Or does the real explanation for the near-universal avoidance of
research reports (beyond the circle of those who produce them) lie in
the fact that there is no practical purpose to be served by wading
through pages of dense prose? That is, once outside the rarefied realms
occupied by scientists and academics, is it possible that there is
nothing of real utility to be extracted from reports as primary sources?
Finally, might the answer rest in the fact that it has become sufficient
for most people just to hear or read the occasional references in the
media to "researchers have found that . . ." or "research has shown
that . . ."?

It will not surprise you, we are sure, to learn that our answer to all of these rhetorical questions is a resounding *"no!"* We think that there are false assumptions behind some of the questions—and the answers they imply. More important, we believe that anyone who accepts such explanations has adopted a naïve and even dangerous view of the knowledge that is required to function as an informed citizen, much less the understanding that is important to live an examined life.

Taken in sequential turn, the following are our own assertions concerning the hypotheses previously mentioned for the neglect of research reports. Specialized training in how to do research is not required to read reports in many fields; the media are saturated with references to findings (or alleged findings) from research, and journals crammed with reports are easy to find (even on the Internet); this is a culture in which many people revere the processes (and fruits) of science; practice in an enormous range of vocations and professions—from teaching, nursing, and social work to parenting, sales, and agriculture—can be informed by what is contained in research reports; and, finally, we think that limiting yourself to what other people tell you about research findings means giving up an important part of your independence—and responsibility.

Some people, both professionals and laypeople, are served by intermediaries who translate research into prescriptions for action, such as the agricultural extension service and many professional magazines. For the vast majority of people, however, if they are to use research-based knowledge to improve the quality of their work, the decisions they make, and their understanding of the world, only television and the popular press can serve as sources. We think that the accounts of research results provided through such media sources are sometimes useful but are also often insufficient—or even misleading. In any case, limiting yourself exclusively to interpretations of research by other people is unnecessary. You can read and understand original reports in many areas of inquiry—and draw your own conclusions.

Our efforts to persuade you on that final point wind through the seven chapters that follow. One particular discussion, however, serves as a useful entry point, so we pursue it here as the final note of introduction. Whatever we might hold to be true about research—its benign and beneficial nature, and the surprising extent of its accessibility to the layperson—there is no denying that among many people, it has acquired a very bad reputation indeed! That negative public image, we believe, is the real answer to the question, "Why don't people read research?"

There are two levels at which a degree of public disaffection serves as a barrier to the use of research reports as a source of information. The first is engendered by the recondite nature of the reports themselves. At a second and deeper level, however, are the doubts that some people have about the processes of research itself, including the appropriateness of privileging research-based knowledge over other sources of truth.

The two barriers have their roots in quite different and seemingly unrelated problems. One might, for example, have great difficulty making sense of reports but maintain a fervent faith in the use of "scientific" information as the basis for wise social policy. One might also have considerable facility in reading research but believe that other sources of truth must be given priority. Whichever barrier is operative, the end result is the same—avoiding any firsthand encounter with research.

❖ PROBLEMS WITH REPORTS

The first barrier, the supposed inaccessibility of reports, is at least well understood and is a widely shared experience in our culture. For that reason, let us begin there. Of all the impediments to reading research, there are four that adhere directly to the documents themselves: specialized jargon, perceived level of intellectual demand, lack of self-evident validation, and difficult retrieval.

People simply do not understand why reports cannot be written in plain English. For the outsider, reading becomes a problem of translation as well as one of comprehension. The problem is more than mechanical, however, because the impenetrability of specialized language leads to skepticism about the motives of researchers and, thereby, to a devaluing of results. The fact that there are rational ways to defend the use of unique system languages in different disciplines (a point we explain in Chapter 6) does little to remove the perception that reports are full of jargon and therefore too difficult to read.

A related problem rests on the belief that one needs both specialized training in academic subject matter and exceptional cognitive skills to understand the information that reports contain. Not only is it presumed, then, that you have to know the territory in technical terms, but you have to be smart as well. The former confuses what is sometimes helpful with what is always necessary, whereas the latter confuses innate intellectual capacity with acquired know-how. These misunderstandings make lack of self-confidence an endemic problem, and they are the first hurdles to overcome in teaching people how to read research.

Next, nearly every novice comes to the reading task with two unspoken questions: "Is this good research?" and "How am I supposed to tell whether it is or not?" Unhappily, there is no guarantee to accompany each research report that can certify the quality of what is contained therein. As we explain in Chapter 3, certain indicators warrant greater confidence in reports from particular studies. Use of those signs, however, is neither as simple nor as definitive as we might wish, and many potential research users are left with the question, "If I can't tell good from bad, how can I trust any of it?" Unanswered, that question alone deters many people who might otherwise look to research for helpful information.

Finally, although research reports have become widely available from a number of sources, learning to operate modern retrieval systems to find studies on a particular topic does require time and, in most cases, some initial assistance. Although research is not hiding under a rock, it rarely falls into your lap, either. It might be men who hate to ask for directions when driving a car, but almost everyone hates to admit that he or she is utterly lost in a library. This fact is one more reason that, once filed away on library shelves, research reports are more likely to gather dust than gather consumers.

Now that you have an understanding of some of the problems that are intrinsic to the nature of reports themselves, we want to turn your attention to barriers that are more (if not wholly) associated with how people understand the research enterprise itself and research products in general. These difficulties are of a different order, but one of their common consequences is the erection of a barrier between people and research-based knowledge. If the processes of research are not trusted to feed a reservoir of important truths, why would we expect anyone to spend time reading reports?

❖ PROBLEMS WITH RESEARCH

The problems with research arise from six perceptions, some widely held and others found more exclusively within certain social groups: complexity of results, conflicting results, trivial topics, impractical studies, absence of commitment and caring, and conflict with other sources of truth.[1] The first of these, complexity, is a characteristic not only of research-based knowledge structures but of the way scholars think.

As Cooper (1996) recently observed, in the social sciences, "the emphasis in research is as much on 'why,' 'when,' and 'for whom,' as on 'whether or not'" (p. 31). For people on the outside, however, exceptions and contingencies serve only to muddy the waters. The characteristic "it depends" conclusion found in so many reports, as essential as it may be to the precision of science, serves to undermine the perceived utility of results, if not confidence in the whole enterprise.

President Harry Truman is reputed to have once asked if someone could find a one-armed economist—so that he would not have to hear another "but on the other hand." We could excuse a great many parents, teachers, and businesspeople if they expressed the same desire with regard to what they hear researchers saying about how best to raise children, teach students, and sell products.

Closely related to complexity are the apparent conflicts among research findings. How often have you heard research being cited by advocates on opposite sides of a debate? Researchers know that differences in the results from apparently similar studies usually are a function of subtle differences in how the research was done. The most common sources of equivocality in findings are (a) how the problem is conceptualized; (b) small alterations in procedures of measurement, treatment, or analysis; and (c) the ever-present problem of differences in the members of sample groups (both within and between studies) that serve to contaminate observations and to confound results. Explaining that to a layperson, however, is a thankless and probably impossible task. Researchers simply have to live with the reputation that they cannot agree on anything, and with the way that image undermines the credibility of their reports.

Next, for many people, there are two knocks on the utility of research that have status as folk wisdom. These popular assertions hold that the things researchers choose to study often are no more than mere trivia and that most of the findings reported in scholarly journals have no application to anything in the real world.

The first of these perceptions is related to a genuine characteristic of most studies. Increments of knowledge are won through a step-by-step process within which great leaps are a considerable rarity. Small bits of insight have to be woven together into the structure of larger webs of understanding. Taken as a single event, which is how any one report must necessarily appear to an outsider, what is attempted in most studies must seem at least unambitious, if not trivial. That perception hardly encourages a wide readership by people searching for magic bullets to cure problems.

Related, but far from conterminous, is the familiar complaint that research performed by out-of-touch intellectuals is too esoteric and without practical application. The problem here might involve the perception of triviality, but the real target of concern lies more in another direction—the gulf between knowing that something is so and knowing what might be done about it. Putting the results from some kinds of research to work requires engineering, development, and dissemination—all processes for which many researchers have no particular talent and even less motivation.

There are, of course, applied studies that directly serve improvements in the human condition (and they are, or ought to be, exempt from such criticism). You will hear more about the distinction between investigations motivated by the need to know (*basic research*) versus the need to improve (*applied research*) as you work through the following chapters.

In that process, you will encounter our proposition that the tidy dichotomy of basic/applied does not always serve us well, the distinction often having nothing to do with what researchers actually do or how knowledge really grows. Nevertheless, it is absolutely true that in many studies, the investigators have no idea at all about how their findings could be put to work, although they might have complete faith in the proposition that, over time, knowing how things work always turns out to be advantageous. It is little wonder, then, that left to envision their own applications, readers whose expectations do not include a long-term perspective have little patience with what they find in many reports.

Researchers who have the good fortune (or bad luck) to achieve elected or appointed positions in which they can participate in the making of public policy quickly receive instruction about most of the shortcomings previously noted (Cooper, 1996). It might take longer, however, for them to discover that there is something more personal to learn about how others perceive researchers and their reports.

Many researchers (although not all) work within a culture that values *objectivity* (the ability to insulate inquiry from personal opinion and attitude) and the virtues of writing without evidence of affect or political commitments. In the culture of public service, however, the opposite applies. Decision makers often deliberately choose terms that will arouse the emotions that lead constituencies to agree with them. Consequently, those who speak the language of dispassionate evidence are regarded with deep suspicion—as cold, disinterested, and lacking in the virtue of conviction.

As they are commonly written, research reports are the last things that most people engaged in the politics of policy development want to hear. Those who insist on using affect-free language are regarded as having covert motives. Why would anyone seek public support for a decision by being neutral?

That distrust of detached objectivity is not limited to legislative bodies, school boards, and other formally constituted groups. Wherever there are contests of ideas, many people look for evident commitment, sincerity, and passion as indicators of credibility—all things for which most (although not all) types of research make little or no provision.

Finally, there are groups within our society, most notably those holding views associated with various forms of social conservatism, whose members deny the privilege of evidence validated by empirical research. As a matter of personal conscience, they give first priority for making decisions, in the public arena as in their private lives, to some other source of truth. That source may be tradition, authority, political ideology, scripture, or any other system of thought that demands adherence to doctrine.

For the members of those groups, the question is not how to best use research but whether research should be consulted at all. For that small (but often fervent and highly vocal) segment of our society, the answer to that last question, on many of the most perplexing issues we must confront, is an unequivocal "no." For them, research provides no source of certain guidance and represents, at best, an alien doctrine.

It is less common for research in the physical and natural sciences to be a target for the kinds of criticism we have noted in these pages. Social science research usually bears the brunt of most (although not all) of the negative perceptions. Among the several reasons for that disparity is the simple fact that disciplines such as astronomy and botany have less to say about problems of professional practice, public policy, and the conduct of everyday life. For the different domains of research, one price of seeming to hold immediate social relevance is close and critical public scrutiny.

❖ SUMMARY

Our motive in recounting powerful reasons that people sometimes avoid reading, or considering, research certainly was not to discourage you. We simply want you to advance with a realistic understanding of the status sometimes accorded research. It is often mixed, and it is sometimes ambivalent. On one hand, research is worshipped in a society drunk on technology and the misplaced notion of the inevitability of material progress. On the other hand, research is sometimes reviled as out of touch, impractical, inaccessible, and arcane.

We have our own opinions about these issues, and by the time you reach the last chapter, they will be no secret. To honestly reach your own evaluation, however, it is necessary for you to encounter some research firsthand—science, up close and personal. That is why we wrote this book, and that is why we have invited you to learn how to read research reports.

In the pages that follow, we will argue not only that you *can* learn how to read research reports of many kinds, but also that you *will* find it profitable to do so. We believe that what you learn from them can have both utilitarian value, as guidance in making personal and professional decisions, and existential value, as a means for making you more fully aware and appreciative of the world—both the one around you and the one within you. In the end, however, the most convincing evidence regarding these assertions will not come from our enthusiastic endorsements but from your own experience. Even if you are skeptical about our claims, as long as you are willing to invest some time and effort, we have all that is necessary for a sound working relationship and a fair test. Hear us out, give it a good try, and evaluate this book in terms of what actually happens to you. Let the games begin!

❖ ENDNOTE

1. These problems are ubiquitous and generic, cutting across the research enterprises of most disciplines. They have been described by researcher Harris Cooper (1996) in a thoughtful analysis of his experience as an elected member of a local school board.

2

The Research Report

This chapter is divided into two major sections, both of which present information about research reports. The first section deals with the many valuable things that can be found in research reports beyond the obvious—the results. The second section discusses what a research report is and what it is not.

❖ FINDING VALUABLES IN RESEARCH REPORTS

Reading Reports: When to Do It

The purpose of this guide is to help people become more confident and skillful at both reading research reports and *digesting* (understanding and appraising) what they find. Our audience includes such people as undergraduate and graduate students, school teachers, health care professionals in clinical settings, social service workers in the field, and administrators of public and private institutions. In fact, readers might include anyone who has an interest in finding reliable facts and information that could help him or her solve problems or do his or her work more effectively. But what exactly is it that you can find in research reports?

The section that follows addresses that question in some detail from our perspective. Our first response to the "What can you find in research reports?" question, however, is to point out that it is not our perspective that matters most—it is yours! Put simply, different people, under different circumstances and with different needs and interests, find it useful to read research reports for many different reasons. Some of those motivations we could not possibly imagine, much less predict.

What you learn from this text might open the door on a rich resource of facts and ideas, but only if you decide to step over the threshold. What research-based knowledge can do for you is an individual matter that depends on the personal perspective you bring to what you read. Our purpose in this section is to suggest the breadth of exciting possibilities that can be served by reading research and to honestly clarify some of the limitations to that process.

Along with that opening injunction to give first consideration to your own needs and interests, we are compelled to offer another caution. For many of the purposes served by research-based knowledge, it might be more efficient to locate what you need through the use of some other form of scholarly writing. In fact, given the investments of time and energy required, reading research reports fails the test of cost-benefit analysis for most people most of the time. As we will explain, if people want to act intelligently, there are much better ways to inform themselves than by reading original research reports.

That frankly negative assessment for the very enterprise that is central to this book is tempered, however, by one salient fact. If you are reading this, it is unlikely that you are an ordinary layperson or that this is just an ordinary occasion. Students, academics, providers of professional services, and all sorts of individuals with responsibility for making decisions about important human affairs are quite likely to find occasions when reading research is an entirely reasonable use of their time. We presume that, for whatever reason, you are one of those people.

It might be a platitude, but it nevertheless happens to be true: *Knowledge is power.* And one kind of knowledge, a compelling kind that often has legitimate claim to precedence over other forms, is created by scientific research—the fruits of which are found in research reports.

Reading Research: When to Consider Using Alternative Sources

The familiar dictum about the power of knowledge applies particularly to the practical utility of research-based knowledge, the kind of knowing that begins with research reports. That observation, however, leads us to reiterate the caution about efficient use of time, for it is one that we hope you will recall when it is needed, long after you have closed this book. Whatever you are looking for, be it the power of applied knowledge, the cultivation of personal intellect, or the simple pleasure of satisfying curiosity, *do not do unnecessary work.* Use the form of scholarly literature that yields the most of what you seek for the smallest investment of time.

One form of scholarly work is discovery—the use of systematic investigation to explore the workings of our world and ourselves. Inquiry of that sort, commonly called *research,* creates a type of knowledge that can be useful in the conduct of human affairs. Accordingly, when some people read research reports, they do so with an immediate and practical need. Although curiosity and the human impulse to understand how things work do motivate some excursions into the literature of research, in most cases, the impulse is more pragmatic.

For graduate students, academics, research workers, and some technicians in applied professions such as medicine and engineering, reading research reports in their full and original form is imperative and unavoidable. Outside of those groups, however, reading reports is not the only means of access to the power of research.

Many sources provide the intermediary service of standing between the accumulation of research reports on a given topic (often referred to as the *research literature* or the *body of research*) and potential consumers of what is in those reports. The authors who provide that kind of service—including journalists, textbook authors, writers in professional journals, trainers and development workers, designers of curricula, and scholars who prepare reviews summarizing groups of reports—write materials that convert technical accounts into understandable facts and informed speculation. In other words, they put research into formats that allow most people to more easily locate, consume, and use the knowledge contained.

Where resources created by such intermediaries and translators exist, they should be the first place to look when you want reliable knowledge. Reading research reports makes sense only when you have reason to go beyond what is easily accessible. At the least, those generic resources are the place to begin any search. You will learn quickly enough whether they contain sufficient detail to satisfy your needs and interests.

To illustrate this point, imagine you are a sixth-grade classroom teacher working in an urban elementary school. Faced with 30 pupils of mixed racial, ethnic, and social/cultural backgrounds, you are particularly interested in finding ways to help them explore their diversity and all of its positive meanings. Part of that teaching agenda is your desire to engage them in learning how to work together effectively in ways that make use of their different backgrounds and perspectives.

Your situation would not be unusual for any teacher at any level of education. The commonplace nature of such pedagogical needs makes it highly probable that you already know about cooperative learning strategies for teaching, a format that can accommodate instruction in many subject areas. If you wanted to know more, however, about the particular uses of cooperative learning in classrooms with diverse populations, would it be reasonable to turn to research reports involving that topic? The answer for most teachers should be a firm "no" or at least a more tentative "not yet."

There is a veritable mountain of research on cooperative learning, a substantial subset of which deals with questions and problems related to cultural diversity in elementary and middle-school classrooms. That research literature, however, has been reviewed and summarized in many excellent articles appearing in professional journals designed for teachers and school administrators. In addition, much of it is treated in chapters within numerous textbooks on education. Even the curriculum guides produced in large school districts might make careful use of the research reports on cooperative learning in laying out objectives, methods, and content for school lessons.

The research-based knowledge to be found in the cultural diversity literature would provide, at the outset, all of the encouragement and initial direction you could possibly use. However, what if, in the course of using cooperative strategies in your classroom, you encountered problems or questions that are not addressed in those generic sources? For example, what if you wanted a means to assess, by quantitative or qualitative means, the impact of a social studies unit on the attitudes of your students toward social responsibility in their community?

It happens (at this time) that such measurement and evaluation problems are mentioned in general sources, but only rarely are any details provided. There are a few research reports, however, that tell stories of attempts to study exactly what interests you—the impact of cooperative social study units on the attitudes of school-age children. Locating and reading those reports now becomes an attractive option.

Your purpose as a teacher might be served not only by what the researchers found but also by learning how they went about the task of finding it.

Put another way, starting from scratch by designing your own means of assessment would require you to do all of the work, and it would probably expose you to all of the false starts and wasteful errors that the report authors already have faced and overcome. Reading and borrowing from them—their findings, ideas, methods, suggestions, and cautions—now seems comparatively prudent as an investment of your time.

There are, of course, an endless number of circumstances that are quite different from our cooperative learning illustration. Some of those conditions might make direct use of reports an absolute necessity, especially when such reading is a course requirement in an academic degree program. Our caution leaves you to weigh the costs and the benefits, with the firm reminder that the use of more generic research-based sources often is the most efficient and effective way to find what you need.

Reading Research: What Can You Find Besides Findings?

We return now to the initial question for this chapter: "What can you find in research reports?" You might have already noted our use of the particular phrase "facts and information." That wording was deliberate and not just a peculiarity of expression.

By using constructs such as "facts and ideas" or "facts and information," we intend to encourage a distinction between facts, as ordinarily understood, and more generic kinds of information. For example, research studies provide ample support for the assertion that school children involved in cooperative learning perform at least as well on achievement tests as pupils taught by more didactic methods. Although we can expect that further inquiry will refine and qualify that point (cooperative learning might work better, or less well, with some children than with others), it seems to be a highly probable outcome in any classroom. That is the kind of fact on which teachers can reasonably base decisions about instruction.

In contrast, a point of information in the same studies is that many teachers have reported to investigators that it was particularly helpful to observe colleagues who use cooperative learning strategies before attempting that kind of teaching on their own. That assertion was not confirmed (or even examined) in the studies, but readers often find it interesting and include it in their own subsequent thinking about the topic.

Another important point of information, gleaned from contrasting the descriptions of cooperative learning in a number of studies, is that in actual classroom practice, the strategies designed by teachers assume a variety of forms, each with its own virtues and limitations. No single study has been directed at such instructional variations, but they are made evident by browsing studies devoted to other aspects of cooperative learning.

What we want you to notice in all of these examples is that both the facts (formal findings from studies) *and* the information (informal observations and ideas that turn up in study reports) would be of potential value to anyone interested in cooperative learning.

When research reports offer facts, even some that meet the most stringent tests for truth (often, the power to predict what will happen in another place, at a different time, and with other people), rarely are those facts the only important information the reports contain. Indeed, for many purposes (for many readers), such factual findings, which were the primary objective for the investigators, are the *least* informative and useful part of the report.

We could fill pages with arguments and assertions about the nature of truth, what does and does not qualify as scientific fact, and how to distinguish between reliable information and informed speculation. We will not do so. We do ask that you bear with us, however, through several paragraphs that serve as a bridge to the question with which this section began: "When reading research, what can you find besides findings?"

From inside the world of scholarship, issues dealing with truth are vital. Many of the disciplines in the physical and biological sciences, for example, employ research and the discovery of facts in a manner that operates additively. One fact after another is gradually established as reliably true and then is fitted together with other facts to assemble increasingly complex and complete pictures of how things work.

In such fields, reliable facts—the truthful findings described in research reports—are the coins of academic commerce. In applied fields that make direct use of such sciences (e.g., medicine and engineering), the main contents of primary interest in a research report are usually the conclusions—what the data allow the author to assert is true.

Other disciplines, particularly those in the behavioral and social sciences, do not present the same picture of cumulative assembly of facts into truth *structures* (theories) that explain how things work. In sociology and psychology, for example, inquiry yields reliable facts that might be limited to individuals or to groups that share a common characteristic or a specific contextual circumstance. In such areas of science, it is quite uncommon (although not impossible) to find scholars attempting to construct comprehensive models consisting of closely fitted, verified, and completely generalizable facts.

The kind of science that produces a series of informative, yet independent, pictures is characterized as *ideographic* rather than *nomothetic* (a series of closely related pictures that are informative only to the degree that they fit together to form a whole—a theory with the power of prediction). Scholars have different standards and expectations for these contrasting kinds of research, and so must readers of the reports produced by the two traditions.

That brief side trip was intended to underscore one point: Just as so-called facts have different meanings and uses within different kinds of science, so too will they have different kinds of importance to consumers of research. The classroom teacher in our earlier illustration, for example, would not have expected to find universally applicable truths about cooperative social study units for culturally diverse students in urban sixth-grade classrooms. Educational research simply does not deal with the world in that way.

Indeed, you might not even have been interested in what researchers found to be true for the particular groups of students, teachers, and schools used in studies of cooperative learning. Instead, what you probably would have wanted was some information or ideas that might be useful when applied in your own situation. For example, how investigators defined the construct of *social responsibility* might have been helpful, as would descriptions of the different methods used to gather information about student responses to cooperative learning units (none of which would have been reported as findings). Most teachers would be hoping to get lucky and discover in an appendix a copy of an instrument used to gather data, as well as information about how well it could be expected to function with children of the age group represented in their own class.

We expect that a great many of you are much like those teachers who are sometimes interested in findings—the facts as they were established by the investigation—but more often are interested in other things contained in the reports they read. Also, we suspect that many of you will be seeking information in research reports from the ideographic sciences: from studies done in the disciplines of anthropology, psychology, and sociology, as well as in applied areas such as business, education, health and social services, sport coaching, and professional development.

Here is a short list of some of the "other things" people are often looking for when they read research reports. Please understand that these items only illustrate, and do not exhaust, the great panoply of useful information that can be discovered. The treasures you find (besides the findings) are determined not only by what you need and what you find interesting, but also by how carefully you search and how open your mind is to the unexpected.

- Other research reports on the same topic
- New terminology and possible key words for retrieval
- Explication of the question and its origins
- Description of the context for the study
- Methods for observing and recording
- Interventions used
- Discussion of findings or development of conclusions
- Implications or recommendations for improved practice

Other research reports on the same topic. If you are in the search mode, looking for reports that appear to deal with a particular topic, then the most important finding for you might not be located in the main text of the report but in the reference list. Before explaining how that might be valuable to you, however, the subject of references leads us here to a brief detour for the purpose of clarifying how they are handled in most research reports.

Today, most research reports do not use footnotes as a way of displaying references used in the main text (although that old tradition does persist in a few disciplines). Instead, sources from which the author has taken quoted material, or simply cited as relevant to the study, appear in a reference list usually attached at the end of the report.

In contrast, a bibliography is a list of related references that the author believes the reader might wish to consult but that are not directly cited in the text of the report. Although they might be quite useful when you are searching the literature, bibliographies are found infrequently in reports.

Returning now to the discovery of additional research reports, it is possible that by reading through the reference list you will discover other reports that appear, on the basis of title at least, to be even more directly related to what interests you than the report at hand. The question of relevance sometimes can be clarified by consulting the main body of the report. Often, there is a section near the beginning in which the author discusses already existing research in the study area. Another part of the report in which related research is subject to examination is in the section titled "Discussion," which is usually near the end of the document. In both locations, what is said about a particular reference can give you a better clue to its relevance than does the title it bears.

New terminology and possible key words for retrieval. New words do not always signal new ideas. In an enterprise like research, with a rich and expanding vocabulary, one frequently encounters unfamiliar terms that turn out to be nothing more than functional synonyms for things or ideas that already have well-established names. That kind of word churning is inevitable in a lively science that is pushing against the boundaries of what is known.

Sometimes, however, new words signal new constructs. Whether they are just new to you or are genuinely fresh additions to thought in an area, acquiring more powerful conceptual tools allows you to think in more complex ways. Such improvement in your understanding of difficult problems is one of the most valuable outcomes from reading research.

A related target for your attention when reading, particularly if you are still interested in retrieving additional studies, is the language itself. Different researchers commonly employ different terms for the same thing. The reason might lie in differences of disciplinary background, time, place, funding source, or personal writing style. Sometimes, such variety in labeling has no apparent rationale whatsoever, which contributes to the confusion and irritation of anyone trying to retrieve reports.

Messy nomenclature is a fact of life, however, and wise readers keep a list of terms assigned to their target topic, or to any topic that appears closely related. Those words can then be used as *key words* (descriptors) when consulting indexes and computerized retrieval systems. By approaching any collection of literature with a variety of terms commonly employed by investigators doing work in the same general area, you improve your chances of discovering valuable reports, even when the words used in the titles do not clearly suggest that the study might be of interest.

Explication of the question and its origins. In a report's introductory paragraphs, through presentations of background literature and by means of the closing discussion of results and conclusions, the investigator reveals how he or she understands the research question. The same sections also delineate why the question is important, what already is known about the answer, and how the scope of the question has been defined and limited for the purpose of the study. Attending closely to this process of *explication* (an effort to situate the question in the ongoing dialogue of scholarship) is likely to teach you a great deal about your topic of interest.

One of the things you might learn is that despite similarities of terminology, the author was concerned about a question or problem far distant from your own interests. Also, you might discover that your own initial definition of the subject was incorrect, incomplete, or just too simplistic. Finally, it is not uncommon when reading a report to discover that what really interests you is somewhat different from what you originally had imagined it to be. All of these discoveries are useful things to learn.

Why the question was important (and interesting) to the researcher, how it fits into the results from other studies, and, quite literally, where it comes from might constitute important things to learn. The phrase "comes from" encompasses answers to questions such as "Who initially raised this question, and why?" "What has been discovered so far?" "How has the question itself evolved?" and "What methods of investigation have been employed, and how well have they worked?" The answers to such questions add up to what is called the *provenance* of the research question, a word that refers to its "origins," or, in more formal terms, to its certification as a legitimate object of study.

Getting a sense of the provenance of the question that interests you is one of the essential steps in learning about it. Moreover, establishing the pedigree of the research question usually is attended to very carefully in a report.

Description of the context for the study. Research in the social and behavioral sciences always involves someone, somewhere, doing something that is observed and recorded—whether that observation is direct or through intermediate artifacts such as a questionnaire concerning parental attitudes, records of patients' participation in therapeutic exercise, or a videotape of a worker's hand motions on an assembly line. Immediately, then, good reports direct the reader's attention to the where, what, when, and who of the study. Those contextual factors are the bridge between the researcher's observations and your own experience. If your interests are specifically related to sixth-grade children, then discovering that the report actually deals with a study of college sophomores might make it less attractive.

Before you make the determination, however, of whether it is worth reading a study that deals with people, places, or conditions different from those of your primary interest, we remind you that such reports can still be valuable. At the least, the reference list, the formulation of the research question, and the means of gathering data might provide information that transfers perfectly into your collection of useful ideas, even if the people and places do not.

Methods for observing and recording. You might have no intention of ever engaging in research yourself, but surely you will be observing events within the context that concerns you. One of the lessons you can learn from a report is how to watch the things that matter and how to do so accurately and efficiently.

Studies often involve creating a record of what is observed in some sort of *code* (numbers, words, symbols, or even electrical traces on a magnetic disc or tape). The recorded code (collectively called *data)* is retained for subsequent inspection and analysis. To accomplish the process of creating data requires very careful decisions about *what* to collect and *how* to record it. Those decisions can tell you a great deal about how to be a good observer, as well as what you might wish to record for yourself when working to solve a problem. Consistency and accuracy are not just necessities in research; they are concerns whenever people want to obtain a reliable account of what is going on.

Interventions used. In experiments and quasi-experimental designs for research, something is done to intervene in the normal course of events. Often, the targets for such action (commonly called the *treatment)* are people. Such interventions, always carefully designed and described in detail in the report, might be precisely what you are looking for. They are significant not because you intend to do a study but because experimental treatments often represent possible alternatives for acting upon problems in the real world of your own work.

How well (or poorly) the treatment works in an intervention study is a function of many variables, not least of which is the particular measure of success that is employed. For that reason, if you happen to value outcomes that are somewhat different from those covered by the measures used in a study, an intervention might still be worth trying, even if it did not prove to be highly successful. Likewise, if your own situation differs from the context of a study in some important way, you still might be interested in adapting an experimental strategy for your needs, even if the intervention was unimpressive when tested under the conditions of the study. Finally, authors often identify the problems encountered with their effort to intervene on a problem, thus allowing you to make improvements on the application in your own setting.

In summary, even when the data fail to provide a clear answer to the research question, it is possible for the reader to discover valuable facts, information, and ideas in the report. Defects in treatment procedure, observation of the wrong outcomes, or even improperly defined questions might not advance the cause of science (although they sometimes do), but they certainly can be useful in deciding what might be done about practical affairs of concern to the reader.

Discussion of findings or development of conclusions. We have emphasized the fact that you can learn from aspects of a research report other than the findings. It is important to stress that point because it is one too often missed by beginners—to their great disadvantage. Nevertheless, to the extent that the research question truly interests you, the findings are the centerpiece of any report and deserve your closest attention. Moving from what was observed (findings) to how those observations should be understood (conclusions) is one of the most difficult points in writing any report, especially because it is all too tempting for researchers to reach the conclusions they expected (or would prefer) rather than those that are dictated by what was actually observed. The wary reader watches the transition from findings to conclusions with special care.

Nothing, however, can be more exciting (and encouraging) than to discover that someone has given clear definition to a problem that exists in your own practice, invented a solution, and demonstrated (convincingly) that it worked. Although you should respect the fact that results do not always transfer perfectly from one setting to another, there is surely no better place to start inventing a better mousetrap than with the plans for one that actually worked.

Implications or recommendations for improved practice. Not all reports contain a discussion of the implications that findings (or conclusions based on the findings) might have for improving practice. Some research is motivated, at least in the short term, by intellectual curiosity and not practical needs. Nevertheless, within the types of research most likely to be consulted by readers of this handbook, it is rare to find one that lacks any clue about how the results might be put to use.

Some studies, of course, are motivated by an immediate need to find a solution for a problem. Reports of such research often have a complete discussion of the results as practical concerns, and they might even have a section that contains explicit suggestions for improved practice. It is always true that the match between the study context and the people, places, and conditions that concern you must be considered. Nevertheless, among the types of research that are designed to maximize the transferability of results, you might discover some with robust findings that support generalization to settings such as your own.

We have observed that even when researchers are primarily concerned with the basic problem of figuring out how the world works, it is quite common for them to close their report with a note about possible applications of their findings. Sometimes, this information is for the consumption of their funding source; researchers always have to reassure their benefactors that their line of inquiry has some potential (at least in the long term) for bearing practical fruit. At other times, however, it seems clear that the author simply has been seduced by the sudden realization that what has been found just might make a difference if someone could figure out how to put it to work. That someone, of course, could be you.

At this point, having urged you to believe that valuable information and ideas can be retrieved from research reports, it is necessary to dispense with one vital matter before proceeding to the obvious next question—"How?" We must share a common understanding of what a research report is before we can answer procedural questions about what to do with one.

❖ WHAT IS A RESEARCH REPORT?

The question posed in the heading of this section was central to our writing of this handbook, and it will be central to how you can use our text to help in your search for facts and good ideas. Just as there were limits to what we intended to write about, there will be limits to the ways you can use this book. The definition of what is (and is not) a research report establishes those boundaries.

In our most general use of the term, a *research report* is defined here as a written document that gives the history of a research study from start to finish. The particular characteristics of the history provided in a report vary with the kind of inquiry involved and with the conventions for writing that have evolved for investigators working in that area of scholarship.

Any attempt to give a more specific definition of a research report, in a way that takes into account all of the individual variations required by each kind of research, would fill many pages and would probably be unreadable. In contrast, a definition such as the one in the preceding paragraph, which was written to be sufficiently generic to cover all traditions of inquiry without being explicit about the unique characteristics of any one of them, ends up seeming bland, imprecise, and not very informative.

Nevertheless, we had to have a working definition in hand as we began work on this book. In the end, we found that what worked best for us was a middle-ground definition, set out in this section, that would not be completely satisfactory to any research specialist. It has the virtue, however, of including a large slice of the territory that is common to all forms of research reporting. If you are going to follow our arguments, understand our instructions, and consider our advice, then it is essential that you understand exactly how we answered the question "What is a research report?"

Research Reports: A Middle-Ground Definition

A research report must give a statement of the question pursued by ·the investigator, as well as its provenance within the research literature. In addition, it must provide a reasonably complete description of all operations performed to gather, organize, and analyze data. An accounting must be made of the findings in a manner that clearly reveals how the outcomes of analysis respond to the research question and, in turn, how they form the substantive basis for any conclusions, assertions, or recommendations that are made.

All of this sounds quite pedantic and stuffy. A shorter version certainly sounds less ponderous and will be easier to remember as you read.

A research report gives the history of a study, including what the researcher wanted to find out, why that seemed worth discovering, how the information was gathered, and what he or she thought it all meant.

What Fits Under the Umbrella?

At this point, some of you have no doubt begun to wonder about the extent to which different kinds of research can be accommodated under the umbrella of our middle-ground definition. That question is not as trivial as it might sound on first encounter. For example, if we say that a research report is a clear, concise, and complete history, then do historical studies produce documents that qualify as research reports? More important, will using this handbook help you read and digest articles in history journals? And what about books and articles dealing with philosophic inquiry, or accounts of careful study in areas such as aesthetics and ethics? Will they be considered in these pages?

Our response to all these questions is "no"—we did not have those forms of scholarship in mind when we wrote this book. We have attended here to the kinds of quantitative and qualitative research that are *empirical* in nature, by which we mean inquiry that requires actually observing and recording (as data) entities, events, or relationships that appear to the investigators' senses when they study a particular aspect of the world. Reports of inquiry that involves only thinking about the world (no matter how systematic and precise that thinking is), as distinct from inquiry that involves directly examining that world, are not the subject of this text. If you find our comments or advice helpful when reading such nonempirical reports, we will be pleased but also surprised.

About Publications

Looking back at the second paragraph of this section, you will see that the word *history*, as we use it here, simply means a reasonably complete accounting of what was asked, done, found, and concluded in the course of an empirical study. You still might ask, however, what was intended by our stipulation that research reports be "written documents."

In general terms, we intended little more than might have been indicated had we stipulated that the report be published. There are, however, some important distinctions to be made among different kinds of printed sources.

The publications that concerned us in writing this text were those research reports that appeared in what are called *refereed journals*. Such journals are the primary outlets for research in areas of professional or disciplinary scholarship. Books, monographs, conference proceedings, and a variety of periodicals do sometimes contain original research reports, as do computer-based archival systems such as ERIC or MEDLINE. Those sources, however, usually differ from refereed journals in one important respect. Publications that are not refereed do not provide the author with the services of peer review or the reader with the quality assurance produced by that process. Through peer review, the manuscripts submitted to a journal are read by established scholars in the topic area and screened for quality of both the research procedures employed in the study and the history provided in the report. Although such adjudication does not guarantee the absence of errors, it does go a long way toward ensuring a minimum standard of quality for what appears in a journal.

Furthermore, feedback from peer reviews often allows the author to revise and resubmit the report. The opportunity to use criticisms and suggestions made by competent peers as the basis for revisions can produce improvements that bring a manuscript up to the journal's qualitative standard and lead to subsequent publication. Through this process, peer review again works to the advantage of both author and reader.

When we prepared this handbook, the peer-reviewed research reports that appear in refereed journals were uppermost in our minds. Accordingly, although this text might help you read and comprehend any research report, including those found in other print or electronic sources, those were not the "written documents" we had in mind. More to the point, some of the procedures and recommendations in this guide are specific to the nature and format of reports found in refereed journals, and they might have little utility with other kinds of documents.

Criterial Characteristics: What Has to Be in a Report?

To close this brief section, we want to return to our middle-ground definition and parse it in a way that might help you to begin recognizing the essential elements in all genuine research reports. We do so with a reminder that different research traditions have different orderings and emphases for the elements, as well as different terminologies.

The characteristics present in most research reports are as follows:

1. Research reports contain a clear statement of the question or problem that the investigator addressed and that guided decisions about method of inquiry throughout the study. Most commonly, the question or problem was defined prior to data collection. However, when the question or problem was defined during the course of the study, its source and development are fully explicated.

2. To the extent possible, research reports situate the purpose of the study, and the research questions employed in designing the study, in the existing body of knowledge.

3. Research reports describe data collection procedures that were planned in advance (although, in some cases, they might have been modified in the course of the study).

4. Research reports offer detailed evidence that the observations and recording of data were executed with a concern for accuracy and that the level of precision was appropriate to the demands of the research question.

5. Research reports demonstrate that the quality of data was a central concern during the study. The report confirms the quality of data by providing information about the reliability and validity of measurement procedures or about other qualitative indexes related to the particular type of research involved.

6. Research reports discuss how data were organized and specify the means of analysis.

7. The results of data analysis are explicitly related to the research question or problem.

8. Conclusions concerning the findings are reported as tentative and contingent upon further investigation.

9. Conclusions, assertions, and recommendations are stated in ways that make the limitations of the study clear and that identify rival ways of accounting for the findings.

10. The report was made available for review by competent peers who have experience and expertise in the area of the study. (This final characteristic is not found in the report itself but in the handling of it by the author.)

These 10 elements provide an overview of the characteristics of most of the reports that we have defined as research. One of the objectives of this text is to help you learn how to quickly identify whether or not all 10 characteristics are present in a document—that is, whether or not you are reading a genuine research report.

About the Genuine Article

The skill of identifying a genuine research report is important because, as you can imagine, there is a great deal of published material about research studies, research findings, research as an enterprise, practical implications of research-based knowledge, and even about researchers that does *not* qualify as a research report. Included among those materials are most articles in newspapers and popular magazines, the majority of articles in professional journals, and even the contents of most research-based college textbooks.

We make this point not to disparage any of these forms of communication. They can be serious, accurate, insightful, and even important contributions to discourse about particular scientific issues. They are not, however, research reports, and that is not a trivial distinction for our purposes, or for yours.

To make the distinction clear, we remind you that research reviews that appear in scholarly journals are usually subject to full peer review, yet they are not, in themselves, research reports—although they might be of enormous value both to people who want to make use of research and to active researchers themselves. In other words, some very serious writing about research topics is *not* contained in research reports.

For this book, we generally ignored that latter genre of research-related publication. The single exception is the one used in the illustration above—the research review. Because research reviews are such a powerful adjunct to the reading and use of individual reports, we include a short section in Chapter 5 on reading and making use of research reviews.

In some fields, it is common to encounter printed materials (and sometimes entire publications) that represent borderline cases. The content of such items clearly meets some of the criteria for a true research report but just as clearly does not meet others. In almost any area in which you are searching for facts and useful ideas, you will encounter examples of such mixed cases. The most common form is a brief description of a study, with particular reference to the findings, reported (often at some length) as part of a discussion of some issue or problem.

Even though this handbook does not attend directly to such items, it should help you read and think about them, particularly with regard to how much credibility you are willing to award them, given what they do not include. Although all sorts of research-based publications can be useful in the search for ideas, their credibility among serious scholars often is low, and for good reasons. Incomplete reports do not allow us to judge the adequacy of the methods used in the study and, thereby, the credibility of any conclusions derived.

In a similar vein, your own confidence in the assertions made in such publications should be tempered by the grains of salt with which you must season what you learn. Accounts that have only some, but not all, of the vital elements present in true reports give you a selected version of history. Often, you really need to know the rest of the story.

Having now raised the matter of your confidence in the content of a research report, it is appropriate to address that issue head on. How can you tell whether a given report is a trustworthy source of information? In fact, it is not improper to raise an even deeper question. Are there compelling reasons to believe that the research enterprise itself is, by any aspect of its nature, worthy of our confidence? In one sense, this book is our response to that question. For the immediate purpose, however, you need a more utilitarian answer, so in the next chapter we turn to an examination of the sources of credibility in research reports.

3

When to Believe
What You Read

The Sources of Credibility

Research can be many things and certainly means different things to different people. The question of what counts as research depends on who is making the decision. In everyday life, we all do things that might be considered research. For example, when shopping for a new car, most of us do some investigation. We might talk to friends and ask them if they like their particular make and model, or we try to question someone in an automotive service department. We might check ratings in automobile and consumer magazines, looking at crash test results and lists of available options. We might even surf the Net, seeking comparative price information. All of these actions certainly qualify as serious inquiry and, in the common use of the word, as research.

The research we are dealing with in this book, however, has essential characteristics other than just a careful search for information. The word as used here denotes a multistage process, with formal rules that prescribe the general nature of each step. Research begins when the investigator formulates a carefully defined question and then designs a systematic way to collect information that might provide an answer. How the researcher goes about answering the question determines whether those activities truly constitute research and, more important for this chapter, whether it is sound research.

One hallmark of such formal research is that it is a peculiarly public act. The investigator must prepare a truthful written account of whatever he or she did. Although that document can never be complete in the sense of reporting every possible detail, it must include a description of all aspects of design and method that support the veracity of the findings. Then, when published, the report can be read and evaluated by other scholars working in the same field. No matter how well designed or how useful to the investigator, a study that has been conducted but that does not undergo that final step of public scrutiny by peers will not be treated as genuine scholarship in any field of study. If an account is not available as a *public document,* then it is not research, either in a scientific community or in this book.

Hallmarks such as peer review and public dissemination are related to credibility—the degree to which you can invest your trust in what a research report contains. If you are not familiar with the rules that govern research, either through formal training or by self-education, you must extend a degree of trust to any report you read. How much trust? On what grounds? With what reservations? Those are important and reasonable questions for an inexperienced reader; however, if you are to believe anything, you will have to trust at least something.

The remainder of this chapter is devoted to helping you examine the believability of research—when to give trust and when to be skeptical. First, we begin by discussing the question of who does research, a matter related to both investigators' credentials and the environment in which they work. In the second section, we explore those aspects of the publication process that help ensure the trustworthiness of research reports. The third section provides a description of occasions when you might be particularly wary about trusting what you read. In the fourth and final section, we suggest some useful (and very pointed) questions to ask while reading any research report, and then close the chapter by confronting a fascinating question: "Can any research study be perfect?"

❖ WHO DOES RESEARCH AND WHERE DO THEY DO IT?

As noted previously, many human activities might be considered research in the common sense of that word. Here, however, we are using the term *research* in a special sense to designate a planned and systematic process for answering questions according to rules that are particular to both a field of inquiry and a kind of research. Furthermore, research is a specialized enterprise that requires the skills and knowledge of a trained investigator. Research is a form of intellectual work, and it is done by people, not by computers.

The end result of the research process usually is the publication of a report in a *journal* (a periodical devoted to research reports and articles about scholarship) or *proceedings* (a printed collection of reports, often called *papers,* that have been delivered orally by the investigators at a meeting of scholars). Again, such published reports are written by people—authors who have a particular audience in mind. That fact is evident in the highly specialized nature of what they write, and it also provides one of the reasons for writing this book. Research reports are anything but an easy read and, for the nonspecialist, some basic guidance can smooth the way.

As we indicate later in this chapter, other formats that researchers sometimes use for public dissemination of their work—such as monographs, books, and the Internet—can present certain limitations on the trustworthiness of the report. Whatever the outlet, however, if research is not retrievable, it cannot be useful either to you as a reader or to us as writers. For this book, *research,* as we noted in Chapter 2, has to mean published (either in print or electronically) research.

Although we have defined research in a particularly narrow sense of the word, and although we will deal primarily with studies published in journals and proceedings, it suits the purpose of this book to do so. The distinction between journals and proceedings, and other print media such as newspapers and magazines, is important for this book because (as explained in Chapter 2) journals provide some form of quality control, usually by means of peer review, over the reports they contain.

It is quite common for researchers to present their work in oral form at a meeting of academic peers and then, with the benefit of critical feedback, submit a revised version for review and possible publication in a journal. As you will learn later in this chapter, the review process that is used to determine the suitability of a manuscript for journal publication often is somewhat different (and more rigorous) than the procedures used to screen papers for presentation at a meeting.

With all the attention to peer review and selective screening for presentation and publication, it is apparent that researchers write their reports first and foremost for other researchers. To put the matter directly, it is highly unlikely that the author of a research report was thinking about explaining his or her study to a layperson, not even to an intelligent and well-educated individual like yourself. Helping you to overcome the difficulties produced by that situation is the function of this book. Who does research, and who tries to read about it, matters a great deal.

Who Does Research?

Most people who do research have completed their training at a university by studying for the Ph.D. or equivalent doctoral degree. This training occurs in all kinds of academic departments—behavioral and social sciences, biological and physical sciences, humanities, and engineering, as well as in some professional schools. Most of the universities that offer doctoral degrees are large and incorporate graduate education as a part of their primary mission.

The graduate student preparing for a career that will include responsibility for research combines course work and apprentice training in a wide range of inquiry tasks as he or she prepares to become an independent scholar. Ideally, the student learns to do research under the guidance of one or several advisors who are themselves active investigators with ongoing programs of study. That arrangement allows faculty to provide students with both a variety of training experiences and a gradually increasing level of responsibility for participation in actual research. Often, this means that early in graduate education, the student performs routine tasks within studies but later advances to the point of helping conceptualize, design, and execute a complete investigation. At the end of the typical graduate program, the student completes a *research dissertation,* which is a final test of the ability to conduct scholarly inquiry independently and make a genuine (if modest) contribution to knowledge in his or her field.

In many fields, doctoral graduates move directly from their training institution into research and teaching positions at other universities or colleges. In some fields, however, it is more common for the new graduate to complete a period of postdoctoral training with a senior scholar at another institution—sometimes at a university, but frequently at a research center with governmental or private sponsorship. Such additional training permits the novice researcher to learn new techniques, obtain new perspectives, develop writing and grant-seeking skills, and further mature as a scholar.

Where Do Researchers Do Their Work?

Research occurs in a variety of settings. The most visible location for inquiry is in institutions of higher education, particularly in the large research-oriented universities. Such institutions provide professorial employment for scholars working in a wide variety of fields. Smaller or more specialized universities and colleges support comparatively modest research enterprises and typically do so in a smaller number of academic areas.

Some university research is conducted in special laboratory facilities, but other studies take place in unspecialized settings or at natural field locations. For example, educational research might be conducted in schools, biological research at field sites such as a local river or a distant jungle, business research in a corporate center, and social work investigations in homes and community centers. Whether on the campus or off, however, if research is performed under the auspices of the university, it is governed by that institution's regulations.

Anyone who does research as a member of the university community is subject to the ethical standards and qualitative controls enforced by academic faculties and the graduate school. A research project can involve an astonishing variety of personnel, ranging from a single investigator to a research team consisting of several faculty members, postdoctoral scholars, graduate students, technicians, and, in some cases, even undergraduates. It is essential that everyone involved in a study march to the same institutional beat.

Although universities train researchers in their doctoral programs and provide the setting for a great deal of scientific inquiry, much research is conducted in other venues. Such settings include military, governmental, industrial, and philanthropic agencies, as well as a host of specialized business entities ranging from research and development laboratories to polling organizations. In the following paragraphs, we briefly discuss some of the most important of these nonacademic sites for research.

We are all aware of the advances made in military technology and equipment over the past half-century. The United States and other major military powers support centers devoted to research and development. Because of the attention received in the mass media, the most widely known kinds of research performed at such locations involve the development of military hardware. The public often is less aware of research that focuses on such factors as the psychological dimensions of warfare, ranging from studies of the biological mechanisms that control a pilot's ability to perform tasks while inverted to changes in personality that can occur when a soldier is made a prisoner of war for an extended period of time. As these examples suggest, military research includes a significant concern for inquiry into the basic nature of both human and material phenomena, as well as more applied topics that lead directly to the creation of weapons.

In addition to funding military research and development centers, the federal government supports sites for other forms of specialized research, some of which are at the forefront of inquiry in particular fields. An example familiar to most people is the Centers for Disease Control and Prevention (CDC). Researchers there conduct epidemiological and experimental studies related to the spread of diseases throughout the world. Some of those investigations have received wide public attention because of the AIDS epidemic and books like *As the Band Played On* (Shilts, 1987), which provide descriptions of how CDC scientists do their work.

Federally sponsored research occurs in other laboratory settings, such as facilities at the National Institutes of Health (NIH). Reports from the NIH often attract attention in the media, and it is probable that most of you have encountered at least some of them. Research sponsored by governmental entities reaches into every aspect of our environment.

One of our acquaintances is a geotechnical engineer employed at a Canadian research center. She conducts studies with colleagues working at other governmental research facilities throughout the world. Focusing on the impact of ocean floor drilling on marine ecology, much of her data is collected aboard ship, with core samples later being analyzed in laboratories onshore. All of the research steps have to be coordinated with scholars and technicians at her own research center, as well as with collaborators in other countries. At the end of that complex process, her research is submitted for publication, where it will become available to support advances in marine science around the world.

In yet another arena for research, businesses conduct studies that are designed to further their own interests, either by contract with investigators at a university or—just as the military does—by creating centers where research can be done in their own laboratories. Such studies take any of several forms. One example is represented by companies in the computer industry that do research on microprocessor technology involving teams of chemists, physicists, engineers, and computer scientists. Their ultimate goal is to produce the next generation of microchips, for which the interaction of investigators from a variety of fields is essential. This type of research is often conducted under tight security in order to complete product development in a manner that yields advantage over competitors.

Another type of business-sponsored inquiry is also sensitive to the corporate bottom line but involves marketing products that already are moving into production. Effective sales campaigns require detailed studies of customers—their needs, how they can be reached with product information, and what features might influence their purchasing decisions. Studies of this kind are intended to generate information that is strictly proprietary. Because such investigations ordinarily are not circulated through academic journals, they would not be considered research in the sense used in this book. Some studies sponsored by corporations, however, do address basic questions that have important theoretical implications. These studies often go through the cycle of peer review and ultimately are published in scientific journals.

Much of the research that reaches public attention occurs in the settings just described. Other types of organizations, however, do sponsor (or, less commonly, conduct) scientific studies. A good example is the research supported by foundations. Most philanthropic foundations concentrate on relatively narrow and specific purposes, such as providing legal services for the poor, and have little cause to conduct or sponsor research. Some, however, do require specialized information, program evaluations, or development work, and for such purposes often contract for research services made available by universities or commercial organizations.

There are a few exceptions to the general rule that foundations sponsor rather than perform their own research. Resident scholars at the Carnegie Foundation, for example, conduct research on educational issues, and both the Heritage Foundation and the Brookings Institution maintain staffs that study social and political issues related to their organization's particular interests. Research of this kind might be published in scientific journals, but it also might be disseminated through foundation-supported books, monographs, or special reports.

In the latter instances, it is important to remember that the studies and findings described in such publications have not been served by the processes of peer review. Again, by our strict definition, they are not research reports. The fact that the studies were performed by trained (and perhaps distinguished) researchers is not sufficient to qualify them for that status.

Even further removed from university and governmental sources of research are organizations found in some areas of commerce that are made up of businesses that band together to fund studies for the overall benefit of the industry. Among the most visible of these are the Tobacco Institute and the National Dairy Council. Such organizations disseminate findings through the media and use studies to lobby for legislation favorable to the business interests of their sponsors. As you can imagine, investigations performed or funded by such organizations do not always achieve status as true research.

As a final example of the many places where research is done, we consider a specialized research enterprise with which we are all familiar—polling. We categorize corporations that do this kind of research separately because of their ubiquitous nature in everyday life. As we watch television news and read the newspaper, we see polls on nearly every topic of public interest, not least of which are predictions about whom we will vote for in any upcoming election.

Polling is conducted for many media outlets by companies that do the actual work of designing studies, devising samples, and conducting interviews. Some of these companies, such as the Gallup Organization and Louis Harris and Associates, are household names and play a large part in what we know about national trends and the attitudes of our fellow citizens. To develop techniques for conducting studies of such complexity, some of these organizations also have conducted research on theoretical problems that involve sampling methods and polling techniques. Research of that kind not only influences their own work but often is published in academic journals devoted to topics in measurement, statistical analysis, and social science.

The topic of polling is of interest in the context of this chapter, however, not because of the genuine contributions that have been made to science but because it represents a perfect example of an activity that people often confuse with research. In the absence of thorough reporting in a research format and subsequent peer review, the polling results (and interpretations) you read in newspapers or see on television have the credentials of news journalism, and not one bit more.

In a typical news report, you are told nothing of a poll's sample size and composition, data-gathering techniques, or, in many cases, the exact nature of the questions asked. Even more important, you often are left ignorant of the margins of error for the statistics used and the considerable reservations that polling technicians might have about the validity of their results. Such factors control results and shape conclusions, which is why such information is so scrupulously reported in true research reports.

Polling specialists know, for example, that telephone surveys require sophisticated methods if they are to yield results of value. Moreover, these experts are likely to know what individuals in news organizations are unlikely to know—that inquiries about what people will or will not do at some future date (a common form of news polling, as in surveys of voter intentions) yield data that are so unreliable that they are virtually worthless in predicting future actions.

Journalists do not raise questions about such technical matters, nor are they qualified to do so. What the public receives in the typical news report of poll results is an unknown mixture of perfectly valid scientific survey work and pseudoscientific mumbo jumbo—and never enough information to distinguish which is which.

A very small number of newspapers and magazines have the resources to employ a trained science writer for reporting about research (and their work can provide information that is both accessible to the layperson and completely accurate). With those few exceptions, however, if you want the credibility of scientific research, print and electronic news journalism must be regarded as unreliable sources. All of this information provides a good reason for learning how to read and understand research reports (and reviews), at least in the areas for which you have a special interest.

Returning now to the discussion of the places where research is conducted, it should be apparent that inquiry conducted in one setting often influences studies performed at another. In large measure, this influence is the result of the network of publications that binds scholars together within and across disciplines, no matter where they do their work. There are, of course, other sources of influence over the research performed at any given location. For example, by establishing priorities that determine which research proposals will be funded, governmental agencies frequently exert powerful influence over the research conducted at universities.

The world of research consists of people working at richly interconnected locations, a fact that accounts for the speed with which discoveries are disseminated and applications developed. As we discuss later in this chapter, however, this same complexity of settings, sponsorship, and sources might also be important in determining how much credibility you should award to a particular research report. All of the research done at all of the possible locations is not equal.

❖ BELIEVING WHAT YOU READ IN RESEARCH:
    THE FOUNDATIONS OF TRUST

To make use of what is found in research reports, readers must have at
least a degree of confidence in the quality of work described and the
accuracy of conclusions drawn. That is what we mean by the word
trust in the context of this book. We want to believe that studies presented at a conference or published in a journal were performed com-
petently and reported honestly. Furthermore, we want to believe that
there would be a reasonable level of consensus among other scholars in
the same field as to what the findings mean. Yet none of us can be an
expert in all or even many of the areas in which we might wish to be
informed by research. What can give us cause to trust and thereby
believe what we read?

The Review Process for Presenting and Publishing Research

Fortunately, the system by which research is selected for presentation and publication provides an initial foundation for credibility. An
understanding of those processes will help you in deciding how much
trust you can place in the reports you read (or the studies you hear or
read about secondhand).

The first time many researchers make their work public outside the
confines of their own workplace and their immediate circle of colleagues is when they present at a meeting of academic peers. These
occasions often take the form of a special symposium or conference
called to share research on a particular topic of current interest, or the
annual meeting of a scholarly organization.

Such papers usually are delivered orally (at a few conferences, it
still is common practice to distribute manuscript copies to the audience) or through poster presentations that involve both graphic displays and informal interactions with visitors. Both presentational
formats provide the opportunity to obtain critical reactions from peers
that are often the inspiration for revisions made before submitting
the report to a journal. To support that process, most academic
organizations—such as the American Sociological Association, the
American Public Health Association, the American Educational
Research Association, and the Society for Neuroscience—hold yearly
meetings at which a major focus of activity is the presentation of
research papers.

Researchers who want to present their work at such meetings submit an abstract, typically one to three pages in length, months before the conference is to be held. Abstracts are reviewed by a panel of other investigators working in the same field. The reviewers then make a recommendation on whether the study appears to be of sufficient high quality and significance to assume a place in the conference program. The conference organizing committee then makes final decisions about which submissions will be presented based on the peer recommendations, the space and time available, and the presence of similar studies with which the submission can be clustered for efficient program design. Even after the selective attrition produced by such screening, most of the papers can be afforded only 10 to 15 minutes of presentation time or limited space in a poster format—and such restrictions allow the investigator no more than a brief overview of procedures and a quick summary of results.

Although most research submitted for presentation at academic meetings is at least reviewed in abstract form before being accepted, the review process for journal publications typically is more extensive and rigorous. As discussed in Chapter 2, journals that publish reports of original research are often referred to as *refereed* publications because independent reviewers, or referees, help the editor determine which submissions meet the standards of the journal and merit publication. Reviewers are chosen both because they are considered to be experts in their field and because they have the skills required to write detailed evaluations, including advice for improving reports while they still are in manuscript form.

When an editor receives a manuscript, he or she ascertains the focus of the study and the type of research design involved, and then sends it to several reviewers familiar with that particular kind of study. The number of reviewers involved, typically two or three, depends primarily on the procedures set by the journal's *editorial board,* a body composed of scholars who establish policy and give advice to the editor and publisher. The number of reviewers can also be influenced by whether the journal has section editors who can provide reviews in their areas of scholarship, and, finally, by whether the editor feels competent to pass judgment on the quality of the study.

Reviewers for a journal, most of whom will be professors and all of whom provide their services on an uncompensated basis, receive a number of manuscripts each year (or as often as each month if they have competence in an area of high research activity or serve a busy journal with high rates of submission). The author's name will have been removed, and, at least in theory, the reviewer is "blind" to the source of the manuscript under consideration. The journal provides directions for the review and, in most cases, standard response forms that put all reviews into the same general format when returned to the editor. Both general and specific comments are required, and attention typically is given to factors such as significance of the research question, methodology, data analysis, quality of writing, and organization of the manuscript.

Each of the authors of this book has reviewed for several journals and found that the nature of the review depended not only on the particulars of the system used but also on such intangibles as the editor's personal style and the unwritten traditions that accumulate around a journal. In our experience, the most stringent reviews were required by journals that provided the clearest (not necessarily the most lengthy) instructions, asked for an explicit recommendation on the suitability of the manuscript, and expected that judgment to be supported with specific reasons.

After all of the reviews are returned, the editor makes a decision about the next step. The options vary with the journal but ordinarily include rejection, acceptance, acceptance contingent on specific revisions to be made by the author, and an offer of re-review (but no commitment for acceptance) if particular defects can be corrected. The author is notified of the editor's decision and, in most cases, receives at least a portion of the reviewers' comments. The anonymity of reviewers is usually carefully guarded by journal procedures. If the manuscript is rejected outright, the author still can use reviewers' comments either to revise the report for submission to another journal or simply to improve future studies.

Some manuscripts are accepted exactly as submitted but, in our experience, that is a rare event. It is more likely that the editor will ask for at least some of the revisions suggested by the reviewers. Those changes might involve providing more detail about the methods used, clarification of the research question, revision in the way the findings or the conclusions are presented, or reorganization of the report to improve readability. Although required revisions can even extend to such substantial changes as reanalysis of data using more appropriate procedures, the vast majority of requests deal with more routine mechanics of writing a thorough and lucid report.

Often, after the author has attempted to make the required changes and resubmitted the manuscript, it is returned to the original reviewers for further comment. That cycle can continue until the editor decides either that the manuscript is ready for publication or that the author will be unable to produce a report that meets the journal's standards. The latter decision, which is rare after the first round of revision, occurs when fatal flaws in study design are made apparent by the process of rewriting the manuscript.

In sum, the tradition of peer review within journals is a vital part of the self-regulation and quality control exercised by investigators in an area of active scholarship. Refereed journals profit from their peer review procedures in two ways. First, many of the reports are improved through changes suggested by competent reviewers (and skillful editors). Second, among the reports submitted for consideration, the peer review process functions to identify and eliminate some that contain fundamental (and irremediable) flaws.

That is how refereed journals provide readers with a measure of reassurance about the quality of their contents. We must caution you, however, that it is not safe to believe that peer review operates with flawless precision as an absolute guarantor of quality in published research. The effectiveness of the peer review system can be no better than the quality of function produced by each part, and, despite the best efforts of editors and reviewers, judgments fail and mistakes do occur. Taken across journals, editors, and reviewers, there is enough residual variability to give all readers cause to be wary and to exercise one final step in quality control—by forming their own judgment about the adequacy of what they read.

Journal Selectivity

In every field of inquiry, some journals use more stringent review procedures and are more selective in what they accept for publication than others. Along with important factors such as circulation and quality of editing, it is selectivity that serves to establish the reputation of scientific journals. In deciding where to send their work for review, researchers must strike a delicate balance between their desire to have the most prestigious outlet possible for their work and their need to get their report into print—and thus available for the perusal of scientific colleagues. In the end, however, more pedestrian concerns can tip the balance in favor of one journal over another. Such pragmatic matters as the nature of the audience the author wishes to reach, or the average time lag between submission and the decision to accept or reject a manuscript (which differs substantially among journals), might be the deciding factors.

On the journal side of the equation, the number of manuscripts received in relation to the space available determines the competition faced by each submission. One journal might receive so many submissions that it can publish only 5% of the manuscripts received. Another journal ultimately might print more than half of the manuscripts received. The differences between the two publications might not be great, and they are unlikely to be immediately apparent to a novice, but they are there, and they are likely to involve issues of quality and, thereby, trust.

Journals that are more selective are more prestigious among researchers (and in the academic community generally) simply because of the difficulty of having a report published in them. Beyond that, however, the matter of selectivity is of genuine importance to anyone who reads research because it is related to the degree of trust that can be placed in the contents of any journal. The nature of that relationship is complex, however, and we want to be very clear about how you should understand it. Excellent studies *do* appear in relatively unselective journals, and defective studies (or incomprehensible reports) *do* slip through the best screening efforts of selective journals. Nevertheless, if readers want to stack the odds in favor of locating sound research and intelligible reports, they should consider the source of publication as one factor when deciding what to read—and what to trust.

Every journal editor has had the experience (which is fortunately infrequent) of rejecting a manuscript only to see it later published elsewhere, sometimes unchanged from its original form. Conversely, however, it is not uncommon for authors to extensively revise manuscripts based on comments from reviewers at one journal and then submit the study to a new journal that provides a fresh review—and acceptance. All of these complications make the whole matter of selectivity and journal reputations less tidy than we might wish. Certainly, the guarantee of quality provided by most journals is something less than absolute.

If you are unfamiliar with the journals that serve a particular area of research, you can obtain some initial assistance in estimating their relative quality by consulting publications that list basic housekeeping statistics for individual journals. Such statistics include such figures as acceptance rates for submitted manuscripts and numbers showing where and how frequently that journal's articles are cited by scholars publishing studies in other journals.

For example, through publication of the *Journal Citation Reports* (available on-line at larger libraries), The Institute for Scientific Information (ISI) provides a large array of descriptive statistics that reflect the operation of more than 600 journals. Among the statistics calculated by ISI for each journal is one called the "Impact Factor," which serves to estimate the relative influence exerted by the average article in a particular journal over scholars working in the same or adjacent areas of inquiry. In addition to helping readers (and authors) appraise the relative quality of journals, these sources aid bibliographers in establishing and maintaining their journal collections.

Aside from such purely quantitative sources for formulating judgments, people who do extensive reading of research reports usually develop a more personal sense of the qualitative hierarchy among journals—although it too is likely to be based in some measure on reputations for selectivity. Without this depth of experience, however, and especially if you are new to the task of reading research (or new to a particular field of inquiry), figuring out which journals deserve greater respect and trust will always be difficult. We wish there were an easy basis on which to make that determination, a "truth in publishing" rating of some kind, but such certification is not available.

In subsequent chapters, we provide some detailed information about particular hallmarks of quality to look for while reading reports. With that advice and some practice, you should be able to accumulate a strong sense of the trustworthiness that is characteristic of each journal. For the more immediate purpose, however, you can obtain a preliminary sense of the confidence that is warranted simply by learning more about the journals you encounter. For example, you might ask the following questions, for which a "yes" answer suggests a stronger and more reliable publication:

- Is the editorial board composed of names you recognize as leading scholars in the field served by the journal?
- Are the reviewers (a list of whom usually is published once each year) active researchers who are employed at universities known for research in the field that interests you?
- Is it the judgment of others to whom you talk—professors, colleagues, librarians, graduate students—that the journal has a strong reputation, high editorial standards, and at least a modest degree of selectivity?

That last point, discussing journals with others, is particularly helpful at the outset. If you do not want to be in the position of treating all research reports as though they were equally credible, there is no alternative to that strategy. Even with assistance, learning to recognize and understand the hallmarks of trustworthy research takes time. Of course, the simple standards of good writing, consistency of editorial style, attractiveness of format, and freedom from mechanical errors provide practical, if not completely adequate, reasons to reach for some journals and not for others.

As useful as such predilections might be, we hope that you will always keep them flexible and hold them subject to change. There are good reasons for that advice, the first of which we have already mentioned—journals with generally strong reputations occasionally publish reports you think are poor, and a less well-regarded journal might contain a study you judge to be absolutely first-rate. Beyond that, however, is the fact that journals do evolve over time with the people who edit them, the organizations that sponsor them, and even with the vitality of the academic field they serve. Use good journals to find good research—but hold your prejudices gently.

Beyond the quality controls provided by journal publication, there are relatively few other sources of reassurance for the beginner who asks, "Does this report deserve my trust?" There are, however, three instances when published research presents characteristics that are commonly associated with sound scholarship: (a) reputation of the author(s), (b) source of funding, and (c) sponsorship. No one (and no combination) of the three can be regarded as an absolute guarantee of high quality. At the least, however, they are positive signs and can be used to identify reports that offer a reasonable chance of returning a profit for your investment of reading effort.

Reputation of the Author(s)

The academic credentials of the author (in the case of multiple authorship, this applies primarily to the first listed or "senior" author)—as established in such general factors of reputation as public recognition; academic honors; appointed positions of power, influence, and prestige; association with major discoveries; and length of track record as an active investigator in the area of a report—naturally lead any reader to expect trustworthy work on topics of importance. Although the final judgment about quality must be based on what is in the report, not on who wrote it, good reputations are generally acquired by people who do good work and who are likely to have attracted both excellent coworkers and substantial resources with which to support their research. If you are in the happy position of being able to choose from among a number of reports to begin a search for reliable information, it is not unreasonable to look first for familiar names.

Source of Funding

When a study is supported by funds from a prestigious government source—such as one of the National Institutes of Health, the National Science Foundation, or the Office of Educational Research and Improvement, or from one of the major private philanthropic organizations such as the Ford, Carnegie, or Pew Foundations—there is some reason to expect sound research on important topics. Again, although there certainly is no guarantee that your trust will never be violated by a shabby study that managed to attract money from a usually discriminating source, the probabilities are in your favor. Such sources demand submission of extensive research plans, process those plans through rigorous and often highly competitive reviews, and, in the end, support only a small fraction of the applications received. Any study that survives the grant application process, wins financial support, and, when finally written as a report, passes through the screening review of a selective journal certainly deserves your attention. What you actually find inside the covers determines whether it also deserves your trust.

Sponsorship by a Research or Professional Organization

Although not common, scholarly organizations sometimes find it appropriate either to provide direct support for a particular study or to endorse the report of a study funded by other sources (often reprinting and circulating the report as a service to members). Whatever the nature of the endorsement, association of a scholarly organization's name with a study usually can be taken as a hallmark of research of particular significance and high quality. The American Association for Higher Education, for example, has sponsored vital survey research that documents practices in American universities. The association makes that archive of information available through a series of reports on special topics (e.g., see Wergin & Swingen, 2000). Although such prestigious sponsorship does not, in itself, provide an absolute guarantee of quality in research, it can be taken as a positive sign, if only because such organizations have so much to lose in the form of public respect if they are careless in their endorsements.

Our previous discussion of selectivity might seem to suggest that research can be neatly divided into the categories of good and bad, but that was not our intention. Although qualitative variability in research is a fact of life, research reports do not distribute into a simple dichotomy of adequate and inadequate. Not only are there degrees of quality represented *among* studies, but, *within* a single study, there are often exemplary elements that can be very instructive, surrounded by less laudable aspects of design, execution, or interpretation. In a world with such shades of gray, learning to make critical judgments takes time and is an ongoing process that will never be completed. Until your ability to discriminate has begun to grow, it makes sense to use refereed journals as the place to look for research you can trust.

To jump-start your ability to sort sense from nonsense in research, we identify some warning signals in the next section that you should attend to whenever they turn up in research reports. As you will see, the technical adequacy of study design is just one of the factors that might cause you to be skeptical about the trustworthiness of a report.

❖ REASONS TO SUSPEND TRUST IN RESEARCH

The review process does provide a filter, ensuring that reports are carefully scrutinized before publication. In addition, however, you should always make your trust tentative and contingent on the specifics that you find in the report. A variety of warning signals can indicate the presence of unresolved problems. In the majority of instances, such problems pertain to one or more of the following factors: technical aspects of method, sampling, replication, conflicts, carelessness, and errors of interpretation. As you read our discussion of those factors in this section, keep in mind that like the matter of journal selectivity, the issues here are not perfectly clear-cut. A warning signal is an indictment, not a conviction.

Technical Problems

At the end of this chapter, we argue that no study is perfect. Every study has at least some limitations inherent in the design and analysis.

In many instances, the author was perfectly aware of any problems and drew them to the attention of the reader. If the report was published in a journal, the reviewers either considered the difficulties unavoidable or regarded them as counterbalanced by an otherwise strong design.

Although we urge you to take an "innocent-until-proven-guilty" approach to any study, you must remember that the devil is always in the details—in this case, in the specifics of what the author did. It is for exactly that reason that research reported in newspapers, popular magazines, or even in documents originating from public relations offices of universities or other research centers usually cannot be judged for technical competence. You simply are not given enough detail on which to base an evaluation.

It is impossible for us to provide a complete overview of all the technical problems that can be encountered in the course of planning and conducting a study. Chapters 7 and 8, however, provide a useful introduction to some of the most common failures. Although those chapters focus primarily on research reports themselves and how to read them with a critical eye, often the flaws detected in the report are no more than a reflection of defects in the design and execution of the investigation.

In addition, references in the annotated bibliography in Appendix A provide a much broader survey of the technical demands to be confronted in different types of research. We urge you to explore several of those and, if you have not done so already, to consider enrolling in an introductory research methods course at a college or university. A course that focuses specifically on designs used in the field of your primary interest would be ideal, but any sound beginning is better than none at all.

You should not expect to master all of the technical issues that bedevil the many kinds of research, even after reading this and other books, or even after taking a course. There is simply too much to learn. The number of research strategies used by scholars has grown tremendously over the past several decades. This proliferation of methodology has provided new ways of answering questions and resulted in substantial advances in many fields. At the same time, however, it has made research skills increasingly specialized. Today, understanding generic models of research, although still a useful first step, will not make you competent to judge the quality of many published studies.

As you read all reports, the following points are the first things to notice. If they are not clearly defined, you should regard that fact as a warning signal.

- The specific variables being studied
- The rationale for conducting the study
- The treatment or intervention, if there is one
- The number and characteristics of the subjects
- The interactions of the investigator with the subjects
- The setting for the study, particularly for the collection of data
- The methods used to collect data
- The analysis used to determine the results

How the author handles each of these basic elements in a study is a matter for your interest and concern.

If there is a technical problem, it might present itself in any of several ways. Sometimes, the difficulty seems obvious because you happen to have acquired the skills or experiences necessary to detect a particular flaw. At other times, you might experience an uneasy feeling about what the author did or even about what is not included in the report. Whatever the case, when something seems amiss, you have to shift your reading strategy from looking for general concepts and the broad story to searching out and examining the details. If you can identify the specific point that seems troublesome, that makes it much easier to obtain the advice of a consultant.

Of course, a technical problem might not be fatal to what you find informative or useful in a study. Furthermore, problems do sometimes occur in the way a study is conceptualized or in the way research questions have been posed, neither of which is a technical matter. Nevertheless, the wary reader knows where problems are most likely to be hiding—in the dense thickets of the technical details.

In the next section, we turn to another factor in research procedures that can be a source of difficulties that make trust difficult to sustain. Sampling is, in itself, no more than a technical operation, and it is not a process that appears in all forms of research. Where it is required, however, it is invariably fundamental to the design of a sound study, and it is usually fraught with difficult decisions. For that reason, sampling is discussed as a matter apart from the more generic order of technical problems noted in this section.

Sampling

Rarely is an investigator able to observe or measure every possible instance of the phenomenon being studied. Instead, a small number of the set (whether people, objects, events, or situations), called a *sample*, is carefully selected, and its characteristics are used to estimate the characteristics of the true (and much larger) population. If all other things were equal, the size of that sample would determine how much trust we could place in the results from any study for which it was used. The larger the sample (again, if everything else were equal), the more comfortable we would be with the proposition that it represents the population. The smaller the sample, the more wary we would be. It is rare, however, for everything else to be truly equal. For that reason, size is not the only factor in the adequacy of a study's sample, and, in fact, it is often not the most problematic.

The task of *sampling* (the process used for selecting the group of instances that will represent the larger population) lies at the heart of many investigations. The central problem in sampling, of course, is to be sure that the sample group truly represents the population and is not distorted in any way by the nature of the selection process. In many studies, how the investigator selects the representatives (people, objects, situations, and so on) that will stand in for all those that cannot be examined influences both the success of the investigation and how useful the findings are to you.

Different types of studies use different sampling procedures and sample sizes, but, for all studies, the objective is to create the sample in a manner that does not allow extraneous variables to influence the findings. For example, if a researcher is studying the effect of a new drug on levels of blood cholesterol, he or she would probably want to select subjects who have an initial cholesterol level in the appropriate range and who are not using a prescription medication that might interact with the drug being investigated.

Likewise, if a researcher is interviewing juveniles who are continually in difficulty with the law in order to understand the factors that lead to their behavior, those individuals selected for study clearly will influence the results. Thus, the criteria used to determine which offenders show habitually delinquent behavior (and are thus eligible to enter the sample) are an important consideration.

In both of these examples, blood cholesterol and juvenile offenders, there are a host of other variables to consider. Age and gender, for example, would certainly require attention in the construction of sampling procedures. Failure to do so could easily make the results less believable, no matter how well other aspects of the study were executed. Men and women, like older and younger people, simply are not the same with regard to either blood chemistry or the dynamics of social development. The sampling problem can be easily solved (for example, by deciding to study a cholesterol drug only in older males), but it must be confronted and, in real life, the solutions rarely are easy.

The adequacy of the sample also is important because it determines whether or not it is reasonable to believe that the results found in the study would hold for any other situation or group of people. Using the results of a study to guide action in a setting that is different from that in the study—called *generalizing* the results—is the most common reason for practitioners in any area to consult research. They are searching for ways to improve what they do.

You, too, might be looking at research studies with the hope of finding information that will improve some function you must perform or choice you must make. As you read, however, ask yourself whether the nature of the sample and the situation in which the study took place are sufficiently similar to the circumstances you face. If they are not, what appeared to be true for the sample used in the study might not be true for your situation. Results can be depended upon to transfer only when the sample has a reasonable match with the point of application. But how similar do the study and your world have to be?

No two situations, of course, will ever be exactly the same. And no two groups of people will be identical in every respect. Only you can judge whether the match is close enough (considering those things that might really matter) to believe that results might transfer from research to reality. The report might contain either some cautions or some encouragement about transfer of results, but, in the end, the call rests with the potential user.

In some cases, the decision is an easy one. If infants were the subjects in a study of the utility of a health intervention, and you are dealing with infants of about the same age and general characteristics, you would have no immediate reason not to think that results from the study could guide your own work. What if, however, the study involved infants from socioeconomic settings quite unlike those for your infants? Then, you might trust the study but not the transferability of results—because of the sample's characteristics. Alternatively, you might decide that the variable of socioeconomic background could not have exerted a significant influence on the results. That decision would require expertise and familiarity with the factors that matter in infant health, and only the research *user* can provide that sort of expert judgment.

As you might have detected, the two primary problems in sampling—getting a carefully controlled sample and the generalizability of results—can be at odds with each other. Limiting the sample can reduce generalizability, but obtaining a wider and less restrictive sample might not control for important variables. In a sense, many investigators have to walk a high wire between these two considerations, balancing one concern against the other as carefully as possible. How skillfully the researcher meets the conflicting demands of sample construction is a major factor in how you regard the results of the study. In some cases, their procedures might have produced a sample with uncontrolled characteristics that obscure the results. In other cases, the sample might seem free from contaminating characteristics but be so unlike what you face that the results are useless for your purposes.

Lack of Replication

Repeating a study in different settings or with different subjects, a process called *replication,* is an important factor in creating trust for the results of research. A single study can provide no more than a suggestion about how the world might work. If it is a strong study with a large sample, perhaps it can make a strong suggestion; however, reliable knowledge still depends on replication.

When a study is replicated and the results are similar or change in predictable ways with changes in sample or setting, trust grows accordingly. Similarly, when replications are attempted and the results are mixed, move in unpredicted directions, or simply do not appear as in the original investigation, there is good reason to be cautious.

As vital as replication is to the orderly process of scholarly inquiry, you should understand that there are powerful forces at work that too often serve to bring study results into the public eye before they are adequately supported by additional trials. Being first to publish an important discovery can have enormous consequences for the career of a researcher, and the urge to have results reach print grows accordingly. Also, every journal editor would like to have the first report of a significant finding in his or her publication, and the urge to accept (or even recruit) manuscripts with clearly preliminary results grows accordingly. Finally, news reporters must, by the very nature of their work, find ways to break the "good news" of scientific advances before their competitors, and the temptation to ignore investigators' calls for replication grows accordingly. The end result of all of those forces has been a great deal of public confusion about what is true and what is not, with consequent erosion of confidence in researchers and the very process of research itself.

Several years ago, a study of the process called cold fusion caused a great controversy in the scientific community (see Simon, 2001 for a discussion). A university public affairs office announced that physicists at that institution had observed the phenomenon in a laboratory experiment. If true, this would revolutionize the power industry—and make both the investigators and the university very wealthy. Some of the subsequent discussions in the media suggested that fossil fuels and nuclear power (based on the process of fission) were things of the past.

There was a problem, however, with the results. No one could replicate them. The failure to replicate observations from the original experiment left only one conclusion: The initial study was flawed.

If the first study had undergone the usual process of peer review for publication or presentation, it is possible (although not certain) that the fatal problem would have been identified and a great deal of wasted time and unfortunate publicity avoided. Whatever the case, replication provided the final court of appeal, and cold fusion remains an unrealized dream. When the research enterprise works correctly to resist the inevitable pressures to rush ahead faster than the evidence allows, it is the combination of peer review *and* replication that can give readers the best possible reason to trust research findings.

Conflicts

Another warning signal appears when you discover that someone doing, sponsoring, or disseminating research has a direct conflict of interest. Such a conflict occurs when obtaining a particular finding would have influence on their political aspirations, finances, career, or on a product or idea in which they have some vested interest. It is quite normal for researchers to expect, or even hope for, a particular result. Outcomes that follow one's expectations or predictions certainly are more congenial than contrary results. It is when the benefits become tangible rather than just intellectual that there is reason for special caution.

University researchers, of course, usually are independent agents, free to report whatever they find, even when their research is funded by an organization that does have some vested interest in certain kinds of results. If such studies are to be submitted for review and publication like any other study, there is at least a modicum of protection for the investigator against any external pressure, and that should be reassuring to the reader.

A different situation can occur when the results are released directly (and solely) by the sponsoring organization. Under those conditions, the reader has reason to be cautious, particularly when the details of the study are not made available. Although the intentions of an organization might be entirely honorable, the very fact that particular results might yield substantial benefits opens the door to selective reporting, if not spin-doctoring.

Lobbying groups, for example, rarely give (or are competent to give) an objective accounting of the quality of research they have sponsored, and they often employ selective reporting of results to their advantage. At a time when we see corporations, politicians, and even government agencies using the media to disseminate findings from studies they have sponsored, everyone has reason to withhold his or her trust. We are not cynical, but we have seen enough misuse of research to make us realists.

Finally, more subtle conflicts of interest have their roots in the inadequately controlled (and insufficiently recognized) biases of the investigator rather than in financial gain. When theoretical commitments, belief systems, or ideological dispositions are allowed to influence the process, research can become nothing more than a tool for advancing a personal agenda—that of the researcher. We do not believe that such contamination is common within the enterprises of social science, but it does exist, and you should be aware of that fact.

As human beings, researchers come to their work equipped with the normal full array of personal predilections and beliefs. They know, however, how vital it is to be aware of those dispositions—and how to limit (if not eliminate) their possible influence. For your part, as a consumer of research reports, the best way to detect bias is to pay attention to any language that suggests the author has an ax to grind. Value-loaded terms or phrases, overstated conclusions, and tortured logic are as much warnings of conflicting interests as are obvious connections between the investigator's (or sponsor's) tangible profit and a particular outcome.

Carelessness

Although our experience indicates that it is rare, readers should be aware that sometimes researchers, reviewers, and journal editors do things that are just plain careless. A warning about that problem is signaled when, for example, the number of subjects in the sample given in one section of a report is not the same as that indicated in another. When columns of numbers do not add up to the total shown in a table, when the author obviously did not use the same methods to collect data from all subjects, when citations made in the body of the report do not also appear in the list of references (or vice versa), or when the paper is so vague or unclear that it is impossible to understand some vital aspect of the study (such as sampling procedures)—then the warning flag is flying.

Spotting an instance of carelessness in a report does not mean the entire study was flawed, but it should make your trust more tentative. Errors of that kind can indicate an overall attitude on the part of an author or editor, a disposition to just not care about being careful with details—and, more often than not, that attitude encourages fatal mistakes.

Of course, we do not mean to imply that any time you do not understand something in a report, it indicates some act of carelessness. In fact, as we argue later in this book, until you develop considerable skill in reading research, it is highly unlikely that you will understand everything you read. Detecting blatant carelessness, however, often is not rocket science, and careful attention to details (plus use of your common sense) can afford a useful degree of protection right from the outset.

Errors and Poor Scholarship

Where carelessness ends and honest errors begin can be hard to determine in a research report. A genuine error is made when the author consciously makes a decision that detracts from the quality of the study. In that sense, the problems of technical adequacy and sampling, already discussed, contribute most of the instances. Errors of interpretation, however, are in another domain. Understanding the findings sometimes can be as difficult as devising a sound plan for obtaining those results.

As you might expect, the problems of reaching a sound conclusion based on the results of a study are further compounded by the sometimes subtle difficulty of explaining that outcome in the report. For example, if a researcher determined from data analysis that babies received better maternal care from their teenage mothers when they received a particular type and frequency of social worker home visitation than when there were no visitations at all, what would be the correct conclusion? At the least, the investigator would have to think very carefully about which factors in the visitation operated to produce the desired outcome, an area of interpretation in which errors might have serious consequences for future practice.

Beyond that difficulty, however, would be the task of communicating the finding of the study to readers. To suggest in the report, for example, that social worker home visitations produce better infant care than no visitations would be an error. The study dealt with teenage mothers, not mothers in general, and examined a particular type of intervention, not all possible forms of home visitation. When the data do not support the conclusion, there is good reason to suspend trust in the study—even when the error might be the inadvertent result of inadequate writing.

As we are using the term here, *poor scholarship* is different and not nearly as subtle as a technical error or an inadequate interpretation of results. This problem occurs when errors in the study or, more commonly, in the report of the study are so egregious that they impugn the investigator's most basic understanding of research as an activity of science. That happens, for example, when the author greatly exaggerates the importance of the study, extends what can be concluded from the results far beyond anything the data support, or suggests applications that betray a complete misunderstanding of the linkage between scientific theory and practice.

We cannot provide a set of rules that will help you recognize all possible instances of poor scholarship, but it has been our experience that a modest amount of practice in reading reports allows most beginners to recognize serious violations of the scholarly canons when they see them. After you gain a sense of how cautious good scholars are with regard to claims about what constitutes reliable knowledge, poor scholarship tends to stand out in sharp contrast.

Although we have presented in this chapter some of the most common reasons to be cautious, if not to suspend your trust altogether, we also want you to remember that, as discussed in Chapter 2, many less-than-perfect studies provide valuable information. The watchword is caution. Watch for danger signals, but do not toss out useful information by treating all flawed studies as though they were worthless.

In some cases, you might determine that the study has a number of strengths but it also has clear limitations (often drawn to your attention by a conscientious researcher). That is not an unusual circumstance, and it will be encountered frequently by anyone who makes extensive use of research. The keys to maintaining the right level of confidence are reading with care, paying attention to details, recognizing warning signals, and knowing your own limitations (and getting help when you need it). The following chapters are designed to help you cultivate exactly those skills.

❖ SUMMARY

You now have in hand a number of points to consider when deciding how much confidence to have in a research report. Clearly, the most important factor is whether the document has been peer reviewed at some stage of its development. Because none of us can be expert in all areas, everyone has to lean, at least to some extent, on the judgment of others who are knowledgeable. Evidence of successful replication is another powerful factor that can inspire confidence. Together with the review service of a respected journal, it is repeated trials of a finding that offers the most substantial reason to place your trust in what you read.

In Exhibit 3.1, we have summarized the questions that to us seem most directly related to reader confidence. The exhibit contains a dozen questions that you should habitually ask after the first reading of a research report. The ease with which you answer the questions will depend on your background in the area of the study and your familiarity with the research method used.

Exhibit 3.1 does not include all of the questions that might be useful with a particular study; these questions are intended as no more than a broad survey of what might be important to ask about research in general. With other tools presented later in this guide, however, they offer a sound and workable place to begin formulating your answer to the essential question, "Can I trust this?"

Can Any Research Report Be Perfect?

Having completed an introduction to the matter of quality and trust in research, we want to add a coda that is more personal. We have come to believe that no study is perfect, and, certainly, no research report is above all possible criticism. In the sense of being free of all

Exhibit 3.1   A Dozen Questions to Ask When Reading Research

1. Has the paper been peer reviewed for a refereed journal?

2. Is evidence of replication available to support the results?

3. Is a conflict of interest evident for the person(s) doing, sponsoring, or disseminating the study?

4. Can the research question(s) asked be answered with the design and methods used in the study?

5. Is evidence of technical problems apparent in design, methods, or analysis of the data?

6. Are sample composition and size adequate to address the research question(s) asked and to support the conclusions reached?

7. Are the conclusions offered supported by the findings?

8. Is there any indication that the investigator was careless in conducting or reporting the study?

9. Does the author make statements about the study that appear to be examples of a poor understanding of scholarship?

10. Is the author conscientious in frankly drawing your attention to limitations imposed by the design or sample, or by compromises made to circumvent problems?

11. Did you find that the report was complete enough for you to form a judgment about each important aspect of the study?

12. Do you understand all of the report, or, in all honesty, do you require assistance with some elements?

limitations, researchers strive for perfection in study design, but they usually have to accept a compromise on that ideal—doing the best they can, given the nature of the problem and the extent of their resources.

If reading this chapter leaves you with a set of expectations that no study can meet, we have not served you well at all. Research takes place in a world that is full of messy problems, some of which cannot be resolved given present technology. Small steps in improved understanding are the reasonable goal of most inquiry, not great leaps based on perfect studies. This is particularly true when people are the objects of inquiry, and it certainly will continue to be true as long as investigators themselves are fallible human beings.

If every study involves trade-offs and compromises in scope and design, the same is true in preparing reports. No journal article contains the full story. The constraint of space alone makes that inevitable. We have described many of these trade-offs in design and report in greater depth elsewhere (Locke, Spirduso, & Silverman, 2000). There, we argued that in research, there are reasonable (even inevitable) compromises with the ideal. As a reader, your task is gradually to improve your ability to discriminate between shortcomings that create no more than limitations on what you can learn from a study and those that are fatal to the entire effort. If you persevere with us, we think that the chapters that follow will set you well on the road to being able to make that critical distinction.

4

How to Select and Read Research Reports

This chapter has two major sections. The first deals with how to select research reports from which you can study and learn, and the second addresses how to read them after you have found them. The latter section involves a discussion of the language of research, the value of working with others as you begin, and how to approach the reading task itself.

❖ GETTING STARTED: SELECTING RESEARCH REPORTS

Looking for the Right Read

If you are using this guide in conjunction with a college course or training program, the selection of reports with which to begin will probably be determined by your instructor. For those of you who are working alone or with an informal study group, we have some advice about picking research reports for practice reading (advice that applies, of course, to those of you in college classes after your instructor turns you loose to find your own readings in the library): *Until you have gained some skill and confidence, select studies dealing with topics about which you have some familiarity.*

That recommendation sounds like simple common sense, but we want to expand on what is obvious by addressing some misunderstandings about how (and for whom) research reports are written. Here are some other reasons for our suggestion to initially select studies in areas for which you have at least basic competence. Researchers write reports in the systematic language that is particular to the area of scholarship represented in the study. That fact adds some complexity to the task of locating reports appropriate for the beginning reader in terms of both language and content.

The languages of research. Based on the common language of everyday speech, research languages (sometimes called *system languages*) add a combination of both technical vocabulary and the conventions (style and format) of scientific writing. Because they are highly formal languages, they allow much less latitude for individual expression and, correspondingly, a great capacity for precision and parsimony. The end result is a dense style of prose containing many unfamiliar words. There is little waste of ink in getting to the point, and each sentence is crammed with important meaning. In our ordinary experience, only specialized documents such as technical manuals and insurance policies present anything like this kind of daunting reading task.

As you might guess, system languages are used because they provide reliability in communication. After a system language is mastered, the words in that language mean one thing (and only one thing) to both reader and writer. The problem is that these languages also serve to limit the access of nonspecialists.

The audience for reports. If you are an outsider, some research reports in the social sciences might just as well have been written in a foreign language, which raises a familiar question: "Why don't researchers write their reports in common language so everyone can understand them?" In answer, the virtue of standardization for reliable communication has already been noted, but the issue of economy bears even more directly on the matter of how reports are written.

If reports were written in a common language that was intended to have the same degree of precision and reliability, most research reports would balloon to many times their present length and still might present significant risk of misunderstanding. Beyond that problem, however, lies an even more fundamental explanation for why authors of research reports do not write in a language intelligible to the layperson.

Researchers write for other researchers (or, at least, for people who are insiders to the area of inquiry), and they have little motive to make themselves understood by outsiders. The reports they write are the primary (although not the only) vehicle for a continuing conversation among active scholars in an area of investigation. When their research is published, what they have learned from a study is both added to the archive of knowledge and made available for assimilation (and critique) by their scientific colleagues. As an outsider, reading research reports allows you to listen in on that conversation, but you must understand that you are not the authors' primary audience.

It is not a matter of hostility to nonresearchers. The point is that you just were not the imagined audience for the report. Being understood by fellow researchers is absolutely critical to personal success as a scholar and, of course, to the wider goals of science. Put bluntly, however, research reports are not intended to be intelligible to the rest of us.

Nevertheless, research reports are in the public domain, and it is fully understood by all that many different kinds of people will read them. In consequence, crashing this party involves none of the social sanctions we reserve for uninvited guests at other gatherings. Besides, in many instances, you will not be a complete outsider, a fact that makes eavesdropping on the conversations of researchers a lot easier.

Because part of a research report's language is drawn from the author's area of scholarship (usually circumscribed by the discipline in which he or she was trained), you should be able to follow at least the broad outline of a study if you have an introductory level of familiarity with concepts in that field. Exceptions lie in the area of specialized research terminology—words that deal with investigative processes themselves and words that are consequent to more advanced (or simply more recent) knowledge than your own. For those words that are completely unfamiliar, some new learning—the learning of the terms and the constructs they represent—is required as part of the reading process.

No guide can make all reports transparent for your inspection. Outside the social sciences, where system languages often have evolved into shorthand symbol systems (e.g., mathematics, chemistry, genetics, dance, physics, astronomy, and statistics), anything short of a solid grounding in the subject matter leaves you forever outside most published reports. Other areas of inquiry, however, make much less heroic demands on the reader.

Although they do have indigenous system languages, professional fields such as education, public health, counseling, nursing, and business administration, as well as some of the disciplines in the social and behavioral sciences (e.g., social psychology, anthropology, communication studies, and political science), are much less impenetrable for the novice. This is largely because they use less cryptic shorthand and more carefully selected common language.

We now go back to the matter of selecting studies for your first efforts. It should now be obvious that, given any choice, you should pick studies from an area in which you have some academic credentials. Beyond that point, however, three considerations will further ease the difficulty of getting started. First, studies of professional practice that employ research methods borrowed from the social sciences (education and nursing are good examples here) offer reports that are often perfect for the novice reader. Second, as a general rule, applied studies dealing with practical problems are easier to decipher than those dealing with basic inquiry into the nature of things. Third, and finally, shorter reports make more sense for the beginner than do lengthy accounts (although page count is not always a reliable indicator of complexity), if only because you can get to the end sooner.

If you are working alone and are particularly nervous about your ability to get off to a good start, we suggest that you retrieve both of the studies for which we have filled out model 12-step forms in Appendix B. Then, as you work your way through the next chapter (5), you can use those reports for your first round of practice. By having our record forms to serve as guides on those first journeys, perhaps you will find yourself less anxious about being out there in foreign territory.

Another strategy for locating reports that are appropriate for beginners to read and understand is to make use of published collections, which reprint carefully selected items from research journals. The editors of such books usually choose reports that are high quality, relatively short, easily deciphered by students in introductory courses, and conveniently grouped into categories according to design, method, or paradigm. Here are good examples in several disciplines: social sciences: Lomand (2002); education: Lyne (1999); qualitative research: Milinki (1999); educational psychology: Patten (2002a); and nursing: Peteva (2003).

Reading Research Cooperatively

If at all possible, find a fellow traveler who can share the work of puzzling through your first reports. In a college research class or topical seminar, the instructor's support almost guarantees that you will not end up completely confused or, worse, completely wrong in your understanding. When you are working alone, those are genuine risks. Having one or several partners, however, not only reduces the perceived hazards, it substantially lowers the possibility of getting hung up. It is our experience that the interactive social effects of exchanging understandings—and misunderstandings—have a powerful and positive influence on the process of deciphering research reports. Two or three people working together can puzzle through difficult passages that any one of them, working alone, would never fathom.

As you will see in Chapter 5, much of our advice is based on the supposition that you are not working alone. If going solo is unavoidable, however, there is help (beyond our suggestion that you begin with reports that have been subject to some form of analysis in this text). A good-quality introductory research textbook can answer many of your questions and provide support while you read.

Any of the textbooks annotated in Appendix A can serve that purpose. We urge you to obtain one of those reference sources, particularly if you are not going to be working with others. You should familiarize yourself with both the content of the opening chapter and the topics that are covered in the main text and appendixes. A glossary of research terminology and a detailed index will serve you well as you confront the exotic tongues in which reports are written. If you need only a brief overview of the methods used in quantitative and qualitative studies, an inexpensive (paperbound) and very effective choice would be Patten (2002b). In that text, the author provides no more than basic literacy in research—including the language and fundamental constructs—but does so with crisp authority and tight focus on the essentials.

Finally, whether working alone or in a college class, before you begin reading that maiden study, we urge you to complete a first reading of the next chapter. In it, we provide several sets of special survival tools that have been field tested with hundreds of novice research readers. The evidence shows that these strategies work for almost everyone who uses them to try to master the craft of reading research.

The first set of survival tools includes three 12-step record forms that provide a simple format for mapping your progress and not getting lost (or overwhelmed). The second set includes a number of exercises that require you to explain research reports to other people. The latter serves to test and expand your understanding of what you have read—perhaps much more rapidly than you would ever have expected. With the help of both of these supporting procedures, most travelers can do more than simply survive their first encounter with the wily research report—they can begin to tame the beast. Before you read about these tools in the next chapter, however, we want to pass on some general advice about how to approach the reading of research reports with an attitude that will maximize the benefits you gain from the endeavor.

❖ HOW TO READ RESEARCH REPORTS

This guide contains a great deal of advice concerning how to approach and actually do the work of reading research reports. Later in this chapter, we provide specific strategies, often in the form of alternative ways of doing tasks, so that readers with different needs and capabilities can find procedures that fit them as individuals. This brief section, however, offers some general advice that we have found useful in helping anyone read research in ways that are fruitful and satisfying.

If you have read this far, it will not surprise you to find that we begin our advice about reading research with some issues that are personal rather than technical. By this point, it should be clear that we regard the most fundamental difficulties in reading reports to be matters of attitudes, values, and confidence.

The technical impediments to understanding research are real enough, but they also represent problems that have straightforward solutions. Getting your attitude adjusted about research, however, is more than a matter of learning a new vocabulary or mastering the arcane conventions of research strategy. Laying the foundations for good readership is intensely personal. It often requires some hard work and persistence, and it has to be accomplished before reading can yield full benefits.

Researchers as Writers: Style and Substance

Like everyone else, researchers come in all shapes, sizes, and personalities. Some produce reports that you will find distant and austere—because that is precisely what the authors are like as people. Other researchers would fit comfortably into your living room for an evening of easy and congenial conversation, and that is exactly how they write.

Beyond qualities of personality, however, are the elements of the writing craft itself. Some investigators obviously have mastered the required skills: They are firm and lucid in their discussion of complex issues and adroit in laying out a clear line of history for their study. Others, just as obviously, are beginners at both formal inquiry and its accompanying demand for writing accounts of what they did. They are uncomfortably tentative and in many ways make it difficult for the reader to follow the story of what was done and what it might mean. In that wide range of expository skills, researchers are no different from the rest of us. If you ask them to explain their work, some produce accounts that are easy to follow, and others present pieces of communication that strain your capacity for attention and convey garbled or incomplete images.

Notwithstanding the commonsense observation that reports differ in their style and intelligibility, the enormous variety in research reports, as prose writing, invariably surprises the beginning reader. The fact that researchers are working within the dual constraints of elaborate scientific conventions and a formal language system leads people to expect that reports will be homogeneous in style and organization, and somehow free from the print of the individual investigator. Nothing could be further from the truth.

Writing technical reports is, nevertheless, writing. Nothing in the prescriptions of format and style can insulate readers as people from authors as people. Accordingly, you should be reassured that having a personal response to what you read is perfectly normal and quite appropriate because, in the end, research reports are personal stories. They are not written by robots, and, although they might be written on computers, they certainly cannot be written by computers.

You should always appreciate graceful writing wherever you encounter it. With research reports, however, pragmatism makes clarity, precision, and thoroughness the elements that matter most. There is no requirement that you enjoy an author's expository style or appreciate the elegance of his or her illustrations. If those happen to be your reactions, so much the better. When they are not, what alternative do you have?

Put directly, you are reading research reports because you are looking for facts and ideas, not because you are seeking entertainment. Within reasonable limits, you must put up with whatever is on the page as long as it yields the substance that you seek.

Researchers as Workers: The Matter of Respect

If you persevere in your efforts to read research as a resource, one particular disposition toward the authors will serve you well. You will have to cultivate this attitude as you practice the skills of consuming research, and you might need to sustain it at some personal cost in the face of serious challenge. It is the attitude of respect—basic respect for the person who did the work.

Let us reduce this matter to its simplest terms. The authors of research reports did the work, took time out of their lives, struggled with ideas, labored over writing the report, and, in the end, took the very real risk of going public, laying their work out in print where everyone can read and judge. That does not make them paragons and certainly does not make inferior science or poor reporting into anything better than it is. What it does do, however, is give you an obligation to take them seriously and to show respect for their intentions.

Whatever your investment as a reader, you owe the author respect for his or her investment as a scholar. You will naturally adopt this attitude when reading strong studies reported in clear, well-organized prose. Unless you are unusually fortunate in your selection of reports to read, however, most will fall somewhat short of that optimum standard.

As you read, it is vital to remember that the vast majority of studies, particularly those in the social sciences, are compromises between perfection and the practicalities of time and money with which the researcher, just like the rest of us, must live. Furthermore, you should keep in mind that it is exceedingly difficult to write a completely transparent historical report of complex technical operations, given the space limits imposed by most research journals.

To the extent, then, that research reports can be problematic documents, all research consumers have to invest some serious effort in reading them. Effort alone, however, will not make it possible to understand every report, and certainly not every report in its entirety. Some reports simply make demands that are beyond the beginning reader's capabilities. This problem, of course, is precisely why this guide was written. What you are doing now is learning how to apply your reading efforts (just trying hard will not be enough). You must "work smart" if you are to get as much as possible from accounts of studies that were (necessarily) less than ideal, that were described through the limited medium of the journal report, and that contain some elements you do not (perfectly) understand. That is simply the way things are.

We trust that most of you can tolerate these limitations and that many of you can find ways to thrive within them.

Belief in the author's good intentions, if not always in his or her good execution, will sustain you through the difficult patches in most reports. If you presume that researchers are honestly trying to inform you, it is easier to work at the task of trying to understand what they have written.

The Reader as Consumer: Burdens to Leave Behind

Disrespectful attitudes toward research authors are not just violations of a humane ethic, they are burdens that become handicaps in learning what reports have to teach. Disrespect often is characterized by a readiness to find fault (which, as we will explain, is not the same thing as reading with caution and a critical eye) and a sense of suspicion about the author's motives. The idea, for example, that academics grind out volumes of second-rate studies on trivial topics for the sole purpose of winning financial rewards, status, or job security is not uncommon among both college students and the lay public. Prejudices like that do not enable readers to be attentive and respectful.

In the social and behavioral sciences, we have observed that some readers approach each study with the assumption that it represents a polemical device intended to promote an ideology dear to the author rather than an honest accounting of inquiry. Accordingly, those readers expend a good deal of energy in searching out flaws or refuting assertions rather than trying (first) to understand what is said.

Another destructive attitude held by some readers is the suspicion that the author is playing games with them. They see the report as the playing field for a lopsided contest in which meanings are deliberately obscured, and the reader is challenged to penetrate the maze of jargon and convoluted argument to discover what happened in the study. Inevitably, the result is anger and resentment over every difficulty encountered in the text.

As you can imagine, when burdened with negative expectations like these, people seldom are able to persevere in their efforts to consume research. After initial attempts that are distracted or aborted by suspicion and hostility, some readers retreat into a state of learned helplessness: "I just can't understand all that strange terminology and stuffy writing." Others simply dismiss any study that is not immediately transparent: "The study was a jumbled mess, just completely confusing."

There is no quick therapy for those negative views and their unhappy consequences. If your own thoughts are troubled by nagging doubts about researchers and their intentions, we offer for your consideration a lesson from our own experience. *We have never encountered a researcher who we honestly thought did not want his or her readers to understand and appreciate his or her work.* Furthermore, we have found most researchers to be people of enormous integrity who have thought long and hard about the ethical issues of doing and reporting their work. They intend to do good research, and they intend that work to be understood.

If you can accept these simple observations as a starting point for your own efforts, in most cases, you and the author will connect. Communicating about complex matters through the medium of ink and paper is full of hazards, especially because it is a one-way process. What is required to avoid these impediments is respect on both sides: the author's respect for the reader's desire and need to understand, and the reader's respect for the author's intention to make that understanding possible.

Reading Research as Puzzle Solving

Understanding research reports is not so much a function of reading as it is of studying. We have encountered very few people who can assimilate a report by starting at the beginning and reading continuously through to the end. If you are like our students (and like us), you will have to flip pages forward and back, underline and highlight, write in the margins (if you have your own copy), make notes, draw diagrams, and take breaks to think about what you have read. In other words, you will have to study the report, not just read it.

The myth that reading research is naturally easy for some people because they are smart or good at science is not supported by our experience. Some readers do learn to "read smart" and persist when the going is tough, but the task is never easy for anyone. When you are struggling with a report, you might find it helpful to remember the following story about people who make things look easy.

Ted Williams was arguably the greatest hitter in baseball history. Stories about his prodigious "natural" abilities are legion, but he was far more than just a marvelous collection of perfect nerve and muscle. He was a student of his art and a product of his work ethic. He summed that up with wonderful simplicity when a reporter once asked him why he bothered to take such long sessions of batting practice every day. Sensing the implications behind that inquiry, he looked hard at the scribe and said, "Don't you know how hard this all is?" (Will, 1990).

In a similar sense, an expert investigator doing research is the same kind of performance that, from the outside, appears easy. In fact, it involves a distinctly uncommon kind of intellectual application—close, disciplined reasoning combined with dogged care in procedure. It follows that reading research calls for a parallel effort, in kind if not in degree. There is no easy way to do the *New York Times* crossword puzzle. There is no easy way to read research reports. We hope we are successful in helping you to find the latter as satisfying to finish as the former—but you will come to understand "how hard this all is."

Communication in Reports: It Takes Two to Tango

Write this down and pin it up in front of your desk: *It takes two people to communicate about research.* In the case of reports, there are (at least) two people involved: the reader and the writer. Each bears some responsibility for doing the work of clear transmission and reception.

Whenever you find yourself confused or frustrated by a report, remember that there are two people involved. It is our experience that many of the problems encountered by beginning readers are caused by inadequate writing. In other words, not all of the problems in understanding are yours. Often, the difficulty lies with the authors' problem in explaining what they thought they meant.

That being true—and we assure you that it is—do not get discouraged. Particularly, do not blame yourself. When you cannot puzzle out what something means, take a deep breath, skip over the offending part (perhaps to return later), and try to pick up the story where it again becomes intelligible.

Like any other intellectual task, reading research involves skills that improve with practice, feedback, and assistance. You will get better at reading, just as researchers get better at writing. Neither of you has to feel uniquely at fault when communication breaks down. All of us are in this together.

Graphic Tools: Most Travelers Need a Map

People differ considerably in the way they represent ideas in their minds. However, we find that virtually all who are just beginning to read research profit from the process of making a map of the events reported in a study. By "making a map," we do not mean anything highly technical and certainly not anything particularly artistic—we mean only a rough flowchart on which are displayed the major steps of the study in temporal sequence. An example is shown in Figure 4.1.

Although drawing little boxes and connecting arrows might feel a bit too mechanical for some readers, we urge you to at least give it a try. Some of our students are more comfortable leaving out the graphics and just listing key words as reminders of the order of events. If that is how your mind works, please be our guest. The important thing is to create some sort of map that locates each operation within a study.

Examples of such flowcharts accompany each of the research examples in Appendix B, and a map of the report is one of the items on the 12-step record forms presented in Chapter 5. Just remember that the point is to help you keep track of what the author is describing. Style is of no consequence. If it works for you, do it.

In mapping the history of a study, the most common fault among beginning readers is a compulsion to transfer every detail in the story to the chart and to get every relationship exactly correct. *Don't try to do that!* Include on your map only what seem to be major steps, and make corrections or additions as the story (and your understanding) unfolds.

The advantage of a box-and-arrow-type diagram is that it easily accommodates events and ideas that are not part of a linear sequence. You can just write things in as connected items wherever they fit into your own thinking. Using the comic-strip artist's convention of the text balloon is a nice way to distinguish such reminders and comments as attachments to your map of the main elements in the study design, as shown in Figure 4.2.

On Getting Hung Up: Do Not Get Stuck on the Wrong Things

It is perfectly natural for beginners to be unclear about what is essential and what is peripheral for understanding a report. Some things just do not matter if your purpose is to ferret out facts and useful ideas. Other things do matter, but finding their exact meaning can be put off until a broad understanding of the study has been acquired. Here are four ways to avoid getting hung up on things that do not

Figure 4.1   Flowchart ("Stress management workshops as workplace interventions: Impact of periodic refresher follow-ups")

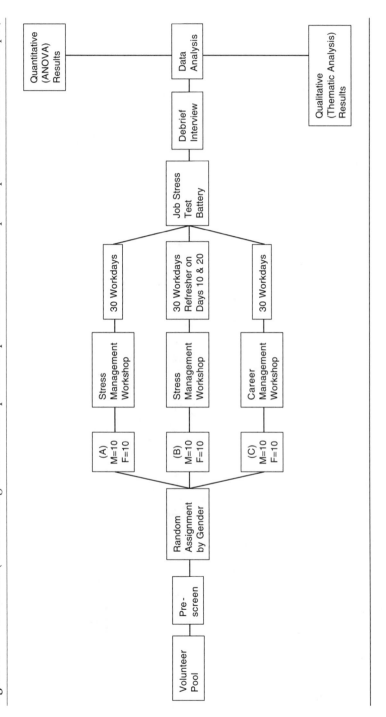

Figure 4.2 Expanded Flowchart ("Stress management workshops as workplace interventions: Impact of periodic refresher follow-ups")

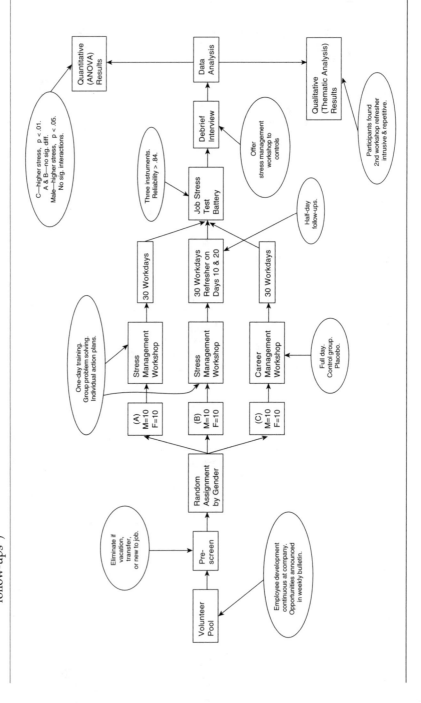

matter, that you cannot find out anyway, or that can be put safely aside until later.

1. *Don't get stuck on* understanding unfamiliar words. If you run across a word you don't know, first look around in the text to see if the author explains the term. If you cannot find a definition in the text, try looking up the word in whatever reference aid you have—a dictionary, a research textbook with a glossary, or even a thesaurus. If someone is handy who might be familiar with the term, ask for an explanation. If none of these easy strategies work, make a note to remind yourself to pursue the matter later, and get on with the task of reading. You just have to pick up the story at a point where the offending word is no longer essential.

It might sound unlikely to you, but we find that there are few instances when a single unfamiliar technical term brings reading to a complete halt. Just remember that in reading a text written in a technical language that is not your own, it is inevitable that there will be problems of comprehension. You have to puzzle them out or, failing that, flag them and get on with the task. Giving up is not a useful option.

2. *Don't get stuck on* what is not there. It is not possible to write a truly comprehensive history of a study in a report, particularly given the space limitations imposed by research journals. Accordingly, authors use their judgment about what readers will find essential and leave the rest out of their account. If you encounter a point in the report that seems to demand a particular piece of information, and it is not there, what do you do? Our advice, again, is to make a note reminding yourself to return to the problem later, and get on with the job. Do not let what is not there bring you to a halt. There usually is enough that *is* present to engage your useful efforts.

Quite often, you will find that the blank is filled by information in a later part of the report. Alternatively, you might come to understand that you do not really need the point to extract the facts or ideas for which you are hunting. Finally, it is absolutely true that some reports do reach print with important points left out. You can write or call the author (we are quite serious about that strategy), but, absent that assistance, you can take only whatever is intelligible without the missing part and leave the rest.

3. *Don't get stuck on* statistics, which by far are the greatest impediment to the novice in reading quantitative studies. There is a good rule of thumb to use with statistical analyses of data: If the technique is

unfamiliar, *look in the text and not in the table!* In any sound report, somewhere will be found a plain-language description of anything found in the analysis that really mattered (in the investigator's mind, at least). In many cases, that bit of text should allow you to proceed with intelligent reading—even if not with full appreciation of the elegance (or appropriateness) of the researcher's statistical analysis.

Where there are plain numbers reported (sometimes as raw data and sometimes as descriptive statistics, such as totals, averages, ranges, and frequencies), it is sometimes quite possible to puzzle out the logic of the analysis even without an understanding of the technicalities involved. Ready assistance is available in some excellent books about statistics that were written for nonstatisticians (several of these are listed in Appendix A; among them, we have found Dodge, 2003, and Pyrczak, 2001, to be particularly helpful for beginning students). Also, the data analysis chapter(s) of an introductory-level research text can often serve to get you past a stumbling block. If you are still stuck, however, after looking for raw numbers, searching out the author's plain-language description of important findings, and using whatever reference aids you have at hand, your only option is to use a time-honored convention—*skip over the statistics and keep on reading.*

Don't let skipping something like statistics panic you, and certainly do not let it make you feel guilty or inadequate. Statistics have a practical purpose, but they are not magical incantations that hold mysterious power. They are just tools.

Trust our reassurance here. The basic purpose of most statistical operations can be figured out with the help of a beginner-level textbook or the help of a friend or mentor. If you encounter any form of quantitative analysis that is more obscure than that, it can safely be skipped over in your reading. Perfect understanding of any analytic technique is rarely essential to finding what you want—good ideas and useful information.

4. *Don't get stuck on* the question, "Is this good research?" Of course, you want to learn how to make better judgments about the adequacy of the studies you read. A sure and unerring hand with that skill, however, is not easy to acquire. To be honest, it takes years of experience to quickly discern flaws of logic and imperfections of analysis in complicated investigation. You must trust the integrity of the journal in which the report appears (and the adequacy of its review procedures) and keep the proverbial grain of salt close at hand.

Fortunately, even the novice will be able to spot the difference between simple forms of sense and nonsense. When you do come upon something that seems improbable in terms of your own knowledge and experience, what do you do? Our advice is firm and simple. Make a note to yourself to look into the matter later, and keep right on reading. Good ideas turn up regularly in studies that contain obvious (and not so obvious) defects.

Torturing yourself with the question, "Is this good research?" will soon short-circuit your ability to attend closely to the author's explanations. Quality in research is always a matter of degree, and perfect studies are rare (it can be argued, as we did in Chapter 3, that they are impossible). Hold off making a summative judgment about the quality of the investigation until you have read the whole report. Formative judgments about particular procedures used, or specific assertions made, by the author are perfectly appropriate and useful observations—just do not let them hold you up.

Yes, there are studies in print that contain such egregious errors that they are not worth the effort of reading. It is our experience that such publications are so rare that they represent little serious risk to the novice reader. In any case, people with extensive experience in doing, writing, and reading research invariably come to believe that the distinction between good and bad research is not easily drawn. Our advice is to use your own common sense about commonsense points and to leave the technical arguments and grand judgments to the experts. Get on with the work of finding interesting or useful knowledge and ideas.

The Limits of Respect: Healthy Skepticism

To close this section, we want to offer another caution. There is a difference between respecting the author of a research report and believing everything you are told. First, researchers do make mistakes when writing up their studies (and you would be astonished to learn how often the processes of publication introduce errors for which the author is not responsible). Second, by their nature, reports are incomplete records, and selective history provides a rich opportunity for all kinds of errors (of omission and commission). Therefore, a little skepticism provides healthy protection against the mistakes that do reach print.

As you read, make it a habit to do a few simple checks. Add up important columns of numbers and see if your sum agrees with that of the author. Be sure you are using figures that truly go together (and beware of discrepancies due to rounding), but when problems persist, mark your marginal flag in red! Arithmetic errors are danger signals.

A number of simple error checks require little time to perform and yield confidence in the report. Is the full citation for an important quotation actually given in the reference list? Is every question that the author formally posed at the outset actually addressed and discussed? Does the size of the subject groups remain the same each time they are referenced in text or tables—and, if not, does the author explain why? If the author says there is a statistically significant difference between the test scores of two groups, look at the actual size of the numerical gap and ask yourself, "Is a performance difference of that size likely to be as important as he or she seems to think it is?" Finally, the irreverent question "So what?" is perfectly legitimate, and, in good reports, the author will raise the question for you. If he or she does not, you have the right to wonder why.

None of these small exercises in healthy skepticism requires the skills of rocket science, but what you can learn from them might be important and sometimes sobering. Careless researchers are often betrayed by their inattention to getting small things exactly right. Their credibility in your eyes must suffer accordingly. Where errors are few, finding them (and here we must be painfully honest) does give the novice a heady sense of power. It is innocent fun to catch the researcher occasionally off base in small details, and, we say, go right ahead and do it, if you can.

However, always keep in mind the honest limits of your ability to critique complex investigations. It is likely that there are many judgments you are not yet competent to make. You have no recourse except to have faith in the skills and integrity of the researcher and the journal. Doing so should not make you uneasy, because all of us have to accept the necessity of trusting the expertise of others—no less in research than in matters of medicine or law. We can assure you that in the vast majority of reports published in refereed journals, such confidence is not misplaced.

You can safely navigate the world of research without falling victim to serious deceptions as long as you maintain an attitude of respectful skepticism. The Romans said it in the Latin phrase *caveat emptor*—buyer beware! We say it in less elegant English—"be respectful but always a little cautious."

5

Staying Organized

Studying and Recording What You Read

This chapter is divided into four sections. Each of the initial three sections presents an instrument that can be used to organize your reading of a particular kind of research material. The first section deals with quantitative research reports, the second with qualitative reports, and the third with research reviews. The final section of this chapter presents a series of exercises designed to accelerate and reinforce your own learning by explaining research reports to others.

❖ READING AND RECORDING FROM QUANTITATIVE RESEARCH REPORTS

We know of no magic trick or intellectual gimmick that makes reading research reports an easy task for beginners. What we can offer, however, is a means for organizing the process that will reduce the initial confusion and, particularly, the tendency to become overwhelmed by the flood of details that appears in most reports.

In the process of mastering the skills needed to read research, the act of keeping a simple record of major points, in whatever order they appear in the report, seems to provide a reassuring sense that you are following the story. When that process also demands that you reduce those points to the essentials, using the least elaborate terms possible, your record also can become the perfect note card to support later recall and use.

Refined by years of use with novices of all kinds, the record form that appears on the following pages (Form 5.1) represents a work sheet for studying research reports. Some novices use it for the first few reports and then find the 12 steps so well retained that the paper-and-pencil supplement to their reading is no longer needed. Others use the form only when they want to keep a permanent record of what they find. Still others develop a revised record that better suits their needs. Finally, some use the original form on all occasions when they want to go beyond skimming to the work of closely studying (and recording) the contents of a report.

One point in our experience with learners, however, is a constant: Virtually all novices find that filling out the form is a useful support during the period when they are gradually building confidence in their ability to extract information and good ideas. Most people are not used to reading any kind of text that is so dense with details. Sorting through the thickets of information to identify essential points in the history of a study is the very first skill to be mastered, and the 12-step form is a handy and reliable guide for that process. Put simply, we urge you to *just do it* (at least until you are confident that you no longer need to do so)!

If you have access to a copy machine with enlarging capability, simply make as many prints of the first page (six steps) as you need (reducing all margins to the smallest possible size to provide maximum space for recording). Then, print the second page (six more steps) on the reverse side. You might find that the double-sided sheets are less cumbersome to use and file, although some students prefer the single-sided format because it avoids the necessity of form-flipping while recording. In either case, the restricted space for writing is what will encourage economy of expression in your record.

Of course, typing your own master form for subsequent copying has the advantage of allowing modifications that meet your own needs. Alternatively, you might wish to transfer the 12 steps to a recording system that is more convenient (e.g., file cards or a notebook computer). For most of you, however, it will be best to delay any such modifications until you have had some experience with the original form provided here.

Form 5.1   12 Steps to Understanding a Quantitative Research Report

Directions: Record notes in only enough detail to support recall in the absence of the original document. Except for Step 1, use abbreviations, diagrams, shorthand, and a careful selection of no more than what is absolutely essential to the study. Work on this sheet alone (except for Step 6), and do not be tempted to run onto additional pages.

1. **CITATION.** What study report is this? Record a complete reference citation.

2. **PURPOSE AND GENERAL RATIONALE.** In broad terms, what was the purpose of the study, and how did the author(s) make a case for its general importance?

3. **FIT AND SPECIFIC RATIONALE.** How does the topic of the study fit into the existing research literature, and how is that provenance used to make a specific case for the investigation?

4. **PARTICIPANTS.** Describe who was studied (give number and characteristics) and how they were selected.

5. **CONTEXT.** Where did the study take place? Describe important characteristics.

6. **STEPS IN SEQUENCE.** In the order performed, what were the main procedural steps in the study? Describe or diagram in a flowchart, showing order and any important relationships among the steps.

(Continued)

Form 5.1 (Continued)

---

7. **DATA.** What constituted data (e.g., test scores, questionnaire responses, frequency counts), how was it collected, and what was the role of the investigator(s) in that process?

8. **ANALYSIS.** What form of data analysis was used, and what specific questions was it designed to answer? What (if any) statistical operations and computer programs were employed?

9. **RESULTS.** What did the author(s) identify as the primary results (products or findings produced by the analysis of data)?

10. **CONCLUSIONS.** What did the author(s) assert about how the results in Step 9 responded to the purpose(s) established in Step 2, and how did the events and experiences of the entire study contribute to that conclusion?

11. **CAUTIONS.** What cautions does the author(s) raise about the study itself or about interpreting the results? Add here any of your own reservations.

12. **DISCUSSION.** What interesting facts or ideas did you learn from reading the report? Include here anything that was of value, including: results, research designs and methods, references, instruments, history, useful arguments, or personal inspiration.

We make no claim that the 12 steps included on our form cover all of the significant points in all possible kinds of reports. Most of what we ask you to record deals with essential information that commonly gets lost or jumbled when novices first begin to work their way through research reports. Several steps, however, were included for a different reason. We have found that making you pay attention to some purely routine things is good discipline—precisely because beginners too often are not inclined to do so. Recording a full reference citation, making a flowchart, and carefully noting your own response to a study, for example, fall in the category of routine good habits that will pay off down the line.

It is not necessary to fill out the steps in sequential order as you read. In fact, you will rarely find a study for which that is possible. At the least, you will be sketching in parts of the flowchart for Step 6 from the outset, and that step might not be completed to your satisfaction until all of the rest are finished.

A final word of advice here is the most important: When deciding what to write down in those small spaces on the form, *less is more!* The form is designed with the specific intent of *not* allowing you to record everything that might be relevant to the 12 questions. From the outset, we want you to practice the skill of determining what is vital to the study's history and what is simply an accessory to the story. In this case, do not sweat the details. You always can go back and add things later. If the 12-step form is to serve you well as you gain confidence in your ability to read, please do remember this point.

Because the instructions on the form are necessarily cryptic, we will now walk you through the items with some initial words of introduction, some advice, and some cautions. These, then, are the 12 steps to understanding a quantitative research report.

Doing the 12-Step

1. **CITATION.** *What study report is this? Record a complete reference citation.* "Why," you might ask, "make such fuss over recording a full reference citation, in formal academic form no less, if I am just practicing with a report?" Here, we have the advantage over you, although we will try not to be smug about it. *Everyone* (and this might be one of the few absolutes in the research business) who works with reports eventually finds that he or she needs a reference, immediately, and in

full—and that he or she failed to take the few seconds necessary to jot it down when the report was in his or her hands.

It is likely that you will be no exception to that particular version of Murphy's Law. Off you will go to the library on (invariably) a stormy night to get a page number that you could (and should) have written down. At the time, no doubt, you could not imagine why you would ever need such a trivial detail as a page number, but now you do.

Those of you who are feeling smug about all this because you have the luxury of a computer link to the library, beware of another variant on Murphy's famous dictum. "When you really need to check a citation at cyberspeed, (a) the server will be down, (b) your password mysteriously will have become invalid, or (c) your search will produce nothing that even remotely resembles what you have in your notes." Thus, filling out Step 1 is at least cheap insurance against having to hear us say, "We told you so!"

If you are a student (undergraduate or graduate), the need for full citations will be all too obvious. For beginners outside the academic world, however, it is more difficult to imagine occasions when a formal reference might be demanded. For that purpose, experience is the best teacher.

It has been our experience, for example, that after you begin accumulating research-based information, you will encounter a surprising number of situations when it will be handy (or essential) to answer the question "How do you know?" with something more satisfying than "I just do!" Among the occasions when knowing the correct reference for a report might be to your advantage are exchanges with professional colleagues, employers, reporters, unions, committees, or parent-teacher associations, or the preparation of reports, memoranda, and even letters to the editor.

You will discover quickly that it usually is more effective to say, "I found that information in xxxxx," rather than to use the more common vagaries such as, "research says . . . ," or "I read somewhere that . . . ." To play the showoff, or to try to overwhelm others with technical detail, is, of course, both bad form and poor social strategy. Moments come, however, when nothing serves like the facts in exact detail, and a report's full reference citation is the first fact to know if you want to make effective use of what it contains.

If you have a firm affiliation with a discipline or profession, it is well worth the time required to master at least the rudiments of the citation style used in journals serving that domain. If you do not have a particular professional or disciplinary commitment, the citation system developed by the American Psychological Association (APA) (2001) provides a reasonably clear and convenient format for recording references. Alternatively, you can fill in Step 1 by using the style employed in the report's reference list.

Whatever format you elect to use, be sure to take the time required to make a complete and accurate record. Doing so will allow you to avoid a long, damp trip to the library on that stormy night or yet another hour given to uttering maledictions at your computer and all forms of electronic retrieval.

2. PURPOSE AND GENERAL RATIONALE. In broad terms, what was the purpose of the study, and how did the author(s) make a case for its general importance? This item occupies more space on the 12-step form not only because studies sometimes have multiple purposes, but because precisely how the purpose of a study is framed, and exactly how the component question(s) is posed, provide the motive force that drives all else. In the end, the most sophisticated methods in the world cannot make a study any better than the quality of the question that is asked. It follows, then, that if you can understand the investigator's purpose, you have a good basis for understanding subsequent decisions about study design, as well as methods of data collection and analysis.

When there are multiple purposes, nested experiments, or long lists of questions based on multiple comparisons within a large body of data, you might have to reduce what is recorded to an exemplar that captures both form (how purposes or questions are posed) and typical content. Please do not be compulsive and attempt to squeeze everything into the small space on the record form. That is pointless and a waste of your time. You already have a comprehensive account in the text of the report. What the form requires is that you understand the purpose of the study well enough to write a brief and accurate extract in the space for Step 2. To do so, you need to read with care and attend to small details—not write the Declaration of Independence on the head of a pin.

You might encounter a report in which the author(s) did not specify one or several questions as part of their preplanned design (a research plan often takes the form of what is called a *proposal*). In such cases, there should be at least a general statement of what the study is about that you can record. The author(s) will have formulated more explicit questions as data were accumulated, which means that you will have to return and complete Step 2 after reading the entire report.

3. *FIT AND SPECIFIC RATIONALE. How does the topic of the study fit into the existing research literature, and how is that provenance used to make a specific case for the investigation?* Here, the first place to look is the introductory discussion and, particularly, the section that rationalizes the research question(s) and study design in terms of existing literature. Unhappily (we think), not all investigators write reports in a completely linear way, and you might find that the initial explanation of how the present work fits into what we already know is left incomplete. Almost invariably, this means that the topic will be addressed again in the "Discussion" section that closes the report. Because it might be difficult to follow such divided explanations of how a particular question is situated in a body of knowledge, you might have to delay completion of Step 3 until after reading the entire report.

Among the things to look for in the report are references to previous studies that called for *replication* (as mentioned in Chapter 3, this term means repeating studies with new populations or with deliberate variations in methodology). The study at hand might have as its purpose the confirmation of an earlier finding through replication. Look also for an indication that some item of research-based knowledge remains incomplete, that a theory is in need of empirical testing, or for the assertion that there is a need in some area of professional application. Any (or several) of these might provide clues about the provenance of the research question within the existing literature.

The researcher believed that doing a study would produce something new, something that advanced knowledge or improved our world (or, quite frequently, both), or that would serve simply to scratch a personal itch. That reason lies in the relationship between what we already know, or can do, and what he or she proposed to discover. Your job here is to find that link and to describe it in a brief paraphrase. Do not attempt a miniature review of the literature here—just focus on what the study will add.

4. *PARTICIPANTS. Describe who was studied (give number and characteristics) and how they were selected.* When research is directed at objects or environments, descriptions of the relevant characteristics usually are straightforward (and easy to find in the report). When people are the target, however, what is relevant among their many characteristics may

be less obvious at the outset. Among the factors that commonly do matter in designing a study are number, age, gender, training or experience, intelligence or special abilities, social status, health, physical characteristics, family background, or affiliation with membership groups.

Here, you can record simply what the author(s) treats as important in selecting who or what to study. You can add detail as the study unfolds and your understanding improves concerning which characteristics truly matter.

5. *CONTEXT. Where did the study take place? Describe important characteristics.* The importance of the study context varies substantially, ranging from relatively inconsequential to critical. For the most part, the nature of the environment (physical or social) exerts its influence through conditions that exist where data are collected. A pleasant, air-conditioned, soundproofed testing room or laboratory space is a far different environment than a third-grade classroom three minutes before the bell rings for the end of the day on Halloween.

All sorts of contextual factors can influence the quality of data collected. For example, performing any physical task in the presence of peer observers takes on an entirely different meaning than when executed in solitude. The potential for environmental contamination of data extends to the entire data record, not just to test results or other empirical measures. Participants might not even provide the same basic demographic information ("What is your age?") or facts of personal history ("How often do you eat candy?") when answering the investigator's preliminary questions in their own home, in a university laboratory, at a community recreation center, or on a park bench.

In most reports, it is unlikely that the author(s) will offer a complete description of all potentially relevant aspects of the study context (restricted journal space demands such economy), but you can at least look for clues indicating that context was a matter of thoughtful concern—and perhaps the target of some efforts at control.

6. *STEPS IN SEQUENCE. In the order performed, what were the main procedural steps in the study? Describe or diagram in a flowchart, showing order and any important relationships among the steps.* Although we always urge our own students to limit their first efforts to the small space provided on the form, this is the one item for which a separate sheet might be required. If your 12-step form is printed on two sheets, it might be convenient to use a reverse side. Not only is more space sometimes

required to maintain legibility, but false starts and experiments with alternative ways of laying out the diagram might consume space before you are satisfied with how you have mapped the history given in the report. We have already provided some rationale for using this step as part of the report-reading process, as well as some explanation of the mechanics involved in making a flowchart (see Chapter 4). Further examples can be found in Appendix B.

Describe what seem to be the most important things the investigator did in design, method, and analysis. To just list the headings from a report (Purpose, Research Question, Method, Data, Analysis, Results, Conclusions) is too general to be useful, but to duplicate all the specifics contained in Steps 1 through 5 and 7 through 10 is simply wasteful repetition. A flowchart is intended to deal with only the sequence of major methodological and analytical operations, not with the substance of questions, data, or discussion.

Imagine that, a year from now, you want to be able to glance at Step 6 and have it guide an accurate recall of the general nature of the study. Such a guide should function like a good road map, laying out a clear route from start to finish. A map that is cluttered with too many details often serves to hide the very thing it is designed to capture—how to get somewhere (or, in this case, how the researcher got somewhere). Start simple, adding information only as your comprehension allows you to identify truly important landmarks.

7. **DATA.** *What constituted data (e.g., test scores, questionnaire responses, frequency counts), how was it collected, and what was the role of the investigator(s) in that process?* For beginners, this is the most deceptive step. It appears simple but requires that you make some often subtle distinctions among all the details in a report.

Whatever operations were performed for the purpose of gathering information about people or objects of interest in the study, some trace of what was detected must have been captured and recorded. A single unit of that trace is called a datum, and all of the traces together constitute the study's data. Please note, the word *data* is the plural form, as in "All of the data are . . . ." This usage is not consistently observed by all authors, but it does remain technically correct.

To illustrate, a standardized mathematics achievement test allows us to observe how a student responds to the question "$12 \times 12 = ?$" The answer will be scored as right or wrong, and that indicator will influence the overall score, which sums up performance over a set of such questions. That summed test score, in turn, will be one bit of datum in a study, and the test scores of all students who participated will then be the data (sometimes referred to as the *data set* or *database*) for the study.

The same logic applies to responses on a questionnaire, the transcript of an interview, the count of foul shots made by a basketball team during the season, the amount of cholesterol in a sample of blood, the time taken by a 60-year-old female to respond to a buzzer, or the salaries of social workers in cities with populations of more than 100,000. All are data, the recorded traces of what the investigator could see, hear, taste, touch, or smell—the processes of empirical observation (scientists generally do not restrict the meaning of the word *observation* simply to seeing, as is the case in ordinary usage).

As recorded, these traces would be called *raw data*, meaning words, numbers, or graphics that have not yet been transformed by any subsequent process (for convenient storage or as a step in analysis). Raw data must often be grouped, summed, refined, and sometimes translated in form (as in typing a transcript from a tape-recorded interview) before they can be inspected for how they reflect on a research question.

To fill in this step, you need to puzzle out what constituted data for the study. That requires you to distinguish the nature of the data from the means of observation, recording, and analysis. Do not attempt to record actual data, just describe what form (or forms) it took. After a bit of practice, this will become a simple task.

Finally, make it a practice to notice the part played by the researcher(s) in the process of collecting data. Sometimes they are merely managers of the process, maintaining a distance from their data sources and allowing intermediaries to perform the actual collection tasks. In other instances, they have a far more intimate relationship with both the participants and the collection process—even to the extent of actually being the instrument by which data are recorded, as in the case of taking notes when interviewing a subject. Keep in mind that the position of the researcher might matter. For example, when the investigator is removed from data collection, you must always ask, "How thoroughly can he or she monitor the degree to which the intermediary (a research assistant, for example) observes the protocol for acquiring data?" In the other direction, when researchers record their own data, you should always ask, "How confident am I that in the recording process the researcher did not (or could not) allow personal expectations to influence what he or she saw—or wrote down?"

8. ANALYSIS. What form of data analysis was used, and what specific questions was it designed to answer? What (if any) statistical operations and computer programs were employed? Some data speak for themselves and require little processing to provide an answer to the research question. For example, consider an experimental study of two methods used to maintain patients' compliance with a regimen of prescribed medication. If all 30 patients in Group A have the desired level of medication in blood drawn during the study, and all 30 patients in Group B have circulating levels below the criterion, it is unlikely that any further processing of the data is required to demonstrate that A works (very well) and B does not. (Of course, questions having to do with why this is the case would require analysis of other data, such as self-medication records or interview transcripts.)

Most data, however, must undergo some kind of manipulation to clarify what they might mean. The process of manipulating and inspecting data is called *analysis*. For example, one tool for the analysis of data, *descriptive statistics,* allows us to determine what is typical for a group of scores, and another analytic tool, *mean difference statistics,* permits us to determine (given certain assumptions) how likely it is that what is typical performance for one group truly is different from what is typical for another group.

To illustrate, in a study that employed both methods of analysis, we might take the raw scores of individuals, sum them, and then divide by the number of cases. That, as you probably know, would produce a single number called the average (in technical language, the *mean* of scores in the data set), a descriptive statistic.

In turn, a further analysis using a mean difference statistic could process the data by using the means (and other products of descriptive analysis) to examine the difference between the scores of the two groups. That examination would answer the question, "How probable is it that a difference of that size, between groups like those, could happen just by accident?" If such a chance event was very unlikely, we might be willing to assume that the difference truly was caused by whatever factor we were studying.

As you can see from that illustration, statistical analysis is a handy tool for helping the researcher understand what raw numerical data mean. Some kinds of statistics do involve higher mathematics and use of probability theory. In the end, however, if you understand the general purpose of a statistic, no matter how complex its operation, you know enough to comprehend the story laid out in the report.

The statistical manipulations of the data constitute the analysis, whereas the outcomes of the manipulations are the findings of a study. When the findings are used to respond to research questions, the author(s) formulates answers to the original inquiry—the purpose of the study. Those answers are often set forth as *conclusions* in the report (see Step 10 of this 12-step process).

Not all data are numerical, of course, and that point is addressed in Chapters 6 and 8 (in which attention is given to qualitative research). Whatever form they take, however, data must confront the same demands: they must be recorded accurately, organized efficiently, and analyzed carefully.

To illustrate that commonality, let us leave quantitative research for a moment and look at an example that deals with qualitative research. Consider a study in which 100 pages of type transcribed from audio-tapes of 10 focus group meetings are the raw data. How do you find out what those data mean if the original research question was "Why do working women plan to vote for our candidate in the coming election?" If you want to obtain an answer that reliably reflects the opinions of the people interviewed, the 100 pages of raw data have to be reduced for efficient handling and then analyzed.

The first step might be to identify all instances of expression of beliefs relevant to the question. A second step would then be to develop some form of category system to sort those expressions into clusters of similar belief. The third step would be to inspect the content of all the categories very closely to determine exactly what rule is operating to include or exclude beliefs from each. With that clarification, categories could then be refined by merging some and dividing others. Finally, if some of the categories contain contributions from most or all of the participants, the words from several quotations within each might be woven together to create descriptions of "typical reasons given by employed women who plan to vote for the candidate."

That is just one of the many kinds of analysis that might be used to process qualitative data in the form of text. Likewise, there are literally hundreds of formats for statistical analysis of numerical data in quantitative studies. For Step 8 on this form, the task is to identify what the report says the author(s) did to process and analyze the data (a single operation or a series of steps).

At first, you might be recording names for operations that you do not fully understand. Do not let that bother you. With practice, you will begin to recognize what different kinds of analysis are intended to accomplish, even if the details of their calculation remain beyond your comprehension. As a beginning step, try to identify what the analysis is called (as a procedure) and, in broad terms, what purpose it appears to serve.

9. *RESULTS. What did the author(s) identify as the primary results (products or findings produced by the analysis of data)?* The results are the findings from the analysis of data. If you asked the question "Do people who drink coffee run faster than those who do not?", and a study of imbibers and abstainers shows that the former run the 100-meter dash an average of 2 seconds faster than the latter, you have a result from your analysis and, within the limits of your study design, an answer to your question. There might be (and probably are) many reasons why it could be an incorrect answer, but that is another story for another book. Results are what you get when the observations have been made and the data analyzed.

As you will see in the next step, for the purpose of the 12-step form, you should not regard results and conclusions as the same thing (even though they are inseparably related). The results are findings bare of any comment, elaboration, caution, or tie to the structure of existing knowledge. They are, quite simply, what the data say about the question. Nothing more, and nothing less. If the result is a simple one, a yes or no, or a few numbers, search it out and write it down in the space provided. If there are results from several different analyses, or if the findings require long description, write down a summary generalization and go on to the next step. The idea here is to confirm that you know what the results look like and where they can be found in the report.

10. *CONCLUSIONS. What did the author(s) assert about how the results in Step 9 responded to the purpose(s) established in Step 2, and how did the events and experiences of the entire study contribute to that conclusion?* A conclusion is a distinctly human product. It is not the output of some mechanical operation, such as data analysis. A computer can generate a result, but only a researcher can reach a conclusion. As an investigator, the researcher considers all that has happened, forms conclusions about what he or she believes has been learned, and attempts to communicate them to readers.

At the point of writing about conclusions, the results from data analysis (the findings) are the central source of testimony, but they are not the only resource at the disposal of the author(s). The entire process of inquiry, from formulating the question through the last steps of data analysis, is part of the total experience from which the researcher can learn.

In that sense, the scholarship of discovery is best understood as a process rather than an outcome. Results are the necessary foundation for what is concluded, but, taken alone and without the context of the whole journey of discovery, they frequently are insufficient as a source of new knowledge.

Research-based knowledge, whether in the form of laws, theories, facts, information, or informed speculation, is always situated in a context. The products of research are human understandings that are specific to a particular time, place, set of operations, display of results, and, ultimately, view of the world. *Knowledge does not exist in a vacuum.*

In articulating conclusions—the act of asserting what has been learned—the author(s) steps back from the immediate detail of data and the analysis to reflect on what they mean within the larger context. This need have nothing to do with grand and sweeping generalizations. Most often, it involves returning to the author's (or authors') sense of what is already known to ask: "How does this fit in? What small change might it make in how we understand ourselves or the world?"

Also, in forging conclusions, the author(s) is obliged to consider what has been learned by the *entire* experience of doing the study, not just the results that came out of the data analysis. In so doing, the researcher situates the results in the full historical context of the study.

As a consequence of thinking about results in those wider contexts, if there is a section in the report identified as "Conclusions" or "Discussion," the author(s) might do more than simply assert that the finding answers the research question. If conclusions involve what the author(s) now thinks about the original question, the methods selected for doing the study, and everything the data have to teach, there often is a great deal more to discuss.

Some authors, for example, begin their final appraisal of what was learned by reminding the reader of the limitations imposed by the nature of the study. In some cases, their first conclusion is that the study should be replicated (i.e., be repeated by another investigator using the same methods to produce a new data set). Accordingly, when conclusions are stated, they will be posed in tentative phrasing and made contingent on confirmation through further evidence. In reports, it is also not uncommon to find experienced researchers describing rival hypotheses that might account for what was observed, in ways that are different from the accounting they have offered in the report.

What all of this elaboration indicates is that researchers normally are very cautious about drawing conclusions, and with good reason. Conducting a study is likely to teach any investigator just how complicated the world really is and why data rarely tell a simple, univocal story.

With that in mind, your task here is to search the final sections of the report for the author's (or authors') most general statement of what was learned. On occasion, it takes the form of a personal statement revealing how the investigator now situates the findings in the context of existing knowledge. If the study puts knowledge even a small and uncertain step ahead of where it was at the outset, that assessment should be there, whether formally labeled as a conclusion or not.

Lest you be frustrated by the absence of a clearly stated conclusion about how the findings respond to the research question, we remind you, again, that there might be other important things that can be concluded at the end of a study. Among the most common of these are reappraisal of how the research question was asked, discovery that the machinery of the study did not work as predicted, or the realization that the data simply did not yield results that were sufficiently decisive to allow any reliable conclusion about what they mean. Offered as well-supported, thoughtful observations, those too are conclusions and should not be ignored in your brief summary for Step 10.

11. CAUTIONS. What cautions does the author(s) raise about the study itself or about interpreting the results? Add here any of our own reservations. The cautions of the author(s) are usually easy to find. If the work has been well executed, and if the conclusions are supported by the data in unambiguous ways, researchers feel no obligation for excessive modesty; they say what they think has been achieved. A conservative view about what constitutes reliable knowledge, however, is the hallmark of an experienced scholar. By sharing their reservations in the report, researchers honor the long tradition of careful science.

Even in the reports of novice investigators, it is not uncommon to find explanations of why the conclusions should be held as tentative or contingent on further study. In many cases, the reason for such reservations lies not in the discovery of some technical flaw in methodology but in concern about how well the results might *generalize* (be applicable) to members of a wider population. If, for example, the targets of observation in the study were different in important ways from those with whom many of the readers will be concerned, that is a serious limitation.

What reservations do you have about the design and execution of the study and the assertions made by the author(s)? To think about such problems does not constitute an attack on the study (or the author[s]); it is a way of joining in the conversation about scholarship. That long and lively dialogue is always critical, cautious, and even skeptical. Active researchers know the rules of that conversation, and, by publishing accounts of their studies, they are explicitly inviting you to join in the thoughtful assessment of what can and cannot be learned from their efforts. It is your responsibility as the reader to be respectfully skeptical—and Step 11 is the place to exercise that duty.

12. *DISCUSSION. What interesting facts or ideas did you learn from reading the report? Include here anything that was of value, including: results, research designs and methods, references, instruments, history, useful arguments, or personal inspiration.* This is personal space in which there are no right or wrong responses. Anything goes here, and we can attest that people learn (and value) the most amazing things from reading research reports. Step 12 provides constant testimony to the diversity of what people bring to the role of research consumer. Your own experience, values, concerns, and personal history determine what is written in this space.

Over the years, our students have used this last step to confirm that research yields much more than dry facts. New names for familiar things, useful constructs, unexpected connections between ideas, good references for other purposes, artful ways to draw graphs, confirmation of long-held hunches, elegant exercises in logic, and entertaining discourse about how things work are among the discoveries. Sometimes the treasures located are more distinctly personal, as in finding weapons for arguing with significant others, encouragement to try a new course of action in professional practice, and, of course (always popular among students), evidence that smart people like researchers can do really dumb things and not appear to realize it! All of these valuables and more are among the gems that people retrieve from reading research reports. We hope that in Step 12 you further add to the zesty disarray of this collection by discovering interesting information and good ideas. More particularly, we hope you find valuable things that never could have been anticipated by the authors of your studies—or by us.

❖ READING AND RECORDING FROM
     QUALITATIVE RESEARCH REPORTS

It would have been possible to prepare study and reading guides for different kinds of research. For example, we could have designed forms that specifically reflected the characteristics of an experiment, a mail survey, or even a research review employing meta-analysis. We have not done so for two simple reasons. First, such proliferation of forms (and the needed guidance for their use) would unreasonably lengthen this text. Second, such close attention to the technical differences among forms of inquiry would have undercut one of our most important messages for novice readers of research—*mastering what is common among different research strategies is more fundamental (and vastly more empowering for the novice) than learning what is unique.*

Despite these concerns, we have made one exception to our decision to limit attention to what is generic in research. We think that qualitative research reports demand special attention in this guide for four simple and, to us, persuasive reasons. First, although there are many kinds of quantitative research (in this context, they are often collectively called *positivist* research to reflect their common philosophic roots), they do indeed share important elements—the ones used to construct the 12-step form presented in the previous section. Qualitative research, however, starts with different philosophic assumptions. Although some of the items in our quantitative guide would work perfectly well despite those differences, others would not. More important, we think that the use of a generic 12-step form might mislead you, making it more difficult to understand the important distinctions between the two research traditions.

Second, because qualitative research is relatively new as a way of thinking about inquiry, the tasks of reading and understanding qualitative research reports are often as unfamiliar to research teachers, advisors, textbook authors, and scholars as they are to the beginning readers who constitute the primary audience for this book. To the extent that teachers and advisors might wish to adopt this text for use, it makes good sense for us to share material that has helped students in our own classes venture into this vast and sometimes puzzling research domain.

Third, we expect that some of you are using this text to engage in do-it-yourself education about research. Within some obvious limits, we think that is both a reasonable undertaking and a laudable ambition, and we want to support your efforts. What follows, then, is also intended to be a supplement to a good introductory textbook on qualitative research (see Appendix A for suggested titles) when it is used outside the supportive environment of a formal research class.

Fourth, and finally, unlike most of the reports and reviews that recount studies based on the assumptions of quantitative science, the text of reports based on a qualitative view of the world tend (at first encounter) to seem remarkably accessible—more like good storytelling or journalism. Such relatively easy reading, being more the rule than the exception in qualitative reports, makes it difficult to remember that, as the reader, you must bring clear expectations about what should be in the report. Put another way, it is difficult to know how to exercise the "respectful skepticism" we have recommended in the face of what often seems comfortably familiar or even self-evident.

For that reason, in Chapter 8 we give close attention to the problem of how to read qualitative research reports with a critical eye. Here, however, we can begin that process by helping you understand some basic distinctions between quantitative and qualitative approaches to inquiry and by identifying the elements most commonly encountered in a qualitative report.

Identifying Qualitative Research Reports

Qualitative research includes a large family of loosely related inquiry traditions rooted in both the social sciences (anthropology, sociology, psychology) and the liberal arts (philosophy, history, literature). Each approach differs from the others in terms of such factors as the role of the investigator, the phenomenon studied, and the means of analysis employed. The members of the qualitative family are united at a deeper level, however, by a shared view of the nature of the social world that distinguishes them from conceptions of social research that have been shaped by conventional forms of natural science.

The unique qualitative vantage point on the nature of social reality is described in Chapter 6 as part of the discussion of different types of research. At this point, however, you need a simple, quick, and reasonably reliable way to distinguish between reports of quantitative research and reports of studies that fall within the qualitative rubric. Here are some rules of thumb that help in making that identification. Because of the complexity (and general untidiness) that characterizes social research, as well as the considerable overlap between the two paradigms for inquiry, the rules come with no guarantee for unerring accuracy. A rule of thumb allows you to be right—most of the time.

Rule 1. If the author(s) says the study is qualitative, it probably is. Such a characterization should appear in the title, the abstract, or somewhere in the introductory section of the report. If the study or the methodology is called qualitative, you can be fairly certain that it is. Quantitative researchers, of course, rarely identify their work as quantitative in nature; because that is the dominant paradigm for reports in most journals, the study simply is assumed to be quantitative unless otherwise specified.

The problem with the simplicity of Rule 1 is that the specific label for a particular subspecies of qualitative research might be employed in the report—with the more inclusive term, *qualitative,* being omitted entirely. When you encounter that circumstance, it is handy to have some familiarity with the names assigned to (or commonly associated with) alternative research traditions in the qualitative domain. A list of such labels is found in Exhibit 5.1. Although the listing is far from exhaustive (and new types of qualitative research continue to appear), if the author(s) of a report uses any of these terms to characterize the study, their own perspective as the investigator, the methodology used, or the form of analysis employed, you can be reasonably confident that you should use 12 Steps to Understanding a Qualitative Research Report (see page 100).

Please do not be distressed by the fact that you might have no idea what the words in Exhibit 5.1 mean or what sort of research each label denotes. In Chapter 6, we describe and illustrate several of the qualitative research traditions and indicate where you can find concise definitions of the remainder. You can be assured that all of the terms in Exhibit 5.1 indicate studies or study components that belong under the qualitative umbrella. For the moment, all we want to accomplish is for you to make that simple dichotomous identification—determining that a report is either quantitative or qualitative.

Rule 2. If the results are reported primarily or exclusively in terms of statistical analyses of numerical data, the study probably is quantitative; if the results are reported primarily or exclusively in terms of words, it is a safe bet that the report is of qualitative research. Of course, numbers are sometimes cited in reports of qualitative research, and investigators sometimes use interviews and record the words of their participants when engaged in

Exhibit 5.1   Labels and Descriptors for Identifying Qualitative Research
                    Reports*

- Interpretive
- Critical
- Phenomenological
- Ethnographic
- Participant observation
- Unobtrusive observation
- Fieldwork
- Naturalistic
- Cultural study
- Ecological analysis
- Feminist
- Marxist
- Hermeneutic
- Narrative analysis
- Life history
- Symbolic interactionist
- Foucauldian
- Emancipatory
- Postpositivist
- Postmodern
- Constructivist
- Deconstructivist
- Constant comparative
- Grounded theory

*Note: Some of the terms represent major research traditions, others indicate philosophic perspectives, and yet others are terms associated with particular forms of data collection or analysis.

quantitative research. The operative distinction here is "primarily or exclusively." Rule 2 really deals with alternative ways of thinking about the world, not with whether some numbers or words appear as data in the report.

Rule 3. If the author(s) reports drawing a random (or otherwise "representative") sample of participants for the study, and then writes conclusions as though what is true of the participants probably is true of the population from which they were drawn, you almost certainly have a quantitative study. For the most part, researchers in the qualitative tradition focus on the participants in the study and leave inferences about other people to the reader. Accordingly, it is unusual for any form of random sampling to be used in a qualitative study. A related characteristic is that studies with very large numbers of participants (more than 50) are likely to be quantitative. Smaller sample sizes can be employed in either type of study.

Rule 4. If the investigator shows much concern about being aware of and carefully managing his or her own subjectivity (e.g., beliefs, values, perspectives, biases, past experiences), the study is probably qualitative. If the investigator reports procedures that are designed to ensure his or her objectivity (complete separation from participants or, at the least, tight control over opportunities to influence data or the results of analyses), the study probably is quantitative. In qualitative research, the investigator is often the actual instrument for data collection and analysis (and in doing so might be required to have prolonged, intimate, and sometimes serendipitous association with participants); therefore, awareness of what she or he brings to the study is a matter of central importance. For quantitative researchers, the control exerted by both adherence to tight and prescriptive protocols (scripted routines and procedures) and the use of unambiguous numeric data (the product of precise measurement) make it highly unlikely that the author(s) will feel any need to deal with details of personal subjectivity as part of the study report.

Rule 5. If the report uses data primarily or exclusively to describe how the participants understand what is happening in a social setting, it is probably a qualitative study. If data are used primarily or exclusively to construct an external understanding (usually the investigator's) of what is happening in a social setting, it is probably a quantitative study. The origins of this distinction are complex, but, put in simple terms: Qualitative researchers think of reality as a subjective entity that exists only in people's minds. For the quantitative investigator, reality exists as a phenomenon "out there," something quite distinct from the subjective states (beliefs or understandings) of participants. The quantitative view holds that with proper scientific methods, reality can be directly observed or experienced as a value-free fact. Thus, invisible entities such as minds, meanings, and understandings are not a common focus for quantitative social science.

You might encounter reports of studies that purport to combine qualitative and quantitative research traditions. In some instances, these studies employ a method of data collection that is commonly associated with qualitative research (e.g., interviewing or field observations) *without* also adopting the fundamental assumptions of qualitative inquiry. The qualitative data so produced are then used as adjuncts or supplements to a primarily quantitative data set. Such studies should be regarded as quantitative in nature and read as such.

In other instances of mixed research traditions, the investigator genuinely has tried to incorporate both qualitative and quantitative vantage points for framing the study—either simultaneously or in alternation. Such complex research designs remain the subject of considerable debate among scholars and might better be put aside until you have become familiar with the two traditions, taken one at a time. If, however, you really are anxious to know more about what are commonly called *mixed methodologies,* look ahead to Chapter 6 and Appendix A, where we have described some useful references that focus on those designs for inquiry.

What follows here is a guide designed to focus the beginner's attention on the elements that make qualitative research, research! It might begin with assumptions that are different from those accepted in conventional quantitative research, but it has the hallmarks of system, rigor, and integrity.

If you are not already taking a research course, we hope that you will seek the opportunity to learn more about qualitative research, either by taking an introductory course or by reading any of the basic texts recommended in Appendix A. (Our textbook, *Proposals That Work,* 2000, contains several sections that you might find helpful as starting places.) Until you take one or both of these courses of action, however, the following reading guide and brief instructions should suffice to open the door to this fascinating and potentially useful kind of research.

A 12-Step Guide for Understanding Qualitative Research Reports

As with the other guides for reading, it is vital that you stay flexible about the use of this tool (Form 5.2), both as a map for navigating through the report and as a recording form. Elements presumed by some of the questions simply might not be present in a particular report, or what we have suggested as a secondary concern might be foregrounded as a major aspect of the study. Again, the advice is, "Do

Form 5.2   12 Steps to Understanding a Qualitative Research Report

Directions: Record notes in only enough detail to support recall in the absence of the original document. Except for Step 1, use abbreviations, diagrams, shorthand, and a careful selection of no more than what is absolutely essential to the study. Work on this sheet alone (except for Step 6), and do not be tempted to run onto additional pages.

1. **CITATION.** What study report is this? Record a complete reference citation.

2. **PURPOSE AND GENERAL RATIONALE.** In broad terms, what was the purpose of the study, and how did the author(s) make a case for its general importance?

3. **FIT AND SPECIFIC RATIONALE.** How does the topic of the study fit into the existing research literature, and how is that provenance used to make a specific case for doing the investigation?

4. **PARTICIPANTS.** Who was the author(s) (important characteristics only), and how was he or she related to the purpose, participants, and study site? Describe who was studied (give number and characteristics) and how they were selected.

5. **CONTEXT.** Where did the study take place? Describe important characteristics.

6. **STEPS IN SEQUENCE.** In the order performed, what were the main procedural steps in the study? Describe or diagram in a flowchart, showing order, time required, and any important relationships among the steps.

7. **DATA.** What constituted data (e.g., field notes, interview transcripts, photographs, diaries), how was it collected, and what was the role of the investigator(s) in that process?

8. **ANALYSIS.** What form of data analysis was used, and what was it designed to reveal? What computer program was used (if any)?

9. **RESULTS.** What did the author(s) identify as the primary results (products or findings produced by the analysis of data)? In general, "What was going on there?"

(Continued)

Form 5.2 (Continued)

10. **CONCLUSIONS.** What did the author(s) assert about how the results in Step 9 responded to the purpose(s) established in Step 2, and how did the events and experiences of the entire study contribute to that conclusion?

11. **CAUTIONS.** What cautions does the author(s) raise about the study itself or about interpreting the results? Add here any of your own reservations, particularly those related to methods used to enhance credibility (trustworthiness and believability).

12. **DISCUSSION.** What interesting facts or ideas did you learn from reading the report? Include here anything that was of value, including: results, research designs and methods, references, instruments, history, useful arguments, or personal inspiration.

not panic!" Use the steps that work, flag those that do not seem to apply, and seek out explanations at a later time.

Finally, please remember that this form was designed for the beginning reader. The purpose is to provide structure while studying the report. The form requires attention to what could (and should) be noticed by any intelligent layperson and is not intended as a list of all of the key elements in a qualitative study. Such a comprehensive document can be imagined, but it would not serve the present purpose of giving guidance (and a convenient recording device) for entry-level reading.

1. *CITATION. What study report is this? Record a complete reference citation.* Our argument for the necessity of this first step was already made in the section dealing with the quantitative 12-step form. Just do it!

2. *PURPOSE AND GENERAL RATIONALE. In broad terms, what was the purpose of the study, and how did the author(s) make a case for its general importance?* When reading qualitative research reports, this question is more likely to be answered in a manner that is discursive and informal than is the case with the terse and explicit announcements of purpose found in reports of quantitative studies. In addition, the range of explanations will be wider, sometimes including highly personal motivations that might be discussed quite frankly. In some cases, the study's purpose is defined in one or several explicit research questions. More often, however, the researcher identifies only the context within which interactions are of interest, and particular questions are defined subsequently through ongoing collection and analysis of the data.

Although the deductive purpose of theory testing certainly can be pursued with qualitative means, it is the exception rather than the rule. Typically, in qualitative studies, hypotheses or theoretical explanations are inductively developed from examination of the data. Arguments for the importance of a study often flow from this latter point. If you can discern how participants understand what is going on, you have leverage for developing some sense of the regularities that are involved in a social setting. That might lead to useful explanations for why things happen as they do.

3. *FIT AND SPECIFIC RATIONALE. How does the topic of the study fit into the existing research literature, and how is that provenance used to make a specific case for doing the investigation?* Aside from the fact that the

absolute size of the literature base of qualitative studies is likely to be relatively small for any research topic, most of our suggestions for what to consider here were already made in the previous discussion of Step 3 on the 12-step quantitative form.

4. *PARTICIPANTS. Who was the author(s) (important characteristics only), and how was he or she related to the purpose, participants, and study site? Describe who was studied (give number and characteristics) and how they were selected.* Given our previous discussion about the centrality of the investigator's subjectivity in qualitative research, it will not surprise readers to find that when describing participants in the study, the investigator is included.

Qualitative research is unlike other forms of inquiry, where credibility rests on correct execution of method, allowing the researcher to remain largely invisible in the reporting process (hence, the almost universal use of the impersonal third person in writing reports of quantitative studies). Careful reporting of procedures for gathering and analyzing data *are* important in establishing credibility in qualitative research, but, because the researcher is often the only research tool involved (with no apparatus for measurement and no statistic for analysis), who he or she is and what he or she brings to the investigation matter a great deal. The form provides some suggestions about what might be relevant, but reading the report will surely suggest others.

In some cases, investigators write little about themselves because their background and beliefs are well established by reputation. In other cases, the author(s) simply tells you nothing about him- or herself. In such reports, you have to draw your own conclusions about credibility based entirely on how carefully the study has been conducted. Whether you find that sufficient or not must be your decision. When there is nothing to enter at Step 4, that can be a tough call.

In recording information about the people selected for participation in the study, the task should be more straightforward. The people who participate in the study (usually, although not invariably, as conscious and willing collaborators with the investigator) are central points of interest in qualitative research. The substitution of the word *participant* for the usual designation of *subject* (until recently, it was a virtually universal practice to use the term *subject* in writing quantitative reports) is more than a mere change in the conventions—it reflects a difference in attitude toward the people who cooperate in the study. Referring to them as participants is intended to invest them with more importance as individual human actors than is the case when they are regarded as passive objects of study. That distinction might not always be honored in the practice of qualitative research, but you will appreciate its intended significance much better after reading a number of reports.

At this beginning stage, just be sure you know exactly who is participating in the study because, whatever else might be true, qualitative research reports are intensely and centrally about particular people. If you need more information to complete your response at this step, the advice given for Step 4 on the quantitative form should provide sufficient direction.

5. **CONTEXT.** *Where did the study take place? Describe important characteristics.* Not all qualitative studies take place in a specific context that is crucial to the investigation. For example, neither interview studies nor studies based on documents such as diaries have a locale for data collection that is particularly significant. Even those, however, involve constructing a picture of what is or was going on at some time and in some place. Because context is central in most qualitative research (for reasons that are too complex to address here), what you write in this space truly is important. It will become even more so as you grow in your ability to read these studies with sophistication.

6. **STEPS IN SEQUENCE.** *In the order performed, what were the main procedural steps in the study? Describe or diagram in a flowchart showing order, time required, and any important relationships among the steps.* Your task here is likely to be much less complex than the mapping of an experiment or other quantitative study. In most cases, the major steps of gathering data and subsequent analysis are named in straightforward descriptive prose (the technical detail within those operations, of course, might be substantial and arcane, but none of that need be recorded here). Just follow the rule that your explanatory sketch should be such that, a year later, it could help you recall the general nature of the study and how it was performed.

7. **DATA.** *What constituted data (e.g., field notes, interview transcripts, photographs, diaries), how was it collected, and what was the role of the investigator(s) in that process?* Again, most qualitative reports provide this information in a straightforward fashion. You might also find it helpful to note here any procedures for transforming and managing the data.

This suggestion has particular importance in many studies because qualitative research is characterized by enormous volumes of data and sometimes difficult problems of data management.

The question of the investigator's perceived role when collecting the data can be more important than you might expect. This question applies principally to investigations that involve collecting data at a natural site in the field. Even when interviews at a completely neutral location are employed, however, there remains the question of how the investigator presents him- or herself to the participant (as collaborator, disinterested scientist, sympathetic listener, and so on).

When data are collected through entry into the context of the participant's world, the researcher might be a strictly nonparticipating observer or might elect to engage fully (or selectively) in the activities that are characteristic of the site. Each of these roles influences not only how the participants regard the investigator but what they are likely to reveal about their own perception of the context. Knowing the role assumed by the author(s) during data collection allows the reader to frame what is reported in the kind of social relationship that existed— a factor which we always make mental note of when stories are told.

It is common in qualitative reports to describe the role of the investigator in some detail, although cryptic designations such as *nonparticipant observer, unobtrusive participant,* and *nondirective interviewer* are not always defined the same way. Do the best you can with the information provided, and remember that it is how the study participants think of the investigator that defines his or her role.

8. ANALYSIS. What form of data analysis was used, and what was it designed to reveal? What computer program was used (if any)? If you are a true beginner, you are likely to be in exactly the same position here as you were with the same item on the generic 12-step form for quantitative research. You will have to seek out and record the names of operations that you have yet to fathom. Do not panic. Everyone has to begin somewhere, and, if qualitative research proves to be interesting, explanations of most analytic processes are only as far away as a textbook or a college course. Even better, largely because qualitative analysis does not involve complex mathematics, many reports offer explanations of process that are both lucid and complete.

9. RESULTS. What did the author(s) identify as the primary results (products or findings produced by analysis of the data)? In general, "What was going on there?" One thing about Step 9 is apparent immediately. The space provided for recording results is relatively small—especially given the length of most qualitative study reports! The stingy space reflects something more significant, however, than just a desire to economize on the size of the form. It reflects the nature of qualitative research and a skill you will have to acquire if you are to make use of such reports— the skill of creating brief summaries that extract essential findings without completely losing the human qualities in a story.

Where the purposes of a qualitative study include deriving answers to one or more questions (whether specific or general in nature), there will be a return at Step 9 to those initial interrogatives and some effort to identify responses (although not necessarily identified as "results"). Studies that start with qualitative assumptions, however, might not have a set of explicit questions (at least, not at the outset) and thus often do not have a single set of listed results that is separate from the data. The data tell a story about what is going on in a particular social setting; the entire story is the "result" derived from analysis of the data.

For most qualitative studies, that means letting go of all the particulars that form the full text of the report you have just read. Now you must search out the deeper meaning behind the story—a generalization that often can be represented in your answer to the question, "What was going on there?" To reduce your answer to a few short sentences might at first seem unfair to the study, particularly if you have acquired a rich sense of the complexities involved and how inadequate simple generalizations might be. On that issue, we offer this advice: What you write down as the results produced by the study is not intended as a representation; rather, it is a kind of acronym that serves both to remind you of a much larger whole and to put at hand the key you found most useful in deciphering the code of meaning embedded in the story.

10. **CONCLUSIONS.** *What did the author(s) assert about how the results in Step 9 responded to the purpose(s) established in Step 2, and how did the events and experiences of the entire study contribute to that conclusion?* Before entering information at this step, you should review our comments concerning conclusions in quantitative studies (Step 10). One difference, however, requires your thoughtful attention.

In qualitative studies, investigators might not assert a single set of conclusions that are identified as such. The body of accumulated data, when combined with the results from analytic procedures, forms the substance of a story about phenomena of interest. Thus, when confronted with the question "What do you conclude from this study?", a qualitative investigator often discusses points within the story that seem particularly powerful, provocative, theoretically instructive, or pragmatically useful. Rarely, however, does an author conclude that he or she can assert empirically validated and reliable truths about what has been studied. If those latter outcomes are what you seek in the report, you might have to formulate your own sense of what constitute legitimate and well-supported conclusions.

11. *CAUTIONS. What cautions does the author(s) raise about the study itself or about interpreting the results? Add here any of your own reservations, particular those related to methods used to enhance credibility (trustworthiness and believability).* Because qualitative researchers think about the problems of reliability and validity in terms that are quite different from the meanings assigned by quantitative science, they often use different terminology. The word *credibility,* as used in this question, designates the qualities of trustworthiness and believability. These are characteristics of a study that inspire a sense of trust and belief in the reader.

There are many things a qualitative researcher can do to create confidence in the reader. Some are general in nature, such as being careful and explicit in describing data collection procedures, and some are very specific, such as cross-checking information across several sources of data (a process commonly called *triangulation).* In some reports, the author(s) designates particular operations as ones that serve the purpose of improving trustworthiness. In other reports, you have to consult your own reactions as the guide to sources of confidence (or the lack thereof).

Although quantitative research deals with the problems of validity, reliability, and objectivity, you will find that, in addition to these issues, there is a great deal more to learn about issues related to credibility in qualitative research. The place to begin, however, is with what the author(s) of the report says about his or her own concerns and the reasons for your own skeptical reactions to the story told.

12. *DISCUSSION. What interesting facts or ideas did you learn from reading the report? Include here anything that was of value, including: results, research designs and methods, references, instruments, history, useful*

arguments, or personal inspiration. A primary purpose of qualitative research is to provide the reader with vivid, rich, highly persuasive accounts of human interactions, often in complex social settings. A commonly repeated aphorism about such studies is that they truly succeed when they make what is familiar to us seem strange and what is strange to us seem familiar. Making yourself aware of the points at which the report has achieved that result is an important part of learning to read qualitative research.

Our earlier description of what should be recorded for Step 12 on the quantitative form applies here with equal emphasis. Results, conclusions, and applications are important in qualitative research, but a host of other valuable discoveries are possible for a reader who is open to learning—and to being surprised.

❖ READING AND RECORDING FROM RESEARCH REVIEWS

As promised in Chapter 2, we include here a brief section on the reading of research reviews. The inclusion of reviews in this guide reflects four facts about the research literature: (a) reviews appear in virtually all disciplines and active areas of investigation; (b) reviews often are the best place to begin when you want a sense of what has been studied and learned with regard to a particular topic; (c) for some purposes, good reviews can provide information sufficient to satisfy your needs without having to read the original reports; and (d) reviews are highly diverse creatures (in format, method, and scope) and can be very complex technical literature. In other words, reviews can be enormously valuable and efficient as resources, but the novice reader might require some assistance in learning how to make use of them.

Reviews can often be found in the same journals that publish research reports. In addition, some periodicals publish only research reviews (e.g., *Review of Educational Research* or *Psychological Review*). In yet other cases, reviews are included in or appended to other documents, such as doctoral dissertations, grant proposals, technical yearbooks, monographs, encyclopedias, and research compendiums for particular disciplines (e.g., *The Handbook of Research on Teaching*, Richardson, 2001).

Reviews vary along a number of dimensions: (a) *scope* (number and kinds of reports included); (b) qualitative control over *selection* of studies; (c) *framework* for organizing and integrating studies;

(d) method for *assessment* of studies; and (e) primary *purpose* (most commonly some combination of summary, methodological critique, development of theory, or derivation of applications or implications for practice). As you might expect, reviews also vary in both degree of technical detail and quality of writing—factors that influence the demands made on the reader. Like research reports, reviews are prose documents that range from awkward, obscure, and poorly organized to lucid and transparent expositions that are as economical in format as they are graceful in expression.

Despite that great diversity, at the bottom line, the majority of reviews do share a small set of common characteristics that define the genre. First, all are retrospective examinations of studies done in a particular area or, less commonly, studies that employ a particular method. Second, all reviews attend (albeit in different ways) to the question of what can be learned from the studies examined. Third, most reviews comment on how the findings of the studies (collectively or individually) fit into the fabric of existing knowledge. Fourth, and finally, most reviews give some attention to persisting problems for the conduct of inquiry in the research area and what might be done to improve the yield of theoretically or practically significant knowledge.

A 12-Step Map for Reading Reviews

The reading guide that follows is not intended to serve the same purpose as the 12-step forms for understanding research reports that were previously presented in this chapter. The latter were intended not only as organizational instruments and record forms but also as tools for the practice of specific reading skills. In contrast, we do not suggest that our 12-step map for research reviews should be used as an exercise tool for building competence in reading such documents. As literature, reviews simply are too heterogeneous to support any notion that one can learn how to read them by acquiring a single set of skills.

Instead, we have provided a mapping device that, through a series of questions, will help you identify familiar landmarks common to many review styles (Form 5.3). Even though not all of the 12 questions might apply to each review you encounter, we are confident that enough of them will do so to make the map a useful aid for improving your navigation. Particularly in complex reviews that are dense with detail, having a prespecified set of review functions to look for as landmarks can help you avoid the feeling of being lost or overwhelmed.

Form 5.3   A 12-Step Map for Reading Research Reviews

Directions: Read through the 12 questions in the map below. Then, skim through the review, noting those portions that appear to be related to the questions. Finally, on your second and more thorough reading, record brief answers for each. Some of the items might not apply to the particular review at hand, and some important observations you can make about the review might not be covered by any one of the questions. Accordingly, *you must use this form as a guide to reading reviews, not as a comprehensive and invariant list of significant content.*

1. **CITATION.** What study report is this? Record a complete reference citation.

2. **PURPOSE.** What was the purpose of the review, and how did the author(s) justify the importance of examining the topic?

3. **SELECTION.** How were studies selected for the review (e.g., exhaustive, specified time period, type of design, population involved, methodology used, or some combination of factors)?

4. **QUALITY.** How was the matter of quality handled in selecting studies for review? Was there a screening process, and, if so, what were the criteria?

5. **ORGANIZATION.** How did the author(s) sort or categorize studies for the review (e.g., a theoretical framework, date of publication, nature of results, sample size, type of design, or some combination of factors)?

(Continued)

Form 5.3 (Continued)

6. **DATA.** If actual data are cited, what kind(s) are provided? Give brief examples.

7. **ANALYSIS.** Is there an attempt to identify (if so, give a brief example for each):

   a. problems related to the kind of question being asked in the reviewed studies?

   b. technical difficulties (e.g., with designs, participant selection, or data analysis) in the reviewed studies?

   c. need for additional research to resolve confusion or to confirm tentative results?

8. **INTEGRATION.** How does the author(s) get from individual studies to the level of general assertions or conclusions about the status of research in the topical area (e.g., vote counting, meta-analysis, qualitative criteria)?

9. **SUMMARY.** Where in the text, and in what detail, is the task of summarizing handled (after each organizational section, in a section at the end of the entire document, in the abstract only), and is the summary format brief or extended?

10. **CONCLUSIONS.** What does the author(s) assert as the main conclusion(s) from the review?

11. **APPLICATION.** If the conclusions at Step 10 are credible, what utility might they have (e.g., applications that are theoretical, practical, or personal)?

12. **EVALUATION.** What would you say if you were asked to review this review with regard to importance, clarity of writing, suitability of organization, and degree of credibility?

In addition, the 12-step map can serve as a record form and can be particularly helpful in reminding you to notice important mechanical features of the review that you might otherwise overlook. Because this form is already crowded as a three-page document, we have made little attempt to provide for different kinds of review formats (or purposes). As your familiarity with this form of research document increases, you will have little difficulty in recognizing which items do not apply to some reviews or in creating customized versions of the generic map for your own use.

Navigating Through Reviews With Your 12-Step Map

We tried to make the language of each question as self-explanatory as possible. If you have a classmate or colleague who is using the map to study the same document, you will have an opportunity to discuss any uncertainties that emerge from your first efforts. With that source of clarification, we doubt that any of the 12 steps will create serious difficulty.

Much of our general advice about the earlier 12-step forms also applies to the use of the review version. Most notably, you should be flexible about the order in which you try to complete the 12 steps. Also, if something in the text is impossible to understand (or if one of the items on the form appears not to be present in the review at all), do not panic. Just flag it and get on with the task. Above all, limit your recorded answers to brief reminders of key points. As with the other guides, becoming compulsive about squeezing all of the information onto the form is self-defeating. You can always retrieve the review document itself if you later find that you need precise detail.

Finally, we draw your attention to the brief instructions at the top of the form. Although you might soon acquire the confidence to complete the form at a single reading (certainly, there are short, nontechnical reviews that require no heroic effort), our experience suggests that the strategy of skimming first (reading only headings, introductory sections, and topic paragraphs), followed by intensive reading and use of the form, is good advice if you are not a veteran reader of reviews.

Also, our suggestion about the importance of noting other review features not encompassed by the 12 steps is not gratuitous. We make no claim to have invented the comprehensive format for reviewing all research reviews. This is a navigational aid, not a holy writ. Keep your eyes and your mind open. It is entirely possible that, for your own purposes, other key questions should be added or substituted to create a better 12-step map. Please be our guest.

❖ EXPLAINING RESEARCH: A TOOL FOR LEARNING HOW TO READ REPORTS

In this final section, we present a series of group exercises that involve explaining research to others. The process of "teaching" a report can serve as a powerful device in learning how to read and understand research.

Teaching Is the Best Way to Learn

Anyone who has had to give verbal instruction, either formally as a teacher in a public or private school, or informally as a member of any sort of study group, will not be surprised that the best way to learn (and to test for learning) is to have to teach what you think you know to somebody else. Experience already will have taught them that lesson. It takes only a small shift of context to realize that the same rule applies to the task at hand.

In explaining the study described in a research report to someone else, you are almost certain to learn more about the investigation. Furthermore, if you can accomplish that feat with demonstrable success (e.g., when your listener can give back a reasonably accurate account of the study), it is likely that you really did understand what you read.

Explaining research provides the opportunity to accomplish a number of desirable outcomes. Although the benefits vary by individual, five that we have most commonly observed are noted here:

1. The social nature of the task ensures that you actually will read the entire study. Indeed, if you are normally sensitive to the opinions of others, you probably will work really hard at comprehending any study you have to explain—even to an audience of one.

2. In explaining a study, you will test whether you actually understood what you thought you had assimilated. Impressionistic and subjective evaluations of our accomplishments sometimes outrun the actuality. Having to explain, out

loud and in detail (rather than sketching quickly in the privacy of your own mind), is an unforgiving reality check.

3. If the time consumed by your explanation is limited (our own rule is that explanation exercises must be completed in 12 minutes), you will be forced to identify the essentials in a report. This is a process that requires you to develop a clear conception of exactly what happened in the study.

4. If the test of a good explanation is that the listener can remember the essential elements of the study, then, in devising your instruction, you will have to give close attention to some of the basic principles of sound pedagogy. Among other things, you will have to decide the order of topics to be covered, at each new point answering the question, "What do listeners really need to know *before* they can understand what I am about to say?" Also, you will have to pace the presentation (not going too fast or overloading any part with too many details), devise illustrations for difficult constructs, find ways to make main points stand out vividly, and, throughout, monitor for the "glazed-eye syndrome" that signals when you have lost your audience. By the time you have devised and delivered an explanation that meets even these simple criteria, you will know more about your study than you ever thought possible.

5. Perfect or imperfect, an explanation is the ideal basis for a fruitful discussion of a study. Not only can you get feedback from your audience concerning what seemed cloudy in your recounting of the investigation (and probably *was* cloudy in your mind), but you can have the luxury of exchanging ideas about the study with someone else.

How to Give an Explanation: Rules of the Game

From trial and error over the years, we have discovered some simple rules that allow beginners to get the most out of giving an explanation. Some of them might seem arbitrary or a bit fussy, but, for your first round of reports, we ask you to try it our way. Modification of the rules can come later. As a convenience in writing about this particular exercise, we have given it a name. Whenever we are referring to the explaining exercise described in this chapter, we have simply capitalized the first letter, as in the "Explanation."

Rule 1. Observe a strict time limit of 12 minutes from start to finish. Yes, you could give a more complete account of the report in 13 minutes, but experience has taught us that after you go beyond 10 to 12 minutes, Explanations of research reports invariably begin to deal with nonessentials (things the listeners should read for themselves if they are sufficiently intrigued by your overview).

Rule 2. The audience, whether one or many, should limit itself to listening attentively, asking only for clarification of major points. Comments and discussion should be reserved until after the 12 minutes are up.

Rule 3. You are free to use any visual aids that will help your audience understand or that will allow you to economize on limited (and thus valuable) presentation time.

Rule 4. Never, *ever*, read your Explanation. Look the audience in the eye and talk to them! Note cards or lists of key words (whatever works for you) are fine, but do not insult your listeners by paying less attention to them than you pay to anything else, including your own insecurity about remembering everything you intended to say.

Rule 5. After finishing your Explanation (in under 12 minutes) and the applause dies down, take time to get some detailed feedback about what people did and did not understand. Not only will that help you improve the quality of your next presentation, it might identify spots in the report that you still do not grasp—a sign that you now might need some external assistance. In addition to soliciting feedback, however, go beyond critique of your performance and exchange views about the study with your audience. Audience members might have some insights that will enrich what you have learned.

Formats for the Explanation: Pairs, Teams, and Solos

We suggest that your Explanations should progress through a series of three types, moving from easy to demanding. All three require a minimum of one or two partners who also are engaged in learning to read research reports. You need not worry about reciprocity, however, because it is built into the sequence of explaining tasks.

Type 1: The shared pair. For your first Explanation, use a study that both you and your audience have read. Pairs are perfect for this exercise (although triads also can be used). Each pair selects two reports, and then each member of the pair reads both but is assigned to explain only one. Everyone gets to play the roles of both explainer and listener. In the process, you cover (thoroughly) two studies in an hour or less—feedback and discussion included.

Although it might seem socially awkward to engage in explaining to someone what (ostensibly) he or she already knows, you will quickly discover an interesting fact. For the most part, this problem does not exist. Not only would your partner probably explain the study differently, but beginners do tend to understand reports in distinctly different ways. You can be quite confident that even though your partner has read the study, he or she will not be bored by your Explanation. In fact, for your first attempts, your partner might be wondering whether you both read the same report!

Type 2: The team task. The second, and more demanding, type of Explanation requires a triad of beginners and three studies. There are two levels of the team task. Level 1 requires everyone in the triad to read all three studies. Two members of the group are assigned the task of explaining one study as a team, as in A and B explain Study 1 to C; then B and C explain Study 2 to A; and finally, C and A explain Study 3 to B.

In preparing for the team task at Level 1, each pair is allowed 15 to 20 minutes to consult, compare reading notes, devise simple graphics, and agree on a division of labor during the Explanation process. With the usual 12-minute limit, and a following discussion of 10 minutes for each study, the three studies can be covered in about 2 hours of intensive work. If you add a short break, it will extend the total time but reduce the symptoms of battle fatigue.

Again, you might ask why team preparation is subject to an arbitrary time limit. Certainly, the Explanation could be done more elaborately if there were more time to prepare, but would it really be done better? From what we have observed, our answer for most team efforts is a firm "No!" Although planning time is a variable with which you can experiment, please do try it our way first.

At Level 2 of the team task, you simply increase the pressure on each team to do a good job. The third member of the triad, the assigned listener, does *not* read the study in advance. Everyone reads only two of the three selected studies, keeping him- or herself innocent of one. Thus, following the pattern above, C does not read Study 1, A does not read Study 2, and B does not read Study 3. We think you will be surprised at how much the simple shift to having a naïve listener alters the perceived (and real) difficulty of the task.

Type 3: The solo explanation. Here, it is best to begin with a return to the paired format, graduating to larger audiences only as you gain confidence (and competence). Working alone, you now explain a study that the listener has not read. Everything is on your shoulders, but you get all the glory when the job is well done.

Most people are satisfied to do a few solo trials and then end their Explanation careers. However, those of you who are preparing for jobs that involve using research on a regular basis (academics, researchers, technical authors, staff development specialists, grant consultants) should press on—at least to the level of working with a larger audience. It is in the triad, where each member is the sole reader of a study and then presents it to two naïve listeners, for example, that you will first encounter the problem of meeting the learning needs of more than one consumer within the same time limit. That will test both your grasp of simple teaching skills and the depth of your own understanding of the report.

How to Give an Explanation: Handy Hints From Hard Experience

Hint 1. A 12-step form is a good place to begin mapping out your Explanation, but do not slavishly limit yourself to the exact order of its items. There is no reason why you should not begin your Explanation of a quantitative study, for example, with the results, Step 9 (as in, "I am going to tell you about a study that unexpectedly found that . . ."), or with who was studied, Step 4 (as in, "This is the only study I have found that actually involved asking children what they thought about working on computers in the classroom.").

Hint 2. Most studies contain problematic elements for the reader. Thus, most studies have elements that are also problematic for anyone trying to explain them. Ambiguous terms, incomplete accounts of procedure, missing information, apparent errors of fact, or debatable assumptions— they all are going to be encountered. With these problems, you will have to do what all research consumers have to do (in the short term)—make note of the problem to your audience and get on with the job. If you are willing to explain only perfect studies, you will not get much practice.

Over the long term, if it really matters, you can track down more complete accounts and the clarification, if not resolution, of most deficiencies. For the present purpose, it is far more important that your Explanation be clear and correct than it is that the study itself be perfect.

Hint 3. Being respectful of the author(s) is your obligation, just as it is your responsibility to flag for your listeners the points that fall short of the ideal study or perfect report. All research reports, whatever their flaws or acknowledged limitations, were produced by people who were struggling with the problems of doing good research and the no-less-difficult task of creating a sound written account of it. All were investigating questions that mattered (at least to them), and all had something to say that should be of interest to an audience if given a proper presentation. An Explanation is always more effective when it respects the author(s) and maintains a positive tone.

Hint 4. Always practice with a stopwatch. In an Explanation, nothing is more embarrassing than to discover that you have 2 minutes left at the midpoint of your presentation. Take pride in crafting a presentation that finishes with time to spare.

Hint 5. We are told on good authority that there are three main factors in selling a house: location, location, and location. Likewise, we assure you that there are three main factors in the design of an effective Explanation: simplify, simplify, and simplify. Remember that your first loyalty in this task is to your listeners, not to the author(s) of the report. A researcher's words are not sacred objects, and neither are his or her ideas about appropriate priorities in using space within the report. For example, if you do not really need to introduce a technical term that will be unfamiliar to your audience (because there is a perfectly serviceable common word), then you have no obligation to do so—*even if the author(s) did.* Your simplifications and deletions might mean that the audience misses out on some of the nuances, rich elaborations, technical detail, and secondary analyses, but getting a really clear picture of what happened in the study is worth a lot more. Again, less detail usually means more understanding.

Hint 6. A flowchart of steps in the study makes a good visual aid with which to map progress through your Explanation. It does not help, however, if it contains so much detail that it requires prolonged scrutiny or if it is allowed to distract attention from the main points of your presentation.

The Bad Explanation: Five Fatal Flaws

As with many problems in human communication, a relatively small set of presentation flaws accounts for a large portion of the failures. In our experience, when beginners have difficulty with the Explanation task, one or several of the following are likely to be the cause.

Flaw 1. Reading, and thus insulting (or boring), the audience.

Flaw 2. Not putting things into a sequence that makes it easy to follow the steps of the study.

Flaw 3. Getting hung up on what is not in the report or in critiquing the study before explaining it.

Flaw 4. Trying to explain too much in a limited time.

Flaw 5. Assuming that the listeners know things that they do not know (often a result of not monitoring the audience).

The cures for each of these flaws do not require an advanced degree in communication studies. In matching sequential order, they are the following:

Cure 1. Do not read. Talk to your audience.

Cure 2. Define new terms *before* using them, use a clear temporal order for events, and always ask yourself, "What has to come first if my audience is to follow this explanation?"

Cure 3. Flag problems briefly and then get on with the Explanation.

Cure 4. Simplify complex operations and delete what is not essential for a basic understanding.

Cure 5. Watch for puzzled expressions and glazed eyes. Find out what the problem is and adjust your Explanation. If you have planned to leave several minutes of unused time, small in-course adjustments to the needs of your audience will fit comfortably.

The Purpose of Explaining

At first, the Explanation can be an anxiety-arousing task. There is an interesting therapeutic value, however, in having to listen to other beginners fumble through their first attempts. You quickly learn that nearly everyone faces a learning curve for this exercise. You also will notice how quickly performances improve.

That rapid growth in competence is a satisfying outcome. For some, giving effective explanations (without, of course, the artificial time constraints and other trappings of the training exercise) might even have practical utility in their careers. For everyone, however, as you gradually master the craft, you can be increasingly proud of your accomplishment. It is no small thing to be skillful at giving short, clear explanations on *any* topic, much less research reports.

Learning to give classmates or colleagues good explanations was not, of course, our primary purpose in putting you through the rigors of these exercises. The purpose remains what it was at the outset— helping you learn how to read and digest research. Toward that end, you will have learned some very specific skills.

When you read a report as a veteran of Explanation training, your practiced eye will automatically sort through the details, looking for the essential elements that drive a study. As you work through the story of an investigation, your explainer's ear will listen for the order of things that makes the most logical sense (not necessarily the ordering of the author[s]). Your critical senses will be alert to ambiguities, gaps, and dubious assumptions or conclusions that should be flagged for later consideration. And, during all of this, you will be rehearsing increasingly complete explanations—for *yourself*. When all of that comes as second nature, you will no longer need the assistance of this, or any other, guide to reading research reports.

6

Types of Research

An Overview

B ecause we suggested in the Preface that this chapter could be used
when puzzling through your first attempts at reading reports, you
might have arrived here without completing all of the previous
chapters. That is perfectly appropriate, and you should find that most
of what is contained here is intelligible. As you continue to work
through the book and try out our suggested strategies for reading, it
might be helpful to return to this chapter occasionally as a way of
refreshing your ability to recognize the different types of research
encountered.

Previous chapters of this book contain repeated references to the
idea that there are different types (or kinds) of research. We have used
the generic word *type* to indicate that studies *can* differ from each other
in several ways: (a) the initial assumptions they make about the nature
of the world (producing paradigmatic differences, such as qualitative
and quantitative research), (b) the organization of the study (producing
design difference, such as experimental and correlational research),
and (c) the procedures used to collect data (producing methodological
differences, such as psychometric and interview research).

As you probably will have surmised, the types just mentioned are neither discrete categories (they overlap in all kinds of untidy ways), nor are they an exhaustive list of all the distinctions that account for typological variety in research studies. The three sources of variety noted here, however, contain the most basic elements that characterize alternative ways of doing research—the basic types of inquiry that beginning readers will notice from the outset.

For example, in Chapters 4 and 5, we discussed strategies for reading research reports that, by necessity, required you to distinguish between qualitative and quantitative studies—two types of research that are shaped by different *paradigms* (different sets of assumptions about the nature of reality). Accordingly, you will have noticed on the two 12-step recording forms for research reports that, although the general topics covered at each step do run in parallel, the actual phrasing of the questions sometimes does not. These differences, of course, reflect distinctive elements within the two approaches to inquiry.

Beyond that source of variation lies the fact that each paradigm has spawned a family of alternative types of research (they could be considered paradigmatic subspecies). In quantitative research, distinctly different designs reflect different pragmatic purposes (for example, to create descriptions or to detect associations). Likewise, in qualitative research, strategic variations in design serve different research intentions (for example, production of theory, discovery of participants' perspectives, or social empowerment of participants).

In addition, however, under the qualitative umbrella are types of research that differ for reasons that go beyond the straightforward demands of research strategy. These types reflect different understandings of what constitutes data, how researchers should relate to participants, and what represent acceptable rationales for engaging in social research. Little of that complexity need concern you at this point. For now it is quite sufficient to recognize several of the types you are most likely to encounter in the first tour through the research literature in your own area of interest.

For several reasons, however, the task of dealing with different types of inquiry will not be as daunting as you might anticipate. It is true that different types of research do sometimes produce distinctively different organizations in the reports, and thus pose different demands (and reading problems) for the beginner. As you will discover in this chapter, however, a more direct examination of differences among types of research reveals the paradoxical fact that there also are pervasive similarities. Many variations in research strategy represent different ways of confronting a common set of underlying problems. The nomenclature might differ but, in the midst of variety, you will encounter many familiar ideas.

Before surveying concerns that are generic to many types of inquiry, however, we want to remind you of a point made repeatedly in this text. Although technical knowledge can be helpful in deciphering research reports, you do not need to become an expert in research methodology and design to extract useful information from them. Because we feel strongly about that point, we selected the content of this chapter to provide no more than a simple framework for categorizing studies, as well as the conceptual basis for recognizing a small, basic set of issues pertaining to the conduct of research. If you want more detailed information, the books annotated in Appendix A should provide a helpful place to begin.

❖ GENERIC ISSUES IN RESEARCH

Planning research requires many decisions that ultimately will bear on the quality of the data collected and the credibility of the findings. First among those is the choice of study procedures that relate to the twin characteristics of *validity* and *reliability*. Although those two terms are used in a variety of ways in the scientific community (and synonyms are often substituted in particular research traditions), we will ignore those complexities and define them here in the way that is the most prevalent and that most closely relates to your task of reading reports.

Although the word *validity* generally denotes the condition of being true, researchers use it with regard to two aspects of their investigations. One set of validity issues is internal to a study and concerns whether the research has been designed so that it truly deals with what is being examined. Can the data collected, for example, actually be used to answer the question being asked?

The other validity issue concerns the external question of whether or not the results will remain truthful when subsequently applied to people, situations, or objects outside the original investigation (from our discussion of sampling in Chapter 3, you will recognize that question as the familiar problem of whether or not a study's findings can be *generalized*). The two kinds of veracity are referred to respectively as *internal validity* (Do the findings tell the truth about the question posed in the study?) and *external validity* (Do the findings tell the truth about these questions when they are situated outside the study?). Because it is somewhat less complex, we will begin with the research problems raised by the latter.

The most common circumstance in which external validity becomes an issue occurs when one group of people is examined in the study, but the results and conclusions are applied to another group. What is true for the particular sample of people in the study simply might not be valid for (that is, might not tell the truth about) another group of people—particularly if that group differs in some substantial way.

Medical research commonly presents such problems of external validity. Because studies of this kind are so expensive and consume so much precious time, it can be tempting to extend hard-won knowledge about medicines or medical procedures to people not included in the samples of early investigations. It can also be unfair, misleading, wasteful, or dangerous.

For example, because of the differences between men and women, the National Institutes of Health created the Women's Health Initiative. This broad research program is a response to the fact that many important medical studies in the past used exclusively male samples—with consequent problems of external validity when applications were made to female populations. Using women in medical study samples ensures that problems of external validity that are related to gender do not put women at a disadvantage in obtaining sound health care.

In contrast, internal validity is not concerned with generalizability but with the integrity of the study itself. Internal validity issues range from simple and perfectly obvious to arcane and exceedingly obscure, but, in the end, they all have to do with whether the study has been designed to yield truthful results. To start with an obvious example, if we wish to know whether taking supplemental vitamins increases intelligence, we would not put our subjects on a regimen of multivitamin pills and then weigh them to check for improvement in cognitive function. Weight is not a valid measure of intelligence, although it is perfectly valid as an index of mass (for objects weighed at the same location). The data gathered have to match the question. An intelligence test would serve our study better, although correct selection of a measurement is rarely so obvious.

Four decades ago, Campbell and Stanley (1963) wrote a marvelously lucid monograph that explained many of the problems with internal validity that are possible in experimental studies (and in a number of other closely related designs for research). That little book still is available (an abstract appears in Appendix A), and we recommend it as an economical and pleasurable means not only for surveying the mysteries of internal validity but for learning a great deal about alternative ways of setting up experiments.

A simple example of the many issues of validity discussed by Campbell and Stanley is that of "experimental mortality." That graphic name applies to the fascinating question, "What happens to results when some of the people in a study sample decide to drop out before all of the data are collected?" The answer involves (at least) further questions about the particular people who defect. If all or most of them share a particular characteristic (bored quickly, fatigued easily, and so on), that fact might well influence what is found with regard to the remaining people. In turn, the investigator is left with the question, "Are the subjects completing the study still representative of the population from which they were selected as a sample?" As you can see, issues that deal with internal and external validity create complex problems for researchers.

Experiments, of course, are not the only types of research. The problems of internal and external validity are ubiquitous and must be confronted by researchers in study formats as disparate as questionnaire surveys and field ethnographies. As you read reports from studies with different research designs, you should notice not only the kinds of validity issues that arise but how the investigators attempt to deal with them.

The techniques used by a researcher to collect data—what Campbell and Stanley (1963) call the "instrumentation" of a study—present some of the most common problems of internal validity. Data collection takes a variety of forms, including machines that use computer programs to direct the monitoring of biological processes, survey forms filled out by door-to-door interviewers, psychological tests completed by subjects, field notes from investigators watching children on a playground, and systematic examination of cultural phenomena through the recording of words used in books, television, or movies. All of these are very different methodologies but are subject to the same question: "Do these data provide a truthful reflection of what the study is intended to examine?"

A second question has to be asked about any instrumentation: "Does it collect data in a consistent manner?" That question deals with the second of the two concerns with which we started this discussion—*reliability.* If you take your body temperature with an oral thermometer and get three completely different readings for three consecutive 1-minute stays under your tongue, your instrument probably has a problem with reliability. Of course, it might have shown three identical readings (perfect reliability), but they all might have been incorrect (an issue of validity, because your thermometer does not tell the truth—it *is* consistent, but also a consistent *liar).*

If you consider that example, you will discover a valuable and easy-to-remember rule. If the thermometer produces reliable readings, it still might not be a valid indicator of body temperature. If it provides valid readings, however, then we know that it also must be reliable. That relationship of reliability and validity holds true for all measuring instruments because reliability is a component of validity. In plain language, you cannot tell the truth unless you are consistent, but you can be consistent and not tell the truth.

Clearly, researchers must establish ways of collecting data that are both valid and reliable. A particularly thorough discussion of strategies for achieving those twin goals can be found in Carmines and Zeller (1979).

In many cases, instruments for collecting data can be checked for validity and reliability before they are actually put to use in a study. This is true, for example, of written tests, electronic and mechanical hardware, and rating scales. Often, reports contain descriptions of such verification, including figures that display precisely how close the research tools come to theoretically perfect validity and reliability.

A simple reliability test, for example, is the test-retest procedure that often is used to establish the stability of test results over time. As its name suggests, the same test is given to the same people on two occasions. If the scores for each individual are roughly the same, that can be taken as evidence of the test's reliability. If the scores change substantially (and in apparently random ways) from the first to the second testing, there almost certainly is a reliability problem with the test. Something about the instrument or procedure causes or invites the individual to respond differently at each encounter. The test might yield numbers, but those numbers will be of no use in finding a truthful answer to the research question.

In the case of written tests, another way to check reliability employs alternate forms of the same instrument. Two separate forms of a test are constructed by writing similar, but not identical, questions (they must cover exactly the same constructs and require the same kind of response, but do so in slightly different words). People who score high on one form should score high on the other. If they do not, the investigator will suspect that something is encouraging subjects to respond inconsistently. The cause might lie in the format of the test, the means by which it is administered, the nature of the content, or (most likely) some combination of these factors. Whatever the case, if you cannot rely on subjects to give the same response to questions that differ in only trivial ways, the data will make no sense, and the study itself will become nonsense.

In some forms of research, reliability cannot be tested in advance because there simply is too much variability in the conditions under which data will be collected. Open-ended interviews and field studies of complex human behavior often do not employ instrumentation that can be pretested for reliability (in such cases, the investigator *is* the instrument). Instead, exceedingly careful attention to consistency of procedures across people, contexts, and time; ongoing inspection of recorded data for evidence of unexplained or unexpected content; and persistent effort to maintain high accuracy must provide the support for claims about the reliability of what is captured in the data record.

Validity and reliability are elusive qualities, and few studies are designed in ways that resolve all possible threats to consistent truth. What the reader of a research report has a right to expect, however, is that investigators show awareness of such issues, report what they have done to control the problems, and be frank about the degree of their success in so doing.

As a beginning reader, of course, you will have to depend on the processes of peer review to catch problems with validity or reliability before manuscripts reach print. It should be reassuring to know that suggestions for clarifying such issues are among the most frequent comments that authors receive from reviewers and that inadequate attention to validity and reliability are among the most common reasons for denying publication.

You must remember, however, that standards for validity and reliability cannot be applied as simple absolutes. Given the complex nature of many research questions, reviewers often must ask, "How much lack of confidence in the consistent truthfulness of this study is tolerable?" The answer will be determined by many factors, but everyone—reviewers, editors, researchers, and readers—knows what is ideal. Research should come as close to producing reliably valid results as human skill and effort can devise.

❖ TYPES OF RESEARCH

Research is conducted in many ways. Scholars in each academic and professional area typically make wider use of some methods than others; develop local ground rules for dealing with concerns about reliability and validity; and, quite often, invent technical jargon for the use of insiders. Nevertheless, many of the basic problems in conducting sound investigations are common to all types of research. It is human inventiveness in response to those fundamental difficulties that works constantly to alter the face of the research enterprise.

In the past three decades, the number (and complexity) of research methods has increased sharply, particularly in the social sciences. Where once only a few forms of inquiry were available (and acceptable within the scientific community), many options now exist. This proliferation offers more than just greater freedom for the investigator; it makes possible a better matching of research tools to the demands of each particular question—and that is an enormous advantage.

However, when we hear our students ask the question, "What is the best type of research?" we always know that they as learners and we as teachers still have important work to do. A particular strategy for inquiry is not good or bad in an absolute sense; rather, a type of research is good or bad to the exact degree that it fits well or poorly with the question at hand. You can find our opinions about this subject discussed at some length (Locke, Spirduso, & Silverman, 2000), but a quick review here will serve to ensure that we are all starting with the same assumptions about types of research.

Questions must guide the selection and use of research methods. Although this sounds like common sense, it is not always easy to remember. All of the elegant technical accoutrements of design and method can distract people from the simple fact that it is researchers' sense of what they want to learn, carefully thought out and clearly defined, that, when coupled with appropriate design and methods, becomes the engine that drives everything else. Is this point really important? Our unequivocal answer is "Yes."

It is not at all unusual to encounter studies that have been weakened by the investigator's inadequate attention to carefully thinking through what he or she wants to learn. Such studies are at least as common as those with the opposite sort of problem—soundly crafted questions that are inadequately served by carelessly selected research methods.

The combination of sound questions with appropriate methods separates the powerful from the merely pedestrian in research. There is no "best type of research"—there are only good questions matched with procedures for inquiry that can yield reliable answers. That dictum holds true even in qualitative studies, wherein the starting point for inquiry can be anything in the range between explicit hypotheses at one extreme to nothing more specific than hazy foreshadows of what might be worthy of exploration at the other. Nevertheless, in every study, all of the components must be compatible with the nature of what the investigator seeks to learn.

We will now introduce you to a framework for identifying different types of research. Our system is intended to be utilitarian and certainly is not intended to be definitive. A number of excellent sources provide far greater depth (e.g., Bailey, 1994; Creswell, 2003; Gall, Gall, & Borg, 2003; Krathwohl, 1998; Robson, 2002; Thomas & Nelson, 2001), in some cases devoting entire chapters to research designs that we can only name here. We again urge you to avail yourself of such help when you encounter unfamiliar forms of inquiry. We have abstracted some of these more specialized texts in Appendix A for your reference.

We categorize types of research into three broad divisions: quantitative, qualitative, and mixed method. Figure 6.1 provides a simple map of those divisions and some of their subcategories. This framework was not designed to include all research types or to be an elegant taxonomy. It contains the easily recognizable types that novice readers are most likely to encounter. As soon as you can recognize its various limitations as a classification scheme, you will not need it any longer anyway. As you read research reports, it will be helpful for you to pencil in the new subcategories (or subdivisions of existing subcategories) that you encounter.

Quantitative Research

As we present each type and subcategory, we will discuss the kinds of questions commonly asked, the data collection methods used, and where you can obtain more information about that kind of research. In addition, we will cite a study that provides a sound example. It is not difficult, however, to imagine the kinds of questions that are best answered (and most commonly asked) by investigators using quantitative designs.

Figure 6.1   Organization of Empirical Research

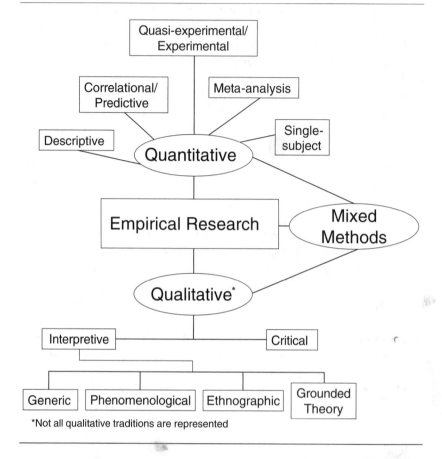

*Not all qualitative traditions are represented

For the central portion of the 20th century, quantitative designs represented by far the dominant type of research in the social sciences. Although other types of inquiry are now in common use, the capacity of quantitative research to describe, predict, and explain social and psychological phenomena has provided a significant part of the foundation on which the modern social sciences have been erected. We begin with a brief discussion of the statistics used in quantitative research. This ordering is convenient because it is the management of quantities that provides hallmark distinctions among the main branches of the quantitative family: descriptive; correlational/predictive;

quasi-experimental/experimental; single-subject; and the recent addition, meta-analysis.

Statistics in quantitative research. Statistics are mathematical tools for manipulating and analyzing numeric data. They range in complexity from the simple average of a group of scores to procedures that require sequences of operations based on esoteric forms of linear algebra before an answer can be derived for the original question.

As you would anticipate, you would need special training to understand the more complicated statistical tools—what they accomplish and how they do it—but, for a surprisingly small investment of study time, you can learn enough about basic statistics to read the "Results" section of many reports and understand what the analysis says about the data. Accordingly, in Appendix C, we provide a user-friendly introduction to some of the most commonly encountered research statistics. How they function in a report is described in terms that make no demand on previous background in mathematics and presume no familiarity with research technology. At the very least, our beginner's guide serves as a valuable supplement to this chapter, a useful introduction to the skills necessary for reading quantitative reports with a critical eye (see Chapter 7), and a guide for selecting additional references.

Most college bookstores have a variety of inexpensive self-study guides, computer-based learning programs, and paperbacks in the "statistics for dummies" genre. Many of these texts provide highly effective ways to obtain a general background for a minimum investment of time. In the more traditional textbook format, however, we think that Pyrczak (1999, 2001, 2002), Dodge (2003), and Holcomb (1998, 2002) are particularly sound and entirely accessible for novice readers (and all six of these references are available in modestly priced paperbound editions). More advanced texts such as Kirk (1995); Pedhazur (1997); Stevens (2002); and Winer, Brown, and Michels (1991) ordinarily are best used in conjunction with statistics courses (or tutorial instruction).

Statistical tools can be categorized by the purposes for which they are commonly employed. As Table 6.1 indicates (in the columns), the function of some statistics is to describe a given set of data (*descriptive* statistics), others are used to examine the relations between or among sets of numeric data (*association* or *correlational* statistics), and still others are employed to detect whether differences between or among groups of data are more than meaningless accidents (*mean difference* statistics).

Table 6.1 provides only the names of various statistical procedures; you will have to obtain explanations of their uses from other sources. When a particular statistic is identified in a report, however, you can use the table to quickly identify the functional family to which it belongs. That, in turn, will reveal something about the type of research involved.

Because the names of statistical procedures are, in some cases, the same as the names of particular research designs (e.g., correlational statistics—which are also called statistics of association, but you are more likely to encounter the term *correlational*—are used in correlational studies to answer questions that inquire about the correlation of variables), people lose track of the distinctions involved. We suggest that you not let that happen. Shaping the question comes first, then the selection of research design, and, finally, decisions about tools for managing and analyzing data. In good research, the three operations must be related by an intrinsic logic, but they are no more the same than are apples and oranges—even when given identical names.

As you examine Table 6.1, notice that it is divided horizontally into univariate and multivariate sections. Analysis of data concerning the single variable factor of intelligence would require a *univariate* (one variable) statistic. If you wanted to examine the impact of nutritional supplements on intelligence and strength, you would have two variables (e.g., IQ test scores and dynamometer readings) and would need a *multivariate* statistic to examine the data. As research has become more sophisticated, this distinction has become more important, and it is one you should begin to notice from the outset.

The following five subsections provide an overview of quantitative research. Table 6.2 presents the purposes and names of some commonly encountered formats associated with three broad categories of quantitative research: descriptive, correlational, and quasi-experimental/experimental. Because they represent special cases, single-subject research and meta-analysis are not included in the table; they are discussed briefly in the final subsections of this section.

Descriptive research. This form of research captures and displays a graphic picture of some aspect(s) of a situation—expressed in numbers. "What is the reading level of 10th-grade students in a rural school district?" "How long does it take for scholarship athletes to complete an undergraduate degree?" "What kinds of magazines are read by adolescent girls in urban areas?" These are the kinds of questions that call for descriptive studies. Although the relationship between or among groups certainly can be described, you will find it conceptually useful

Table 6.1 Names of Common Statistical Procedures

	Description	Correlation (Association)	Differences in Means
Univariate	Mean (μ, $\bar{x}$)	Pearson's Product Moment Correlation (ρ, r)	t test
	Median (Md)	Coefficient of determination (r^2, R^2)	Analysis of variance (ANOVA)
	Mode	Partial correlation ($r_{ab.c}$)	Analysis of covariance (ANCOVA)
	Variance (σ^2, s^2)	Semipartial (part) correlation ($r_{a(b.c)}$)	Trend analysis
	Standard deviation (σ, s)	Rank order correlation (r_s or τ)	Sign test
	Standard error	Point-biserial correlation (r_{pb})	Mann-Whitney U
	Range	Chi-square (χ^2)	Kruskal-Wallis one-way ANOVA
	Confidence intervals		Friedman two-way ANOVA
	Skewness (γ_1)		Effect size
	Kurtosis (γ_2)		
	Standard scores (z, T)		
	Percentiles		
	Percentile ranks		
Multivariate		Multiple regression	Hotelling's T^2
		Logistic regression	Multivariate analysis of variance (MANOVA)
		Discriminant function analysis	Multivariate analysis of covariance (MANCOVA)
		Cluster analysis	
		Principal components analysis	
		Factor analysis	
		Canonical correlation	
		Path analysis	
		Structural equation modeling	
		Hierarchical linear modeling	

Table 6.2 Purpose, Names, and Examples of Research Techniques Used in Quantitative Research

	Descriptive	*Correlational*	*Quasi-Experimental/ Experimental*
Purpose	To describe a sample on a specific variable. Can also describe subsamples on the same variable.	To describe relationships among variables, to predict a criterion variable, or to test a model of the interrelationships among variables used to predict a variable.	To test differences in group means for one or more independent variables.
Names of Commonly Used Research Formats	• Survey research • Political polling • Delphi surveys	• Predictive • Multiple regression • Causal modeling • Structured equation modeling • Path analysis	• Causal comparative • Repeated measures design • Within and between design • Randomize block design • ANOVA or MANOVA
Examples of Research Techniques (for all three research types)		• Data collection with instrumentation for specific variables (e.g., electronic monitoring of brain waves, blood alcohol testing) • Paper-and-pencil inventories • Attitude measures • Surveys • Use of statistics to analyze data	

to assign studies that focus primarily on the analysis of relationships to the following section on correlational research. The statistics used in descriptive research include such tools as measures of central tendency (e.g., mean, mode, and median—these yield descriptions of what is "typical" in a set of numbers, or where the middle is when a set is listed from highest to lowest) or measures of dispersion (e.g., range and standard deviation—describing such characteristics as the number of steps between highest and lowest numbers, or how tightly numbers in a set cluster around a central value).

An example of descriptive research is a report by Coward, Duncan, and Uttaro (1996). They made use of data from a national census of more than 13,000 rural nursing homes. They described nine types of facilities in terms of such variables as availability, size, cost, and the character of long-term care. They drew conclusions about the adequacy of facilities within each type and discussed the implications of their findings for the future of rural nursing homes.

Correlational research. This type of research examines the nature of the relationship between or among variables. Three types will be discussed here: simple, predictive, and modeling. The *simple* form of correlational study employs a statistic that yields a single number (called a *correlation coefficient*) that expresses the extent to which a pair of variables (two sets of numbers) are related—that is, the degree to which we can predict that when measures of one variable produce numbers that are larger or smaller, the numbers for some other measured variable will be similarly larger or smaller. For example, when two sets of test scores shadow each other closely in the same direction, the coefficient will be larger and positive in nature (closer to +1.0). When the numbers closely shadow each other as mirror images (that is, they run in opposite directions), the coefficient will be larger and have a negative sign (closer to −1.0). When the numbers show no particular pattern of association, the coefficient simply will be small (whatever its sign), indicating little relationship (closer to a correlation coefficient of 0.0, the statistical indication that two variables have no relationship whatsoever).

Simple correlational studies are used for questions such as these: "What is the relationship between the number of nurse home visits and outpatient adherence to postoperative routines?" "How do hours invested in practice relate to playing errors in Little League baseball?" "To what extent does educational level relate to the rate of unemployment for men and women?" In each case, one or several forms of correlational statistics could be used to reveal the answer.

As these examples suggest, one of the particularly useful powers of correlational research is that it allows the examination of relationships among variables measured in different units (e.g., pounds and inches, minutes and errors, course credits and months employed). What matters in correlational research is not the actual units of measure but how the relative sizes of scores in different distributions relate to each other (a *distribution* is a list that shows not only the rank order of scores but also the magnitude of difference between adjacent figures).

As an example, Keefe and Berndt (1996) examined the relationship between friendship quality and self-esteem within a sample of seventh- and eighth-grade schoolchildren. They administered tests (with known reliability and validity) for the two variables during the fall and spring semesters. By examining how the relationships (correlation coefficients) changed over time, they were able to make interesting hypotheses about how the availability and quality of friendships might relate to a child's regard for him- or herself.

The second type of correlational design, *predictive research,* is used to improve our capacity to anticipate events. By examining the patterns of association between some set of variables and something that the investigator wishes to predict (usually called the *criterion variable*), it is possible to identify the best possible set of variables to use. Here, an example will serve better than a lengthy explanation.

If you want to know which set of variables best predicts the 5-year survivability of a cancer patient after surgery (choosing from, for example, age, health status, gender, type of malignancy, extent of cancer spread, and postoperative care), a correlation statistic called *multiple regression* would yield the answer. It might well be that all six of those variables used together predict no better than just age and gender when used alone. Whatever the case, the answer can be very important in determining medical procedures and hospital policies governing care for cancer patients.

Prediction research can be particularly valuable when it is necessary to establish priorities for the distribution of scarce resources. Questions such as "For children, which demographic, educational, and home environment factors contribute the most to their reading ability as adults?" allow findings (when properly replicated) to influence educational policy. When available, tax dollars can be invested in programs that are likely to produce the largest improvements in literacy, even though many factors contribute to the development of reading skills.

Vitaro, Ladouceur, and Bujold (1996) published an example of predictive research. They examined the relationships between a number of variables and gambling in young boys. It was not entirely surprising when they discovered that gambling was related to both delinquency and substance abuse. Thus, in practical terms, the results confirmed that social workers should anticipate greater risks associated with gambling among delinquent boys with a record of substance abuse. However, the same statistical analysis revealed that certain measures of anxiety also predicted gambling behaviors—a new and important insight. In addition, when the investigators examined groups of gambling and nongambling boys, they found a number of variables that appeared to discriminate between the two. This combination of correlational study with group comparisons allowed the investigators to inspect their sample from several angles, an approach that can yield rich and sometimes unexpected results.

The third kind of correlational study, *modeling research* (which includes such techniques as path analysis and structural equation modeling), maps in graphic form (often in the familiar format of boxes with connecting arrows) the relationships among a number of variables, displaying the degree to which any one of them can be used to predict one or more of the others. Interlocking questions such as "What is the best set of factors for predicting whether or not a student will graduate from college?" "When placed in a diagrammatic model, how are those contributing factors most logically arranged?" and "How much predictive power is exerted by the various lines of influence drawn among the factors?" illustrate the wonderfully complex sort of problem that can be addressed through the correlational procedures used in modeling research.

The model shown in Figure 6.2 displays a hypothetical set of factors that influences the extent to which adults volunteer their assistance to service organizations. The lines drawn between factors show the direction of influence (what can be predicted by knowledge about a given factor), and the number given for each line (called a *path coefficient*) indicates the degree of influence exerted. In effect, the path coefficients show the power of prediction on a scale from −1.0 to +1.0.

Translated into a set of plain-language statements, the model asserts that how much time people have available is a primary predictor of their volunteer behavior (whether they offer to help at all and, if so, to what extent). The path coefficient of .74 indicates a robust and positive prediction—the more time we have to expend (or believe we

Figure 6.2   Example of a Structural Equation Model

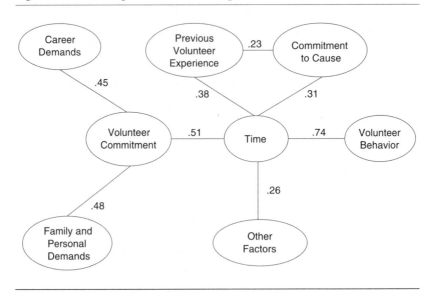

have), the more time we are likely to invest in voluntary service activities.

Note, however, that both the realities of available time and the perceptions of that availability are influenced by other factors, as displayed in the six related latent variables (in the ovals) that directly or indirectly impact time. For example, how much time people believe they have available for such activities as community or charitable service is partly a function of their degree of commitment to the idea that voluntary service to others is an obligation (.51). That commitment, however, is modulated by the very real constraints of career (.45) and family (.48) obligations.

The sense of how much time is available is also influenced by personal commitment to the particular cause at hand (.31). Among the influences that determine our commitment to a service activity is previous experience as a volunteer (the path coefficient of .23 indicates a relatively small, but nevertheless positive, relationship). Did volunteering produce a satisfying sense of accomplishment? Were work conditions acceptable and demands reasonable? If you examine Figure 6.2 closely, you will see that a good experience might exert its influence indirectly by increasing commitment to the particular cause involved, with that, in turn, serving to increase the time devoted.

Alternatively, past experience could have a more direct influence by leading the participant to raise the estimate of time available for any form of service (.38).

Unhappy encounters with volunteering, of course, could have the reverse effect, and the path correlations might have negative signs (bad experiences predicting both lowered commitment and a decrease in the time perceived to be available). As you can see from all of this, statistical modeling can provide useful (and sometimes unexpected) insights into the complexities of how things work—insights that are invisible or only dimly glimpsed from our surface view of relationships.

Modeling research has found a growing number of useful applications in recent years. As an example, Etezadi-Amoli and Farhoomand (1996) used structural equations to develop a model of computer users' satisfaction and performance. They developed a survey form, with appropriate validity and reliability demonstrations, to measure six dimensions of attitude toward computer use. When entered into the equation used for analysis, survey data from a sample of users generated a graphic model that not only arranged the variables in a manner consistent with their interrelationships but highlighted connections that might otherwise have been lost in a swamp of statistics. The model makes graphically clear, for example, that how people feel about computers plays a large role in determining how well they learn to use them. That insight is useful because, absent such evidence, the more likely assumption would be that competence in use is a predictor for positive attitudes—not the reverse.

Quasi-experimental/experimental research. This is a large family of related research designs, and a full explanation of even one would demand far more space than we have available in this introductory text. The feature that ties all of them together is the inspection of data to determine whether two or more groups differ on some variable. The most familiar format is the classic experiment in which the investigator provides some treatment (often called the *intervention)* to one group (the *experimental group*) but not the other (the *control group*). The two levels of treatment (some and none) together constitute the independent variable being manipulated in the study. The two groups are then compared for their status on some variable (usually called the *outcome* or *dependent variable)* that might have been influenced by the treatment.

As you might imagine, the questions being asked, the study design, the statistical analysis employed, and the findings produced can become very complex. For example, many experiments have multiple dependent or independent variables. It is one thing to examine the therapeutic impact of a cold medicine given to a particular sample of afflicted patients, but it is quite another to ask whether there are differences in attitude toward crime, education, and the economy among urban, suburban, and rural voters, when data are divided by gender. There are, however, experimental designs that can juggle the two independent variables (residence and gender) and the three dependent variables (attitudes toward crime, education, and the economy) with precision and elegance.

The family of designs for which the generic term *experiment* is applied in common speech actually consists of two branches that researchers carefully recognize as distinct. The difference between what scholars call *true experiments* and the large subspecies of studies referred to as *quasi-experiments* lies in the degree of control that the investigator exercises over the study. In true experiments, researchers not only choose the treatment, but they also select subjects, assign subjects to groups, and, finally, assign treatments to groups. In its purest form, the true experiment requires that these three manipulations be done through use of random procedures (allowing chance to control selection and assignment).

For example, if an investigator had determined that it would be appropriate to conduct a true experiment to find out whether small, daily doses of aspirin would lower the incidence of heart attacks in a population of older men, he or she would take the following steps. First, the researcher would randomly select a large number of men between the ages of 60 and 65. Next, that sample would be divided by random procedures into two groups. Then, again by a random operation (perhaps the flip of a coin), one group would be designated as experimental (treatment), and members of that group would take one-half of an aspirin every day. The remaining group would be designated as control, and members of that group would take daily dummy tablets (called a *placebo treatment*) made of some pharmacologically inert substance. (If this were a variant of the true experiment called a *double blind*, neither the investigator nor the subjects would know which group was receiving the treatment and which the placebo until all the data had been collected.) Finally, 10 years later, the investigator would count the number of men in each group who had suffered cardiac incidents. The investigator would have had control of each manipulation and would have obtained strong evidence concerning the presence or absence of a causal relationship between the treatment (aspirin) and the variable of interest (heart attacks).

In contrast, quasi-experiments involve conditions under which the investigator does not control one or more of the critical variables and might be unable to use random procedures to select or assign all subjects and treatments. For example, a common form of quasi-experiment is used when it is necessary to study intact groups created by events or natural processes (voters in a rural county of Illinois, people who have been in automobile accidents, or all the students in Ms. Smith's third-grade class). The researcher does not have control over who is selected for study, who is assigned to groups, or, in some cases, which group receives the experimental treatment. Given the logistical difficulty in controlling all of these factors (at least outside the laboratory), it is not surprising that the vast majority of experiments in the social and behavioral sciences are quasi-experiments.

The distinction between the two kinds of experiments is not trivial. In particular, the use of randomization in selecting subjects or assigning treatments has powerful consequences for what can be learned from a study. We will leave to you the thrill of discovering more about this topic from another source at another time (for example, Kirk, 1995; Winer, Brown, & Michels, 1991). We must add, however, that this is a case of the sooner learned, the better served.

Experiments and quasi-experiments are appropriate for the same sorts of research questions; often, the availability of time, subjects, resources, and technology for collection of data determines the choice between the two. A simple question such as "Do employees who receive on-the-job safety training have better safety records than a control group of otherwise equivalent employees without such training?" could be addressed by any of several kinds of experimental or quasi-experimental designs. We would be remiss, however, if we did not note that the complexity of the design selected is not an indicator of research quality. It is far better to use a simple design that fits a simple question than to adopt an unnecessarily complex strategy that yields the same answer. Complexity is costly and multiplies the opportunities to make fatal errors.

An example of a quasi-experiment was reported by Brice, Gorey, Hall, and Angelino (1996). They examined the impact of an eight-session health-promotion program on the subjects' health-related beliefs and subsequent behaviors. Subjects in the treatment group were not selected by random procedures. They were chosen simply because they were available for the program, completed it, and were willing to undergo the 9-month follow-up procedure. The treatment group's scores for the dependent variables of belief and behavior were compared with those of subjects who were on the program waiting list. Careful examination of the two groups revealed few obvious differences in their characteristics, and, given the substantial superiority of outcome scores for the treatment group, the authors seemed justified in concluding that the program had a positive effect.

As we suggested, when contrasting true and quasi-experiments, tight control over subjects, environments, and treatments is often a luxury reserved for laboratory studies. It is singularly difficult to establish the level of control required for a true experiment in the more open and unpredictable conditions of the real world, which is why such investigations are relatively rare. That they are not impossible, however, was demonstrated by Barber and Gilbertson (1996).

In that study, the subjects were partners of people who were both dependent on alcohol and resistant to any change in their behavior. The partners were randomly selected from a larger population and then randomly assigned to four conditions. The treatments were (a) an intervention designed to help the partner, provided on an individual basis; (b) the same intervention for the partner, provided in a group setting; (c) no intervention; and (d) participation by the partner in Al-Anon (a support group for people who are friends, relatives, or partners of alcoholics). Dependent variables included measures of change in drinking behavior, status of other personal problems, and degree of marital consensus. The study found that the various treatment conditions had different effects on different dependent variables (not an uncommon result in multivariate studies). For example, Treatment (a) was the only one to produce positive change in marital consensus.

Single-subject research. This type of research is often categorized as experimental by those who use it to study human behavior. We have listed it here as a separate form of inquiry because it does have distinguishing features that will immediately be apparent to the beginning reader. That the underlying structure and assumptions might match those of an experiment seem less important here than pursuing our purpose—to ease you through the early stages of reading research reports.

Researchers using single-subject designs (a number of alternatives are available) usually are interested in examining the contingencies that shape human behavior. As the name implies, observations are made of a single subject (or of one subject at a time). Typically, the investigator collects data that establish how the subject behaves under normal conditions (called *baseline behavior*), before any treatment is implemented or any change in the situation occurs. Then, the investigator introduces change, adding or removing something that might influence the subject's behavior and recording data that reflect the consequences.

Unlike other forms of quantitative research, it is rare to find statistics used to analyze data in single-subject studies. More typically, the frequency of behavior is graphed across time so that changes such as shifts from baseline, attenuation of effects, and reversal of effects (with removal of treatment) can be noted easily. If data are collected concurrently for a number of such individual graphs, the display of results for even a small set of subjects can be very persuasive. Books by Sidman (1960) and Johnson and Pennypacker (1993) are the standard references for anyone interested in this type of research.

Within the social sciences, there is a virtually endless array of variations on the basic strategy represented in single-subject research. Some of these are widely used to evaluate various methods of modifying human behavior. For example, Maguire, Lange, Scherling, and Grow (1996) conducted a study to examine results produced by an intervention designed to reduce the uncooperative behavior of mentally retarded patients when they have dental work performed. Four adult males who were mildly to severely mentally retarded were the subjects in the study.

A behavioral baseline was established for each of the four participants by recording and graphing the frequency of their resistant behaviors during regularly scheduled appointments (including expressing physical aggression, shouting, refusing to open the mouth, and turning the head away from the dentist). Then, the investigators implemented a treatment for the subjects. The intervention consisted of a number of elements, including having the dentist give an explanation of all parts of the dental procedure, letting the patient touch the tools and ask questions, providing frequent positive reinforcements designed to counteract the negative aspects of the experience, and incorporating breaks to help the subjects manage discomfort. During subsequent appointments at which the treatment was applied, the levels of resistant behaviors decreased sharply from those observed during collection of baseline data. Although the frequency of patient resistance for both baselines and subsequent treatments did show some fluctuation across visits, such a uniform and persistent deflection of rates (coinciding exactly with implementation of the treatment) could not reasonably be attributed to natural variation in the subjects' behavior. The authors concluded that the treatment had been effective in reducing uncooperative behavior in the dentist's chair.

There are a number of interesting variations on the design used in the study just described. In one, called a *reversal design,* the next step would be to remove treatment and to inspect the behavior graphs for a change in frequency, moving back in the direction of the original baseline levels. If that were observed, it would add weight to the argument that the intervention had been the true cause of the patients' change in resistant behavior. Another variation involves the timing of the intervention. If the initiation of the treatment had been spaced across appointments so that Subject 1 received the intervention on the first visit, but Subject 2 not until the second visit, and so on, and each of the behavior graphs deflected downward only as the treatment was introduced (having retained baseline levels until that point), additional weight would have been added to the argument that it was the treatment and not some other condition that was causing the improvement in cooperation. From these examples, it should be clear that for certain kinds of research problems, single-subject designs offer attractive alternatives to more traditional forms of experimentation.

Meta-analysis. In recent years, new methods have been created that allow researchers to combine studies that have the same focus to derive a single result—one that allows for conclusions with considerably more persuasive power than could be provided by any single study. This technique for combining the results from independent studies is called *meta-analysis.* Researchers do not collect original data but aggregate findings from previous studies through the use of special statistical formulae.

Although the statistics might seem mysterious, the basics of the underlying logic are not. In experimental and quasi-experimental studies, the investigator is interested in whether the experimental group, which he or she has "treated" with something (such as special reading instruction, a relaxation program, or a drug), is significantly different from a control group that was not treated. (Researchers use the word *significant* not in the usual sense of *important,* but as the label for differences that are unlikely to be due to chance—i.e., differences probably caused by a treatment.) In the simplest sense, for the difference to be statistically significant, it has to be larger than the average differences among subjects in the control group. That comparison of between-group differences and within-group differences produces a resulting number called the *effect size,* which is the statistical construct on which meta-analysis is based. As we indicate in Appendix C, in the context of experimental research, effect size is an indicator of the strength of the treatment.

In meta-analysis, researchers treat the effect size as a datum—that is, as a score representing the study from which it is derived. The effect sizes from a number of studies are analyzed in ways similar to the standard statistical analysis of data from individuals in a single experiment. If the topic under examination has attracted a substantial amount of interest, it will have produced many studies; if enough of those studies are of high quality, the meta-analysis can determine the average effect size of all the studies taken together. That it can do so regardless of differences in the individual studies (such as sample sizes and methods of data collection) makes meta-analysis a powerful tool.

In some areas of inquiry, for example, a group of studies that has produced only modest results might be concealing the fact that the findings actually are substantial as well as persistent—a fact that can become apparent only through the magnifying power of meta-analysis. If you are interested in learning more, references such as Hedges (1998), Hunter and Schmidt (1995) and Lipsey and Wilson (2000) provide the essential details.

Nichol et al. (1996) conducted a meta-analysis using studies of emergency medical systems (EMSs) for treatment of out-of-hospital cardiac arrests. After carefully selecting the reports to include, they combined results for response time until EMS personnel arrived, bystander application of cardiopulmonary resuscitation, and various types of interventions provided by EMSs. They found that several critical factors influenced survival rates, not all of which were obvious from a reading of the contributory studies when considered individually. Such findings show that we have much to learn by doing research on research, which is the function of meta-analysis.

Qualitative Research

At this point, we have completed our brief overview of issues that are generic to all types of research and our survey of the five basic formats for inquiry within the quantitative domain. We turn now to a different type of inquiry—qualitative research. Before you read the next section, however, it might be helpful to be reminded of three points made in previous chapters.

First, if you arrived here from Chapter 5 (or any other point in the text) because we suggested this section as a resource providing greater detail about qualitative research, you have done exactly the right thing. You should be able to read what follows without difficulty and then return to the earlier point in the text armed with some useful insights into qualitative research.

Second, the general problems of doing good qualitative research will sound familiar. The persistent issues already discussed in this chapter have not been left behind in the world of numbers and statistics. Formulating good questions, matching questions with the appropriate methodology, collecting high-quality data that are valid and reliable, and interpreting those data with thoughtful care still are the name of the game, even when the names given to those problems change.

Third, the change to qualitative research involves more than a change in methods of data collection and more than a change in the form of data from numbers to words. Quantitative and qualitative research reflect different paradigms—that is, they start with different assumptions about the nature of the world, truth, and the functions of research. We will not discuss the philosophic roots of those differences, but we do assert one proposition concerning them. Until you have read and thought about the differing philosophic perspectives that operate in the two worldviews (Denzin & Lincoln, 2000, provides a good place to start), you will not have a full appreciation of either quantitative or qualitative research.

Qualitative research is now represented in many fields of study, and its influence in the social sciences has been growing steadily. In addition, this form of inquiry has been going through a recent period of rapid diversification, with the creation of a number of distinctive research traditions. As illustration, Table 6.3 presents an overview of purposes, commonly used nomenclature, and specific techniques associated with qualitative research. The two traditions, or subcategories, of qualitative research shown in the table will be introduced here in some detail: interpretive and critical research.

Studies broadly categorized as interpretive have found wide use, and, indeed, much of our previous discussion of qualitative research in Chapter 5 pertained primarily to studies that would be classified in that group. The other tradition we will introduce, *critical research,* is less

Table 6.3   Purpose, Names, and Examples of Research Techniques Used in Qualitative Research

	Interpretive	*Critical Theory*
Purpose	To understand a situation from the perspective of the participant.	To understand and critique power within society.
Common Forms	• Ethnographic • Constructivism • Phenomenological • Grounded theory • Participant observation • Interpretive interactionism • Hermeneutics • Case study	• Feminist • Marxist • Critical ethnography • Deconstruction • Postmodernism • Poststructuralism • Foucauldian
Examples of Research Techniques	• Observation and use of field notes • Examination of documents • Interviews	• Analysis of print materials, popular culture, and social structures • Documentation of empowerment activities, often using interpretive research techniques

common, particularly in some disciplines. Its visibility is growing, however, and you are likely to encounter at least one report based on critical theory when exploring the literature on almost any topic of current interest in the social sciences.

Good references are available for all forms of qualitative research. A comprehensive treatment of the qualitative paradigm and its various methodological traditions is available in Denzin and Lincoln (2000). For introductions to interpretive research, we have found Bogdan and Biklen (2003), Creswell (2003), Flick (2002), Maxwell (1996), Merriam (1998), Morse and Richards (2002), and Rossman and Rallis (2003) to be both sound and popular with our students. Truly accessible, introductory-level texts on critical research are more difficult to find, but Thomas (1993) is quite suitable for most purposes.

For readers who are new to the world of research, Robson (2002) might be one of the best resources for beginning their explorations. The author unfolds both qualitative and quantitative approaches to social science in a parallel fashion that clarifies differences and similarities. In its second edition, the book is comprehensive in coverage, strongly oriented toward practical use in designing studies, and persistently understanding about the needs of the novice.

Finally, by now it will be apparent to you that we could not possibly describe all of the variant forms assumed by qualitative research. To meet that need, you must have a true compendium—and, fortunately, there is one. For any short-term purpose, you should locate a library copy of the *Dictionary of Qualitative Inquiry* (Schwandt, 2001). If you have longer-term interests in research, however, purchase of this volume might be unavoidable (priced well under $50.00, the cost of a paperbound edition is not excessive). The book is devoted exclusively to defining the language conventions (a kind label for jargon) of qualitative research. With suggested readings and cross-references given for most entries, this might be one instance when you actually find yourself sitting down to read a dictionary.

Interpretive research. In this kind of study, by acting as the primary instrument for data collection, the investigator builds an extensive collection of *thick description* (detailed records concerning context, people, actions, and the perceptions of participants) as the basis for inductive generation of an understanding of what is going on or how things work (an *explanatory theory*). Often, the purpose of interpretive research is to understand the setting for social action from the perspective of the participants.

Reports can contain richly detailed narratives that are grounded in the data of the participants' own words, as selectively extracted from transcriptions of interviews. Descriptions of context and events are often developed directly from notes (commonly called *field notes*) made in the course of observations at the actual site of interest in the study (a research strategy generally referred to as *fieldwork*). Questions that might be asked in an interpretive study include "How do Native Americans view the criminal justice system?" "How do teachers implement a new state-mandated curriculum in their classroom?" and "What is the experience of teenage runaways when they become homeless?"

Among the methods commonly used by interpretive researchers are interviews, systematic observation of the setting or events under investigation, and analysis of documentary materials (lesson plans, police reports, hospital records, news stories, and diaries). Typically, collection and analysis of data takes place concurrently, with preliminary insights and new questions being used to inform and guide subsequent data collection. Some interpretive research takes the form of case studies (see Merriam, 1998, or Stake, 1995) in which a single participant or site is investigated both in depth and over considerable time. In contrast, research teams, multiple sites, and numerous forms of data collection can make some interpretive studies logistically complex and truly heroic undertakings.

Trustworthiness of data is as vital an issue here as it is in any other form of inquiry. The means used to confront the threats to validity and reliability necessarily take different forms (and have different names) in this research tradition. As you read reports, however, you will have little difficulty in recognizing those familiar concerns.

Results from interpretive studies are reported differently than are those from quantitative research. Prose text rather than tables and graphs give a very different feel to qualitative reports. The similarity to newspaper reporting and historical novels is often striking, and it is in some respects quite genuine because it arises from the author's desire to create a credible and engaging story. The less obvious dissimilarities, however, are what make one research and the others journalism or fictional literature.

Among those differences is the fact that journalists rarely are constrained to make their personal biases and investments in a report a matter of public record, whereas, in many interpretive studies, that obligation is observed with scrupulous care. Journalists are rarely trained in the social sciences and tend simply to describe rather than to analyze what they have observed. For the same reason, they cannot make use of powerful theories in framing and explaining their findings. Also, deadlines play a much more prominent role in reporting than in research and have the inevitable effect of limiting the collection of information. Finally, newsworthy elements (the events and issues that make a good story) often are not the items that have the greatest power to help us understand how and why things happen. Investigative reporters and interpretive researchers share many of the same skills and at their best have much to teach each other. The products of their inquiry are not better or worse than each other, they simply are different—done for different purposes, addressed to different audiences, and shaped by different contingencies.

Here are some examples from a variety of research traditions that have evolved from or been influenced by the qualitative paradigm. We have selected types that are among the most commonly encountered in the social science research literature for applied professional fields such as nursing, social work, education, occupational and physical therapy, public administration, and counseling. The home disciplines of the investigators include psychology, sociology, anthropology, communication, and education.

Generic studies. The term *generic,* used here to indicate a basic or standard form of interpretive research (a nomenclature suggested by Merriam, 1998), refers to qualitative studies with characteristics such as those discussed in this and previous chapters—but without a particular perspective that would immediately mark them as members of a specific tradition. Investigators who do studies like these are seeking to describe and to understand something. In most cases they follow these steps: (a) identify a conceptual model or theoretical framework for thinking about the research problem (usually drawn from one of the disciplines), (b) collect data through interviews, observations, or document analysis, (c) analyze the data through a process that identifies recurring patterns and thematic regularities, and (d) present conclusions in terms that use concepts from the initial framework.

Studies of this sort represent by far the largest number of published reports. Other than the presence of potentially interesting features in design or provocative qualities in the findings, there was little to recommend one selection over any other. Accordingly, we simply drew the generic specimen—Dowson and McInerney (2001)—by lot.

Note, however, that the annotation for this study (as well as those used to illustrate other types of qualitative research) is lengthier by several paragraphs than the preceding examples for designs in quantitative research. That change reflects the more discursive content of qualitative reports (both the use of numbers rather than words and the use of tables for economical presentation serve to keep most quantitative reports lean). In addition, we want readers to grasp the complex notion that in any qualitative study, the investigator is using a more flexible and broadly defined set of tactical possibilities after research is under way. Therefore, it takes a little more space to recount the story— a tale that typically has a few more twists, turns, and subplots than are provided by a tightly designed and faithfully executed experiment.

In a study of 86 male and female pupils at six Australian middle schools, Dowson and McInerney (2001) focused their efforts on identifying and describing the academic achievement goals espoused by the students. The goal descriptions included components in three areas: *cognitive* (what the participants said they thought about their goals), *affective* (what they reported feeling about their goals), and *behavioral* (what they actually were observed doing in relation to their goals). The theoretical framework for the study drew from both achievement and social goal theories.

To establish an initial sense of the range of achievement goals, students first participated in individual conversational interviews. Then, using data from that first cycle of conversations, a subsample of students was interviewed with a more direct focus on particular goals (those involving work avoidance and several forms of social motivation). Finally, two kinds of field observations were undertaken in the classes attended by the participants: (a) structured observations using a schedule based on what had been revealed about student goals during the interviews and (b) unstructured classroom observations that involved taking field notes and engaging in informal conversations with participants.

All data were transcribed into hard copy and then coded for easy retrieval. By inductive analysis (moving from the data to hypotheses or theories), students' statements and investigators' field notes were sorted into categories reflecting similarities in content and context. The categories were refined and then organized according to their relationships with each other. The result was four primary clusters called *goal orientations:* (a) work avoidance—the goal of minimizing effort on academic tasks, (b) social affiliation—the goal of wanting to work together with other students, (c) social responsibility—the goal of living up to perceived expectations, and (d) social concerns—the goal of helping other students.

The resulting description of what students want to achieve in middle school was complex, richly illustrated, and full of surprises. Aside from avoiding work, a persistently maladaptive goal from the adult vantage point, the participants espoused and enacted social goals that clearly constituted important reasons for engagement in learning. Among the conclusions that will catch the attention of any reader was the assertion that social motives, rather than being peripheral to performance of academic tasks, might be salient and highly predictive of school achievement.

Phenomenological studies. Phenomenology is a philosophic perspective that underlies all qualitative research traditions but, when used to examine the meaning of something (an event, role, process, status, or context) from the vantage point of someone (or some group) who actually experiences that phenomenon, both the study and the methodology are likely to be called *phenomenological*. Here you see represented a point we have repeatedly made about the way qualitative researchers think about the world—that reality exists only in the eyes and minds of beholders. In other words, the meaning of "loneliness" can be constructed only out of an understanding of what lonely people say it means. What the researcher thinks something might mean has to be put aside so that he or she can listen attentively to the reports of participants' subjective experiences. It is out of these data that the elements and structure of the phenomenon can be identified and described.

In a study of single and single-again women, Lewis and Moon (1997) asked, "What is it like to be a single woman today?" and "Are the experiences of women who have always been single different from those who find themselves single again after having been married?" A qualitative methodology was selected because the area of investigation was new and the purpose of the study was exploratory and phenomenological in nature.

The report contains both an extensive review of the research literature on the phenomenon of singleness (including the evolving image of single women in recent history) and a description of the authors' own background and connections to the study (their academic backgrounds, professional careers, experience as single women, and sources of interest in the topic).

The study had two phases: (a) 37 single women between the ages of 30 and 65 who had been recruited as volunteers through a newspaper advertisement were divided into small focus groups in which they responded to a series of open-ended questions (the protocol questions were revised after the authors viewed and analyzed the videotape of each meeting, thus progressively sharpening the nature of the probes); and (b) questionnaire responses were analyzed from 39 similar participants who had not been in the focus group interviews. Four of the focus groups in the first phase consisted of women who had always been single, whereas three groups were composed of women who had become single as a function of death or divorce. The semistructured questionnaire used in the second phase was based on recurring themes derived from the focus group data and was prepared in two forms: one for single women and one for single again women.

All interviews and open-ended questionnaire responses were transcribed and coded to allow tallying and comparison. The investigators wrote preliminary statements describing what the participants said they had experienced about being single. Then, working back and forth between the statements and the data set (in an analytic process called *constant comparison*), they produced a final set of themes that represented their findings. After carefully considering issues of reliability and validity, the researchers asserted a single, "overriding" conclusion: *"Single women have unresolved or unrecognized ambivalences about being single"* (p. 123).

They supported that assertion with illustrations drawn from three regularities that appeared in the full data set: (a) women are aware of both the advantages and drawbacks of being single, (b) women are ambivalent about the reasons for their singleness, and (c) although content with being single, many women experience feelings of loss and grief. The reality of singleness as it was lived by the participants was far more mixed than is commonly portrayed in a society that tends either to glamorize or to stigmatize the single life.

Ethnographic studies. With its origins in anthropology, *ethnography* is both a research process (the researcher "does" ethnography in the field), and a product (the reported study can be called "an ethnography"). It is a form of qualitative research used to examine social units, some as broad as an entire culture and some as narrow as a single social unit or setting (a family, classroom, or rest home). The focus is always on the values, attitudes, and beliefs that determine how members of the group behave in the social setting. These are the dispositions and practices we learn to be members of and participants in various organizations and communities, and, although those rules and structures might change over time, they are passed on to newcomers as the shared dimensions of culture (both explicit and implicit) that they are expected to know (and observe).

In the typical format, the researcher gathers data (most commonly through field notes) by direct presence as an observer (and sometimes participant) in the natural setting. The usual objective is to develop a holistic perspective that will allow an analysis of local culture in its full context. The aspect of sociocultural interpretation (including historic, economic, and demographic factors) is what distinguishes classic ethnographic studies from other on-site-observer approaches that generate descriptions of a problem or setting.

There is no particular set of methods used by all investigators, and data collection tactics often evolve as the study proceeds. It is not uncommon for quantitative data to be accumulated along with extensive information that reflects the understandings of the participants (in that latter sense, ethnographic studies are also phenomenological in nature). There is great emphasis on accuracy, detail, and completeness—the agencies of internal and external validity. The final products are descriptions and explanations that illuminate the meaning and function of human actions within a specified setting or a defined social unit.

It would have been easy to select as an example here a study involving ethnography in an exotic cultural context—a village in Mexico, a farming commune populated by members of a conservative religion, or an urban neighborhood with a predominantly immigrant population. Instead, we used our sense of places that would be familiar to the majority of our readers (hospitals, schools, social agencies, small business organizations, churches, athletic teams) to select a study that illustrates the culture present in a local work setting—a place with visible boundaries and recognizable participants.

Francis (2000) set out to ask a simple question about an agency designed to provide case management for homeless people with mental illness: "What is case management, and what, in their own eyes, do case managers do?" As so often happens in qualitative research, however, the question turned out to be far more complicated than the researcher had anticipated. Moreover, the study actually performed in response to those complexities became itself a case study of the centrality of broad social context in understanding local culture. What happened at the agency on a day-to-day basis proved to be as much a function of resource allocation, state and federal contests for power, bureaucratic regulations, and the politics of social systems in which the agency was embedded as it was of how the participants understood their social and professional roles.

Federally funded as a demonstration project, the research site was an agency charged with providing intensive case management for homeless persons who suffer from mental disorder and substance abuse. Immediate administration, however, was under the jurisdiction of the county community health system. Formed into nontraditional teams of service providers consisting of a case manager, a nurse, an outreach worker, a project manager, and a consumer-member (a person with a history of homelessness and addiction), the agency staff placed special emphasis on sharing information both within and across teams.

Over a 5-month period, the investigator collected field note data through daily on-site observation (attending staff meetings, participating in agency activities, and shadowing team members both in and out of the office), as well as through unstructured interviews with 10 informants selected from various roles within the agency. All data were transcribed, coded, and analyzed through use of HyperResearch, a computer program for text analysis.

As soon as on-site observation began, it was immediately clear that participants wanted to talk about how the conflicting regulations of the state, federal, and county bureaucracies made it difficult to provide effective service and retain clients. Thus, the focal question became, Why is it so difficult for this agency to deliver its intensive case management services, and what are the consequences of this difficulty? Although the question was tied tightly to the immediate circumstances of that particular agency, the answer had to be found in the wider sociopolitical context within which it operated.

The county health system had services set up for people who were homeless *or* mentally ill *or* substance abusers, but not all three. The federal funding mandate, however, presumed services for a population with any two or all three of these problems. In the ensuing contest of political wills, the case managers reported a pervasive sense that neither the county administrative system nor the federal bureaucracy was really concerned about whether their clients were actually getting any help.

What evolved was a set of norms that valued (and encouraged) creative evasion of regulations in ways that would make clients eligible for assistance. When such practices failed, clients were left unserved, often after enormous investments of time and emotional capital by case managers. In turn, the accumulation of fatigue and stress began to produce burnout in members of the staff, and, accordingly, the entire organization began to show signs of instability.

These effects were interpreted by the author in terms of classic role-conflict theory, with consequent recommendations for the design of social service agencies. An ethnographic investigation offered far more than a description of what case managers did in a modern social service agency; it provided a demonstration of how an environment made hostile by regulatory conflict can make the most desperately needed, well planned, and adequately funded program go awry.

Grounded theory studies. Although it is employed in studies that reflect a general qualitative orientation (the investigator is the primary instrument of data collection, reality is assumed to be a subjective construct created or negotiated by people, and inductive processes are employed to derive meaning from the data), grounded theory is, nonetheless, a very specific research methodology. At the outset, we need to prepare our readers for what might be two small disappointments. First, no matter which study we select for our illustration, the methods of data collection are likely to sound generally like some of those you already have encountered. Second, although we will describe its purpose and general form, beyond that overview we will not explain how grounded theory, as a specific method, is used to analyze data. The process is complex, specified in great detail, and full of constructs that would be unfamiliar to most readers (Glaser & Strauss, 1967).

Indeed, the method is also unfamiliar to many researchers who freely use the term to characterize any study they have performed in which a hypothesis was derived to explain or understand the data. In the majority of such attributions, however, it is our judgment that, *yes,* they did have a theory, and, *yes,* that theory was derived (more or less) from their inspection of the data, but, *no,* there is nothing in the report to suggest that they actually employed the procedures specified for grounded theory. Incorrect or not, however, that misappropriation of terminology seems to be with us to stay.

The purpose of genuine grounded theory studies seems clear enough—the production (development) of a theory. The theory emerges from the investigators' intimate association with and manipulation of the data (and hence it is "grounded" in the data), and the theory can be used to help understand why the data are the way they are. More to the functional point, grounded theories offer something beyond a descriptive response to the question "What's going on here?" by providing a systematic explanation for both why and how it does go on.

As powerful as they may be, however, such theories can be elusive. Grounded theories are not just lying around in the data waiting to be discovered; they have to be extracted by a theoretically sensitive researcher who guides the data collection process as useful concepts, linkages, and categories begin to appear. Then, the process of constant comparison (going back and forth between tentative explanations and data, searching for confirmation) commonly is used, first to create descriptive categories (a useful by-product of many grounded theory studies) and then as the basis for theoretical assertions that pull things together.

Thus, grounded theory studies do not start with a theory—they end with one. Invariably, the theory is a new one that did not exist before that particular study, because it came out of that particular study. Also, because the theories produced tend to be very specific to the context studied, they often have strong implications for the design of effective practice. What they lack in terms of grand generalization, they gain in terms of applicability.

The central question for the study we selected to illustrate grounded theory (Ungar, 2000) was, "What role do friends and peer groups play in the lives and psychological development of teenagers?" The author of this study was a Canadian clinical psychologist with a practice that included treatment of high-risk adolescents ages 13 to 18. With each of 41 male and female volunteer participants who met the criteria for being high risk (various combinations of poverty, physical and sexual abuse, family violence, neglect, addictions, and mental disorders), two interviews were conducted lasting one to one-and-one-half hours. Most (37) of the participants were or had been the investigator's clients in individual, group, or family therapy, and, in all cases, full clinical case histories were available for review.

In the first interview, open-ended questions were asked from a protocol designed to cover issues related to adolescence, mental health, relationships, social competencies, coping strategies, and experiences of power and control (or lack thereof). In the second interview, questions were shaped by the results from ongoing analysis of data (transcripts) created by the first session. In addition, as a strategy to ensure that the data were trustworthy, participants were asked to comment on the emerging theoretical statements (a process sometimes called *member-checking*).

The grounded theory approach as just defined was implemented throughout the data collection and analysis processes. The result was a theory describing three developmental stages of power as adolescents progressed toward positive self-definitions. This theory suggested a process that was contrary to the widely accepted adult notion that peer groups exert pressure that is one-way and highly coercive, leading vulnerable adolescents into antisocial behaviors. Peer groups were described by participants as forums in which they enhanced personal power through the assertion of a personal identity. In virtually every case, apparent conformity hid the important power the adolescents had within the peer group to be themselves.

At the first developmental stage, the teenage participants described being *stuck* with an identity (usually one given to them by adults such as parents, police, teachers, or other authorities) such as delinquent, troubled, violent, truant, or suicidal. The participants might have had some small degree of agency in choosing their identity, but there were few alternatives other than those assigned by adults.

At the second developmental stage, the participants tried on new identities as a result of the serendipitous discovery and acquisition of another label, often one provided by the different groups with whom they interacted—most particularly peer groups. These unstuck participants became *chameleons,* using their new identities as coping strategies within their difficult life circumstances, allowing them to appear more powerful than they might really feel.

At the third developmental stage, participants reported that they were able to construct self-definitions of their own choosing, which then were accepted and reinforced by peers—and in some cases by family and community members as well. This stage of *acceptance* allowed them to become more resilient and self-assured, proclaiming to the world: "This is who I am. Accept me."

Each of the stages in the developmental theory was grounded in the data, a fact illustrated by description of specific cases and quotations from their interviews. Further, the theory not only was new, it was counterintuitive, running strongly against our adult predisposition to see peer groups as a negative force that often leads hapless youth into delinquency. The reverse appeared to be true for the participants in this study: They used peer groups as means for searching out and assuming new and more positive self-definitions.

Critical research. Investigators doing critical research begin with a number of assumptions that differ sharply from those made by people working within other qualitative research traditions (or within the quantitative paradigm). Most scholars who work from the perspective of what is commonly called *critical theory* value the production of new knowledge through research (although they would insist on defining *knowledge* in their own terms), but only when it is conducted in a socially responsible manner—as they (individually) understand that moral imperative. Again, most of them would regard it as incumbent on the investigator to be concerned with how knowledge is used and, particularly, how that use relates to inequities in the distribution of power and material resources in our society.

The concern for matters of social justice and equity would be extended to any disadvantaged social subgroup: single-parent families, urban schools, minority-owned businesses, former convicts, people on welfare, illegal immigrants, or girls in a male-dominated physical education class. Research, for *most* critical investigators, either must help us understand the sources of inequity (and the social processes that sustain it) or must go beyond that goal to serve as an agent for remedial change by helping to empower members of an oppressed group (usually as a consequence of being participants in a study).

Those two alternatives for doing socially responsible research *both* imply that critical research must be concerned with making a better society—in the first case, indirectly, through improved understanding of social mechanisms, and, in the second case, directly, through empowerment of participants. Even that observation, however, oversimplifies the subtle varieties of critical research as it exists today.

Our use of the italicized word *most* in the text above was intended to clearly signal the qualifier "not all"—that is, we were being deliberate, not simply overly cautious. Critical research is a tradition very much in the making. It is in a state of wonderful disarray. Spirited disputation fills journals and conference meetings, and a heady sense of new enterprise is everywhere. Thus, most critical researchers would agree with our broad characterization of their perspective on inquiry, *but certainly not all.* If you do some background reading in this area (such as Thomas, 1993, mentioned earlier in this chapter), you soon will discover the truth of that assertion.

As you might expect, critical research does not require the investigator to maintain complete objectivity about the study. Indeed, most critical theorists regard objectivity in social science as no more than a polite fiction. That, however, does not indicate a disregard for care and close attention to detail in the planning and execution of a study. Nor does it suggest that critical researchers are not concerned about the quality of data obtained, the systematic use of analytic techniques, or a full accounting of both method and results in the report. They simply believe that all research is value bound and see it as appropriate that they make their *subjectivity* (personal values about the question and commitments about their role as researchers) explicit and public, for both participants and readers.

The questions addressed in much critical research sound similar to those used in interpretive research, although they might signal something about the investigator's social politics. "How do policies in administration of the parole system influence the recidivism rate of adolescents convicted of first-offense, nonviolent crimes?" is an example of the former, whereas "What are the primary vehicles for social oppression of lesbian teachers in the public schools?" represents the latter. Both studies, however, would be concerned with understanding how dominant groups impose their construction of reality and thereby institutionalize disadvantageous positions for stigmatized people. Investigators in both studies might also be committed to finding ways to use that knowledge to confront the inequity.

Often, critical studies that involve a component of social activism include careful documentation of that process. Recording this information is regarded as a particularly important aspect of being a responsible investigator. Because an analysis of the empowerment process often reveals valuable lessons that can inform others who follow, doing so meets the political obligations assumed in critical research.

Methods of data collection in critical research can be closely similar to those used throughout the qualitative domain: interviews, observation, and document analysis. The relationship of the researcher to the participant might be more egalitarian, even to the point of sharing some of the decisions about the course of the study, but, in such investigations, careful collection of data remains a central task.

On the other hand, in this form of inquiry, scholars are persistently testing the boundaries of tradition—even when what constitutes established practice might be no more than a decade old. In some reports published as studies in the critical tradition, the author assumes a stance so far removed from what we have come to expect that he or she is almost unrecognizable as a scholar. Further, even the definition of what constitutes the basic elements of research (design, data, analysis, results) begins to morph into unexpected forms. In the face of such diversity, we offer two examples, representing types drawn from very different locations in this wonderfully messy domain of human inquiry. We hope you regard them as exotic but truly interesting (or, perhaps, exciting) specimens with which to illustrate this type of research.

The tale told by Papineau and Kiely (1996) is unusual in several respects. Clearly, it is about the uses of critical theory, even though the authors elected not to use that term anywhere in the published report. Further, their writing is entirely free of the arcane jargon and philosophical circumlocutions that frequently appear in the writings of critical theorists. In that sense, this is a research report and not a polemic.

That it also happens to be the report of an evaluation study should not concern you at all. This kind of evaluation is as solidly qualitative research as field ethnography.

The story begins with a grassroots community economic development (CED) organization. One of the many similar groups that sprang up in the latter decades of the 20th century, the CED agency that was the focus of evaluation in this study arose through a coalition of community groups operating in an urban neighborhood. Their mission was to promote social change through educative, economic, and social services to single parents, unemployed youths, immigrants, the homeless, and persons on social assistance. To accomplish those ends, they employed a model of action that involved members of the community (including service recipients) as full participants in the development and implementation of solutions for social and economic problems.

Beyond provision of services, however, the members of the CED organization also saw empowerment as a coequal mission. Whatever they undertook (for example, a new employment program for low-income people, or a loan fund to provide capital for starting small businesses), they intended to leave those who received service more self-confident, more skillful in carrying out activities to attain goals, and more inclined to take collaborative action to effect social change. In brief, the target for CED was assistance provided in a manner that would produce empowerment.

After several years of operation, it was no surprise, therefore, when the members of the coalition decided not only that it was time to evaluate how effective the CED programs were in accomplishing their intended missions but that they wanted the process of evaluation to empower *them* as well! Thus, an accurate title for the report of this study might well have been, "Using participatory evaluation to empower the empowerers." It was reasoned that not only would such a process leave the stakeholders in the organization more committed to their work and savvy about getting it done, it would increase their commitment to evaluation results and their utilization.

An experienced evaluation researcher and group leader was employed, and the following design was laid out: (a) the initial plan would be approved by the several boards of directors from the organizations involved, (b) through a small group meeting with all stakeholders (administrators and staff, volunteers, donors, and service recipients), the questions to be addressed in the evaluation would be specified, (c) through a similar process, the instruments (interview and field observation protocols, questionnaires, rating forms) would be drafted, (d) data would be collected, (e) data would be analyzed and evaluation reports prepared, and (f) strategic planning would proceed throughout the organization. Finally, it was decided that the investigator would also document what was done to empower the stakeholders—and how well that worked.

It all happened as planned—for the most part. Things moved more slowly than the ambitious research plan had proposed, and there were a few unexpected defections along the way. For example, service recipients had no time or inclination to do instrument design and data collection tasks, and coalition leaders had no interest in doing data analysis (seeing that as the proper job of the investigator). Nevertheless, the verbatim transcripts of interviews were coded and subject to content analysis. Numeric data from rating scales were consolidated with descriptive statistics. Reports were written and then presented to the CED stakeholders.

And, what were the results? Was the agency serving the needs of its clients and was it leaving them empowered? Of greater interest for us, did the study leave the participants (the organization's stakeholders) feeling empowered—an outcome that is central in critical theory? The answers are "yes" to all of these questions—with very few reservations. There were grumblings about the evaluation taking too long, asking too much work from participants, and being cumbersome in design. Yet, everyone also agreed that it was open and comprehensive, which are exactly the qualities that require time and broad-based involvement.

There was consensus that the organization had been strengthened and its members energized. There were specific findings to indicate that stakeholders emerged with new skills (computer use, instrument design technology, evaluation strategies) and a greater sense of self-efficacy. The positive evaluation results were used to promote the agency within the wider community, and the positive evaluation experience became a model for other grassroots development groups. The report tells the story of competent critical theory research—and offers evidence that sometimes those tales have happy endings.

At this point, you should fasten your intellectual seat belt for a sudden leap to a location that is much less familiar. The work of Cole and Hribar (1995), although clearly an example of serious scholarship and solidly located in the tradition of social criticism from Marxist and feminist perspectives, pushes hard against the limits of any envelope containing what we would define as qualitative research.

The absence of systematic procedures designed to produce empirical data (aside from what is derived from other sources) is but one of the features that might puzzle some readers. The lack of an identified set of participants in the immediate context of a study might be a source of disorientation for others. Nevertheless, this is a specimen that shows where some social scientists are taking the tradition of critical theory.

So, you might ask, "Is this a research report?" The fact that you (or we) might be made more comfortable if we could exclude it from the category of "research," or at least provide it with a less confusing label ("social critique" would have an air of elegance, "polemical essay" would be more abusive than deserved, and "critical commentary" would be too bland to honestly reflect the sharp edges intended by the authors), is not really relevant. Report, article, essay, or commentary, this type of research is something you will encounter in journals. Perhaps at this stage it is less important to characterize what it represents than it is to listen to what the authors have to say.

In "Celebrity Feminism: *Nike Style*—Post-Fordism, Transcendence, and Consumer Power," Cole & Hribar (1995) examined the phenomenon of the "Just do it!" advertising campaign sponsored by the Nike athletic shoe company. Part of that process involved close (and skeptical) attention to the fact that the corporation has been widely celebrated for its apparent role in encouraging women to become more physically active—before it was fashionable to do so. Drawing from a wide variety of contemporary literature, the authors provide ample evidence that Nike has been portrayed as a progressive, pro-woman company with socially responsible policies.

It might surprise some readers to find that the authors' critique of that characterization does not center on the fact that, through the artful "Just do it!" campaign, a transnational company captured an enormous segment of the worldwide market for women's athletic footwear, promoted sales to a level previously unimagined, and made untold billions in the process. Nike receives no direct condemnation for the fact that it was not acting entirely on the basis of altruistic motives. Instead, the substance of the critique centers on two quite different points.

First, through a long argument that we are not competent to abstract or to even annotate, Cole and Hribar make a case for the possibility that in the course of making women feel "empowered" to take charge of their own bodies, the marketing minions (who, in this case, were women) have replaced (or co-opted) traditional feminism (with its activist political and social agenda). Instead, the Nike campaign has promoted a kind of "celebrity feminism" that looks inward to the self (as body and attitude) rather than outward to the problematic place of women in society.

One of the most striking pieces of evidence in that regard is inclusion of the full transcript for the now famous "Did you ever wish you were a boy?" advertisement. We can testify that reading it now leaves one with the impression that Nike was saying, "With a hard, slender body encased in spandex, *and a pair of our shoes,* you can run away from the real weight of women's history."

The second direction of social critique leads the authors to argue that in the "Just do it!" campaign, Nike was speaking with a forked tongue. Like many transnational corporations, Nike manufactures absolutely nothing—it is a pure marketing company. All shoes are produced in Third World countries, and, the authors claim, they are produced mostly by women who are paid low wages and who work under dangerous and unhealthy conditions.

We found the evidence presented to sustain that point much thinner (and less persuasive), but events since publication have worked to confirm the authors' judgment, at least for corporate entities that depend on cheap labor in third world countries. In recent years, a host of brand-name companies have been scrambling to retrieve their good names as responsible citizens by showing fits of concern about workers at outsourcing sites abroad. We make no claim that this report triggered that wave of corporate sympathy, but that is precisely the kind of outcome that critical researchers hope to produce.

You now will have to contemplate the question we raised at the outset: "Is this a research report?" The authors have asserted that from the postmodern perspective (their particular philosophical vantage point), their work constitutes research. We will not contest that point. What seems more important here is that you begin to form your own judgment on the matter.

Mixed Methodology Studies

We have to admit that this is an unfortunate name for a type of research, whether qualitative or quantitative. It gives the impression that if a qualitative study happens to employ a methodological step that produces numeric data (for example, a count that yields the frequency with which a certain response is given to an interview question), it has become a different and special type of research, or that if a quantitative study includes use of a method commonly associated with qualitative research (for example, interviewing participants to ascertain whether or not they liked a particular experimental treatment), the investigation is no longer a true experiment—and must be called something else.

In neither case is any change required; an experiment remains an experiment even with all sorts of supplemental information from interviews and observation notes, and an ethnography remains an ethnography no matter how many numbers are included in the report. Many social scientists have freely intermixed data types and data acquisition methods without feeling any necessity to take aboard the philosophical perspective of a paradigm other than that which served as the principal guide for their research.

Mixed method studies are not created simply by mixing methods from two paradigms. We believe the mixed method label is justified, however, when other, more profound changes are made in quantitative or qualitative studies. When, for example, the nature of the research problem makes it necessary to use both qualitative and quantitative data in developing a more thorough answer, when each kind of data is subject to rigorous standards of quality that are appropriate within its paradigm of origin, and when interpretation links data types together in a genuine synthesis—that represents something that (in our cosmology, at least) deserves being called a distinct type of inquiry.

A number of scholars have given attention to possibilities for such integration of qualitative and quantitative research, sometimes referring to it as a strategy of *mixed designs,* which to us is a more satisfactory label. Miles and Huberman (1994) have outlined four such alternatives. Their options involve either simultaneous use of parallel qualitative and quantitative strategies or variations on alternation between the two. Any of these designs could be planned and conducted in a manner that conforms to our characterization of a genuine mixed method design for deserving status as a distinct type of research.

There are entire books devoted to this topic (see, for example, Green & Caracelli, 1997, or Tashakkori & Teddlie, 1998, 2003). Because most of them involve plowing through some fairly dense material, however, we suggest that you begin with either of two alternatives:

Robson (2002), whose own approach as a critical realist leads him to make flexible use of research strategies and tools in combinations that seem to best fit the particular research problem at hand, or Flick (2002), who has published extensively about the use of combined paradigms for the purpose of triangulation (designs in which the strengths of one approach are used to compensate for the weaknesses in the other).

Our example of a mixed methodology study (Walker, 1996) is relatively straightforward, and it has the advantage of dealing with a mundane activity of daily life with which all readers are likely to be familiar—watching television. The purpose of the study was to examine the behavior of couples that watched television together (the dominant recreational activity in the United States today), how they used the remote control device (RCD) to select programs, and what feelings those patterns of use produced. Individuals in 36 highly diverse volunteer couples were interviewed with a protocol that included questions of two distinct types.

The more structured section contained sociodemographic questions (age, length of relationship, etc.), as well as items concerned with number of television sets, frequency of joint viewing, and happiness with the behaviors and interactions that occurred while watching with the partner. The second, more open-ended section contained questions that related to power: how the couple decided on a program to watch together, how partners got each other to watch programs they wanted to watch, and the nature and intensity of their frustrations with watching television together.

A coin toss was used to determine which partner would be interviewed first. Partners were interviewed separately, usually in their own homes. Interviews were audiotaped and transcribed. The Statistical Analysis System computer program was used for statistical analysis of the quantitative data. The transcripts of qualitative data were read and reread to create descriptions of both the range of responses and the primary themes that typified feelings and beliefs concerning joint viewing. Results involved presenting a synthesis of data types, sometimes cross-checking for validity, and at other times using both qualitative and quantitative perspectives to fully develop a rich characterization about viewing behavior.

The central conclusion was that partners in close relationships "do gender" and exercise power even in their ordinary, everyday behavior and, specifically, in their selection of television programming via a remote control device. Men control the RCD more than women, and women are far more frustrated by RCD behaviors than are men. Both genders have means for persuading the other partner to watch what they prefer, but, in that negotiation, women only rarely win. Unnegotiated channel switching by men was a frequent occurrence in the participant group, and men persisted in doing that even when their female partners were obviously frustrated by the behavior.

The confluence of qualitative and quantitative data confirmed that among the participants in this study, leisure was a source of conflict—conflict between their own enjoyment and the enjoyment of their partner. Women often expressed resignation about the state of things—only 4 out of 36 thought they might be successful if they attempted to change the way their partners used the RCD. The author provided an array of qualitative and quantitative data to support the assertion that such resignation reflected a latent form of men's power over women.

The women became less able over time to raise issues of concern, they anticipated the struggles that would occur if their own wishes were made known, and they predicted a negative reaction to their wishes from their male partner. Joint television watching by the couples in this study was hardly an egalitarian experience, and the uses of gendered power appeared to undercut the very notion that it is a recreational leisure-time activity for women.

❖ CONCLUDING COMMENTS ABOUT TYPES OF RESEARCH

We have briefly surveyed the kinds of research you are most likely to encounter as you pursue the retrieval and reading of reports. Some of the studies you read will combine aspects of several formats. For example, a study might include both correlations and descriptive comparisons across groups—techniques normally associated with two quite different members of the quantitative research family. Another study might use statistical operations to categorize subjects' attitudes toward their jobs and then employ interviews to capture their perception of workplace conditions. Knowing which methods of data collection were used is not sufficient to predict how data will be interpreted and results identified. Data are always at the center of any study, but the paradigmatic assumptions of the investigator on which the study is grounded are what will shape how findings are understood.

All of that serves to underscore a fundamental truth about the nature of research: Tidy categories are the creations of textbook authors.

For the most part, they do not exist in the real world, where disorder, if not a state bordering on chaos, is the general condition. So please do not be shocked by the fact that what you find in the research literature sometimes seems rather unlike some of our descriptions. Simplifying, and imposing a degree of order that does not appear in nature, was our intention. We hoped to lure you in by not frightening you away.

7

Reading Reports of Quantitative Research—Critically

Things to Notice and Questions to Ask

Throughout this text, we have been absolutely explicit about one point. We believe that it is possible to read many research reports as intelligible sources of useful information without first acquiring the technical knowledge and skills required to judge either the research procedures involved or the adequacy of the report as a document. If the ability to make definitive and fully informed evaluations were the mandatory prerequisite to reading reports, this text would be pointless.

On the other hand, we certainly do not believe that ignorance is bliss in this matter. Familiarity with research as a systematic enterprise and a good sense of what to expect within reports of different kinds of research are essential equipment for a reader. Furthermore, from Chapter 2 onward, we have tried to identify simple, nontechnical indicators that reflect the degree of care with which a study was performed and with which the ensuing report was prepared. As with any other endeavor, the quality of workmanship makes a difference in the product.

Chapters 7 and 8, then, are concerned with the critical reading of studies informed by the quantitative and qualitative paradigms, respectively. They are intended for readers who are ready (and inclined) to learn more about the points at which they should ask critical questions and make tough judgments. To dispose of an obvious question that might come to mind, let us be blunt. Is it possible to use this text as a tool for learning how to access research reports without mastering the materials contained in these two chapters? Of course it is. This book was deliberately structured to allow that sort of limited use. But please do consider the following before you decide whether to read on or not.

Having invested your time and energy to come this far, why not acquire all of the skills that we can offer (in this context) to help you discriminate between reports that are undecipherable or seriously incomplete, and those that are merely difficult to read? A useful by-product of developing that sensitivity will be the opportunity to learn more about the distinction between research that has been properly done and research that has not. The additional cost in time will be relatively small when compared with what you already have expended, and the intellectual demands will be no greater than the level you already have demonstrated.

Extending the range of your critical skills does not require great technical facility or mastery of arcane knowledge. Few of the really difficult issues in research reporting are primarily technical. Of course, it is true that advanced training in research design and procedures can yield critical expertise concerning the purely technical aspects of a study, but just knowing the right commonsense question to ask at the right point will put you far ahead of the naïve beginner. Chapters 7 and 8 are devoted to the basic questions that any careful reader can ask, and, to make them even more useful as additions to your research-consuming skills, we have particularly targeted those points in reports at which errors are most likely to appear. At the outset, learning to read with a critical eye means nothing more than learning when to ask commonsense questions about commonplace problems.

Although your personal interests might lead you to study either Chapter 7 or Chapter 8 with greater intensity than the other, it is our assumption that *you will read both chapters and, preferably, in the order presented here.* The rationale for that injunction lies in the fact that the two chapters are complementary and, to some extent, overlapping.

We have asserted throughout this book that some of the standards of quality against which studies can be tested are the same (or are closely related) for all types of formal inquiry. Although that position has been subject to some vigorous debate among scholars, we are going to stick by it here. Thus, if you detect similarities between the two chapters that read as though the same principles have been recycled under different names, you will be correct. Such overlap is intentional and not an accident of writing. Make no mistake, the two traditions—quantitative and qualitative—are different, and profoundly so. Nevertheless, being aware of what they share is an essential part of understanding and respecting each.

Another preliminary injunction is to remind you of a point concerning reports that we introduced in Chapter 3. Length, format, aspects of writing style, and, to some degree, even the content of a research report might have been determined, or at least been influenced, by the requirements of the journal in which it is published. Not everything you find—or, particularly, fail to find—as you read can be laid at the feet of the author. The editorial board of each journal specifies the expected form for all submitted manuscripts, and authors must comply.

Journal specifications can consist (in whole or in part) of standards established by a particular discipline—for example, *The Publication Manual of the American Psychological Association* (2001) or the *MLA Handbook for Writers of Research Papers* (Gibaldi, 2003) of the Modern Language Association—or to other institutional sources, such as the *Chicago Manual of Style* (2003) from the University of Chicago Press. In addition, most research journals publish a guide for authors (variously called *submission guidelines, manuscript requirements,* or *information for contributors*) at least once annually. Many journal publishers also include guides for contributors on their Web sites, where they can be accessed at any time. A quick scan of what any journal requires will give you considerable insight into how the reports within its cover acquired many of their distinctive characteristics.

In the end, however, it is the author who is responsible for all of the decisions about what to write—within the limits established by the journal's guidelines. That process shapes the heart of the report, accountability for which falls to the author—and the author alone.

As a final introductory point, we would like to remind you of another truism that has been repeated throughout this guide. No single flaw makes a report useless for all purposes. Not only is it possible to extract useful information from the report of a study that has severe limitations, but virtually all studies do present at least some shortcomings that are a consequence of practical compromises made by the investigator. As Chapter 3 makes clear, when you find an inadequacy, you have found a reason to be cautious—not cause to stop reading. Inadequate reporting makes it difficult to understand a study, and inadequate research procedure makes it difficult (or impossible) to trust the findings. Neither, however, disqualifies a report from serving as a resource if it contains other ideas or information that can be of use to you.

❖ INTRODUCTION: THE FIVE BASIC QUESTIONS

As you will have learned by now, the first reading of any report should be devoted to a survey of content—how the document is organized, what the study was about, and, generally, what the findings were. If you delve further into the report, it will be because you suspect that the report contains useful information, either in the findings or in some other component of the study. In either case, you will be reading with increasing attention to detail, particularly in those sections that are related to your immediate interest.

As you study the report in greater depth, you will begin to form judgments about the quality of the document and, by extension, to form evaluative impressions about the conduct of the investigation. What follows are simple guides intended to direct your attention to key elements in the report and to sharpen the critical eye with which you regard researchers' stories. Your goal is not to catch them in a mistake, but you should be intent on learning as much as possible from what you are reading. Part of that process is asking tough questions about what you are being told.

Most research reports, whether quantitative or qualitative, contain the answers to five basic questions: (a) What is the report about? (b) How does the study fit into what is already known? (c) How was the study done? (d) What was found? and (e) What do the results mean? We will begin by showing how these basic questions play out in the format and content of the report for a quantitative study. This analysis is followed in Chapter 8 by a discussion of considerations for qualitative research reports.

For quantitative studies, the traditional component parts of a report are shown in Table 7.1. In the sections that follow, we will

Table 7.1   Five Basic Questions Answered in Research Reports—Typical
Section Headings

What Is the Report About?

Title
Abstract
Purpose (also can relate to the following question)

How Does the Study Fit into What Is Already Known?

Introduction, Research Purposes, and Related Literature
References

How Was the Study Done?

Method
    Subjects
    Research Plan or Design
    Instrumentation
    Procedures
    Analysis

What Was Found?

Results
    Description of the Findings
    Figures
    Tables

What Do the Results Mean?

Discussion and Conclusions (often includes reference to the second question)

describe how each part of the report should work to provide an answer
to the corresponding question. Although all reports do not contain the
particular headings used in Table 7.1, and many reports do not present
the headings in the exact order we have suggested, most do include
sections that serve the functions indicated, even if they are given other
titles, are arranged in different order, or involve merged combinations
of several topics.

At the end of our discussion of each major component in the typical report, we suggest what the key critical evaluation questions should
be. For example, about the section dealing with the purpose of the

study, here is one of the questions you should ask: "Is the purpose of the study stated clearly, and is it framed within introductory material that makes it easy to understand?" As you read the section on methodology, you should ask questions such as, "Is there a clear explanation for why these particular subjects were selected?" Regarding the measurements used in the study, you can raise the vital question, "In each case for which it is appropriate, are validity and reliability values provided?"

You might soon discover that other questions seem particularly useful in the kind of reports you select, and those can be added to our initial listing. The primary point, however, is to ask the questions systematically, as a matter of routine, while you work your way through each report. We think you will be surprised at how quickly they become automatic, how informative the answers can be, and how much confidence knowing the right question can inspire.

What Is the Report About?

What the report is about is explained in the title, the abstract, and the section containing a statement of purpose. (The latter serves indirectly as the frame for answers to all of the questions throughout the report, but it more directly determines the response to the first two: "What is the report about?" and "How does the study fit into what is already known?")

The Title

The importance of the title is established by one salient fact. More people will read the title than any other part of the report. Indexing and retrieval systems often depend on the title for key words on which to base the listings for a report, and being listed in the right categories determines whether a study comes to the attention of potential readers. In addition, the interest inspired by a good title can make the difference between large and small readerships. Accordingly, authors who are sophisticated about the mechanisms of retrieval and the interests of their primary audience spend considerable effort to devise title wording that is clear, concise, accurate, and appealing.

At the most general level, the title describes what was studied, at least in terms of naming the primary constructs examined and the type of research involved. Particular parts of the study that are unusual or of special interest (e.g., subjects, means of measurement or analysis, scope of data collection) will be noted. Mention of such specifics, however, is always constrained by the need for brevity. In the end, a good title tells the appropriate subset of potential readers—those who might reasonably have an interest in the content of the report—enough to move them to the next step, which is reading the abstract.

For any study that you consider reading, if the title performs its function well, you will take that next step with some confidence that it is going to be worth your time—and perhaps with a degree of anticipation triggered by the promise of an intriguing element in the study. When neither is true, you already know something about the investigator's limitations as a writer, which you can hope do not extend to the capacity for careful thought.

The Abstract

Almost all research publications require an abstract, usually placed in prominent fashion on the first page of the report. Often limited to a single paragraph, the abstract ordinarily contains a general statement of the research topic, a brief description of the study design and the methods involved, and the most important results obtained. Journals with a strong professional orientation might encourage inclusion of a statement that specifies the practical implications of the findings.

The first function of the abstract is to expand on the information provided in the title. The intention is to allow potential readers to make a quick determination about the match between the study and their interests. The need for brevity (many journals dictate the maximum number of words permissible in the abstract) limits the explanation, but artfully designed abstracts can display most elements that will concern readers (at least, as the researcher imagines them).

Allowing readers to discriminate between reports to be read and those for which title and abstract will be the only parts consumed is the first and most formal function of the abstract. As most of you will have already discovered, however, abstracts have other important uses. One of them is to refresh your memory weeks or months after reading a study. Also, single-page abstracts greatly facilitate the shuffling and categorizing process when you are trying to compare multiple studies within a topic area. Finally, abstracts can serve to keep you superficially informed about new findings in an area of inquiry, particularly when time makes it impossible to read every relevant study in its entirety.

We suggest a firm rule about that latter use of abstracts, however, and urge you to believe that it is violated only at substantial risk. Never use an abstract as the basis for citing or quoting from a study, applying the findings in any personal enterprise (speaking, writing, or making professional decisions of any sort), or even in any careful effort to consider what is known about a particular problem. An abstract is a snapshot that captures only the most vivid elements of a complex process. The picture it provides is devoid of the rich contextual details necessary if you are to use critical questions to evaluate—and to understand fully—the study presented in the report. Not only do abstracts rarely contain material that will help you understand the limitations of a study, they are unlikely to portray fully how significant the findings might be when taken in the dynamic context of an evolving field of knowledge.

Abstracts are enormously useful tools when employed for purposes they can properly support, but they are designed to be no more than the portal of entry into the full report. As with titles, when they invite you in with a clear and reasonably thorough idea of what will be encountered (or warn you off by their unfocused or obviously incomplete nature), they do their job well. As long as you do not ask too much of them, they can also provide a variety of other useful services. For all of these reasons, you will quickly come to appreciate the artful craft required to write a good abstract, and you will assign a mark of somber dissatisfaction to those that mislead your efforts to understand the study.

Abstracts come in a range of varieties and have been roughly categorized as descriptive, informative, and informative-descriptive (Michaelson, 1990). The *descriptive* abstract attends to only the general subject matter of the report, picturing the broad nature of the study. It offers no details about sampling, instrumentation, data, analysis, or findings. *Informative* abstracts add specifics, often citing particular hypotheses tested, statistics that reflect primary results, or even a summary of conclusions. The *informative-descriptive* abstract obviously combines the previous two, with emphasis on placing the details in the wider context of a research topic. Generally, of course, the three lie along a scale of increasing length, although none is likely to exceed a single page.

Exhibit 7.1   An informative abstract

Abstract

The purpose of this study was to examine the influence of parenting styles on 8-year-olds' emotional and cognitive levels. Volunteer parents from an after-school program were observed on five occasions over a 6-month period and categorized as permissive ($n = 53$), authoritative ($n = 48$), or authoritarian ($n = 51$). The 8-year-old children were measured on four emotional variables (stress level, emotional distress, anger, and creativity) based on a laboratory assessment and two cognitive variables (composite measures of verbal reasoning and quantitative reasoning). Data were analyzed by MANOVA. Comparisons among the parenting styles showed that the children of authoritarian parents had significantly ($p < .05$) more stress and anger, whereas children of permissive parents were the most creative. There were no significant differences for any other variables. These results indicate that parenting style might influence some measures of child development but have little impact on other developmental variables.

In all three types, the essential problem is to avoid saying too much, thus cluttering the reader's decision process, or too little, thus depriving the reader of information essential to making the right decision. An example of a typical informative abstract (the type you are most likely to encounter) is shown in Exhibit 7.1. Read it and apply the most basic question of all: Would that abstract provide the clear basis for deciding whether to proceed or to quit?

The Purpose

The most direct answer to the question of what a report is about will be found wherever the author describes the purpose of the study. In some cases, that description is given as a formal statement, as in the first example shown in Exhibit 7.2 (Research Purpose). The second example in the exhibit, however, shows that the tone can be much less formal, as when the implied purpose is simply to find the answer to a question (Research Question). Finally, if previous research or theoretical work has given the researcher some reason to believe that the results of the study will take a particular form, the purpose might be stated as the testing of a hypothesis, as in the third example in the exhibit (Research Hypothesis).

Exhibit 7.2   Three ways to state the purpose of a study

Research Purpose

The purpose of this study was to determine to what extent the duration and frequency of physical therapy influence health care costs following traumatic injury.

Research Question

Does the duration and frequency of physical therapy influence health care costs following traumatic injury?

Research Hypothesis

The health care costs of patients who participate in physical therapy over an 8-week period following traumatic injury were significantly less than the costs of patients provided only 4 weeks of physical therapy.

Whatever its format, and no matter the section of the report in which it appears (certainly near the beginning), a statement of purpose that provides a clear indication of exactly why the study was performed is the final confirmation of what the title and abstract promised. If you have difficulty locating or deciphering the statement of purpose, you have an indication that something serious is wrong—and, 9 times out of 10, it is a problem with the author, not the reader.

Statements of research purpose or a research question constitute broad descriptions of what will be accomplished in the study. In contrast, *research hypotheses* are statements of specific relationships or differences, often expressed in ways that are designed to be tested by statistical analysis. Hypotheses are more specific because they predict the relationship between or among operationally defined variables, often specifying the particular units of measure to be employed. Hypotheses are more often encountered in quantitative studies (they are found only rarely in qualitative inquiry), primarily in correlational and experimental or quasi-experimental investigations. Broad statements of purpose or research questions are more typical of descriptive research—particularly if the study is exploratory in nature—whereas, as you would expect, hypotheses are more likely to be used in areas for which there is a well-developed knowledge base.

Although an announcement of purpose should appear early in a report, it is often not the first thing you read. In the examples in Exhibit 7.2, if you were to appreciate any of the three statements, you would first have to understand that therapies and costs are related variables. That kind of background information is ordinarily provided in the opening section of the report, often under the ubiquitous heading "Introduction." In the present case, this section might include facts from medical knowledge (the impact of physical therapy on the course of healing in tissue structures) or results from previous studies (the impact of therapy intensity on length of hospitalization). The point of such introductions is to show how the purpose of the study is both logical and important. The best of such preliminaries lead naturally into an explicit statement of purpose and provide a basis that draws readers forward into the next section (which usually deals with methods employed to perform the study). The worst introductions leave constructs crucial to understanding the purpose undefined, relationships of interest unidentified, and the importance of doing the study unclear.

For the novice reader, such omissions certainly constitute fair grounds for abandoning the effort. If you are reading a report in a completely unfamiliar area, however, some of the difficulty might lie in your own inexperience with the assumptions (and shorthand expressions) that are characteristic of the dialogue among researchers. In such cases, perseverance (perhaps through several reports of work in that area) might yield greater clarity. If not, you are probably dealing with garbled writing, inadequately conceptualized research, or both.

Critical evaluation: What is the report about? How well did the author communicate what the study was about? Here are the questions you should ask about the title, abstract, and statement of purpose for any report. You can modify them to suit particular research formats, as well as add items to the list that serve your own specific interests and needs, but you owe it to yourself to know the answers if you want to grow in your capacity to read and use research.

- Does the title indicate the important constructs and relationships in the study?
- Does the abstract provide enough information to make a decision about reading the full report?

(Continued)

(Continued)

- Does the abstract suggest the importance of the study?
- Is the purpose of the study stated clearly, and is it framed within introductory material that makes it easy to understand?
- Having read the title, abstract, and statement of purpose, is it easy for you to determine the degree of relevance that this study is likely to have for your needs?

How Does the Study Fit into What Is Already Known?

Several parts of the report can provide information that places the study in the context of previous knowledge. Such information can lead the reader to understand any (or all) of the following: the rationale for the study, the explanation for selecting particular methods of data collection or analysis, and the potential importance of findings. This type of information is most commonly found in the four sections devoted to the introduction, research purpose, related literature, and references. Unfortunately, the use of headings is not standardized in research reports, so you often have to identify the section you are reading by its content rather than by a simple and convenient label.

In certain types of research, the statement of purpose signals a direct connection to existing knowledge, as in the case of replication studies, or those studies that undertake to test a hypothesis or a theoretical model generated by previous investigation. In such cases, the fit between the study and what is already known is made obvious in a straightforward manner and typically at an early point in the document. The other parts of the report within which authors commonly work to connect their study to the existing body of knowledge are found in more variable locations and formats, and they might not be identified by a special heading.

In most reports, the introduction and discussion of related literature are interwoven rather than set apart in separate sections. In that combined format, the major concepts and their relationships are introduced, and previous research is used to explicate the logic of the researcher's purpose. Attention to gaps in the structure of knowledge, conflicting findings, promising leads, and the need to establish the exact limits for previous findings are among the common ways of inserting a study into what is already known.

In some reports, the introduction and related literature appear under separate headings. In such cases, it is common (although by no means universal) to find that the researcher has deemed it important to provide an extensive summary of previous findings as background for a particularly complex study design or a new or unusual conceptualization of the problem, or as a service to readers when the relevant literature is obscure or difficult to retrieve.

Finally, the fourth resource for locating the study within what is already known is the reference list. This part of the report contains full references for all of the documents cited in the report, often including research reviews that can be used to extend the reader's appreciation of the fit between the study and the knowledge base.

The Introduction, Research Purposes, and Related Literature

As indicated in our earlier discussion, the introduction provides context for the purpose of the study. Some of the more common functions are to explain the following:

- What the research problem is
- What the major concepts and constructs are
- How the major concepts relate to each other
- What efforts have been made in the past to solve the problem (citing the related literature)
- Which elements of the problem remain unresolved
- What barriers stand in the way of solving the problem
- Which modes of investigation now seem appropriate
- Why the problem remains viable and how findings might contribute to theory or practice.

Introductions normally begin by explaining the major concepts and their relationships to each other. Often, the author tightens the focus either by expressing the conceptual elements as constructs in which the constituent parts are specified (often as particular measurements) or by giving the constructs operational definitions. For example, suppose a study asks the question, "Do teenagers who are required to be accountable for their automobile-related transgressions (tickets for parking and moving violations, or damage) throughout the years they learn to drive and manage a car have different adult driving histories than those who are not held accountable?" The concepts, constructs, and operational definitions might appear in the introduction as follows:

Concept #1: Accountability—Being responsible for one's actions

Construct #1: Accountability for automobile-related transgressions— Financial restitution, in whole or in part, of accident-related car damage; payment of fines for parking or moving violations during the learning-to-drive phase

Operational Definition #1: The score obtained on the Driver Home-Training Questionnaire (DHTQ)

Concept #2: Driver home training—Acquiring experience in driving following formal class instruction and certification to drive

Construct #2: Driver home-training years—The period of time in which the teenager, living at home and dependent on adults, is instructed, tutored, observed, monitored, and disciplined with respect to the operation of automobiles and the laws that apply in automobile driving

Operational Definition #2: Driver home-training period—The period of time immediately following formal class instruction and acqui- sition of a driver's license, in which the teenager (15 to 19 years of age) is living at home and is allowed to drive a car independently

Concept #3: Driving history—A record of events related to driving and automobile management that occur to an individual

Construct #3: Driving history—Driving events that occur in the period of time following the driver home-training period (that is, indepen- dent, unsupervised driving of an owned or leased automobile)

Operational Definition #3: The score on the Driving History Record, which includes city records of parking violations, moving viola- tions, and insurance claims from ages 20 through 35

Extracted from text in this fashion, the elements of a study have a stark and sterile tone, but, woven into the fabric of an artful introduc- tion, they can acquire the power of logical exposition and even the interest of an unsolved puzzle.

As you can see by the introduction presented in Exhibit 7.3, a good introduction not only inserts the study into the context of what is

Exhibit 7.3   Example of an introduction section

Introduction[1]

(What the research problem is)

Driving transgressions have increased over the past decade (Jarvis, 2003). Compared to the early 1990s more people run red lights, park illegally, drive faster than the speed limit, drive without a current license, drive without liability insurance, drive with expired inspection stickers, neglect to pay parking tickets, and do not take responsibility for unwitnessed "fender benders" or other types of damage (Alison, 2002). Moreover, in each 5-year period since 1970, the frequency of driving-related transgressions has significantly increased (Zorch, 2001). These transgressions contribute substantially to increased accidents, which in turn increase injuries, fatalities, and insurance premiums (Brown, 2000).

Why have these types of transgressions steadily increased? One hypothesis that has been advanced by Root (2002) is that the parents in each generation have provided less and less supervision and discipline for driving behaviors during the time when the new driver is accumulating driving experiences that will shape his or her driving behaviors for a lifetime. As provocative as this hypothesis is, however, to date, no evidence has been provided to support it. Thus, in this study, parental supervision practices were analyzed to determine whether they have indeed changed over the years and whether these practices were, in fact, related to the driving behaviors of the study participants.

(The major concepts and constructs)

It has been shown that children learn accountability for their actions when they are forced to deal with the consequences of those actions (Brown, 1992) and when they are exposed to some punishment that is directly related to the transgression (Phelps, 1991). Thus, teenagers whose parents require them to pay part or all of the cost of traffic tickets from their allowance, or those who are required to participate with the adult owner of the car in all of the inconveniences and annoyances necessary to file insurance claims and have car damage repaired, are learning a lesson in taking responsibility for their actions. Similarly, children who are prevented from driving any car for a period of time appropriate to the transgression, or at least until repairs are completed, learn that it is more pleasant to avoid behaviors leading to car transgressions than to deal with the consequences of those transgressions.

The home driver-training period of time is an extremely important time in the formation of driving behaviors (Filer, 1979). Teenagers, who wish desperately to drive, are dependent upon adults for a car. Driving a car provides social status and mobility for them, both of which are extremely important (Dash, 1989).

(Continued)

Exhibit 7.3 (Continued)

Thus, this is the last time period in which adults can have teenagers' undivided attention regarding driving rules and regulations, both state-enforced and home-enforced. Additionally, the young drivers in this time period are fresh from their school-based formal instruction classes in driving and have just acquired their licenses. At no time will they know the rules and regulations better than at this time period (Fromp, 1978). Being first-time drivers, they also have no previously accumulated bad driving habits. It might be the last time period in which parents have a realistic opportunity to affect their driving habits for future years.

(What efforts have been made in the past to solve the problem?)

Although a few researchers have shown that teenagers who receive formal instruction prior to acquiring their licenses have fewer accidents and fatalities (Johnson, 1983; Lawler, 1990; Smith & Greene, 1996), no researchers have related parental supervision behaviors during the home driver-training period to automobile transgressions, accidents, and fatalities. Some have studied driving history records as they relate to personality traits (Bilter, 1983), socioeconomic status (Church & Reed, 1983), and education level (Wilder, 1989), but none has focused on parental supervisory and education techniques during this critical period.

(What barriers stand in the way of solving the problem?)

The two largest problems that researchers have faced in their quest to determine whether instruction or supervision might have an impact on adult driving histories is the difficulty of finding ways to measure parental supervision techniques and to obtain objective records of adults' driving experiences with transgressions and accidents. Self-report questionnaires that probe behaviors that occurred 3 to 5 years previously are notoriously inaccurate (Peoples, 1975). Insurance records and records of traffic violations and accident reports insurance records have always been difficult to access because they are filed in different agencies and rarely are cross-referenced.

(Which modes of investigation are now appropriate?)

Several events and technological developments have occurred recently that have made this study possible. First, in 1990, a comprehensive 5-year study of parental supervisory techniques related to several types of social behaviors was funded by the American Transportation Foundation (Jones, 1996). In this study, parents and children (up to 20 years of age) were required to keep a daily log regarding their use of automobiles, including for each trip (a) time of day, (b) miles traveled, (c) purpose of trip, and (d) number of

(Continued)

Exhibit 7.3 (Continued)

passengers. Second, in 1991, the Department of Public Safety developed a computer bank that included all automobile transgressions and records of accidents and fatalities. Third, in 1992, the state required all drivers to provide proof of liability insurance and to identify their insurance company (Public Law, 1993). Fourth, the National Institute for Transportation developed a sophisticated computer program that could integrate databases written in several languages and stored in many different formats (Jackson, 1993, 2003). All of these developments made it possible to acquire the driving history records of adult drivers who had been participants in the earlier Jones (1996) study and to relate the parental and teenage interactive behaviors to their later driving behaviors.

(Why the problem remains viable and the solution might relate to theory or practice)

The purpose of this study, then, was to determine whether the adult drivers whose parents required them to be accountable for all automobile-related transgressions during the time that they were dependent upon their parents for access to driving had fewer transgressions, accidents, fatalities, and lower insurance claims as adult drivers than those whose parents required no responsibility for transgressions. If this were found to be true, then greater efforts might be made to encourage parents to use this type of supervisory practice with their teenagers during the home driver-training period.

Endnote

1. All citations given in this example are fictitious, as are the agencies and instruments.

already known (while establishing all of the needed definitions of terms), but it leads you forward toward a discussion of methods. When you find yourself anticipating (perhaps even with genuine interest) the explanation of how the study actually was performed, the introduction did more than just report history—it began the telling of a good story.

References

As we noted in Chapter 2, the reference list might contain materials that serve your needs even when the present study does not. Remember that, in many cases, the list of references includes not only reports, articles, and books related to the provenance of the research problem, but, in many cases, the original sources for particular techniques of measurement, data collection, and analysis—any one of which might be a valuable find for your purposes.

There are other important reasons, however, to get in the habit of scanning the list. From such a review, for example, you can learn whether most of the references are old or relatively recent, as well as what type of journals have published the reports being cited. Information of that nature can contribute to a tentative judgment about the quality of the study. Up-to-date sources, respected journals, and distinguished authors should raise confidence in what you are reading.

Critical evaluation: How does the study fit into what is already known? How well did the author explain how the study fits into what is already known? Here are the questions you should ask about the statement of purpose, introduction, related literature, and list of references. You can modify them or add others that serve your own interests and needs, but you owe it to yourself to know the answers.

- Is the topic of the study introduced in terms of previous investigations?
- Did the author explain what is known and not known in sufficient detail for you to understand how the study fits into the present structure of knowledge?
- Were decisions about the design and procedures of the study explained in terms of what has been found effective (or ineffective) in previous investigations?
- If conflicting findings were noted in the relevant literature, were they discussed and given consideration in the present study?
- Do the references include recent reports from investigators who have established track records for research in the area?

How Was the Study Done?

The "Method" section of a report is intended to explain precisely and thoroughly how the study was conducted. In theory, the goal is to write such a careful account that another investigator could repeat the study exactly as in the original. Although everyone knows that, in practical terms, it is impossible to completely replicate every detail in a study, there is no doubt that providing the reader with an accurate and thorough description of every major procedural step is a perfectly reasonable and achievable standard.

Without such an understanding, it is impossible to estimate how much confidence can be placed in the findings. Furthermore, only through carefully documented details is it possible to consider differences in procedure as the reason for differences in findings among studies that attack the same problem (such discrepancies are not unusual in an area of active inquiry). Given that degree of importance, if you find that you really cannot follow the author's explanation of methods (and you are persuaded that the problem is not merely your unfamiliarity with specialized language and conventions unique to the area of inquiry), the report might be seriously defective.

Before you reach that conclusion, however, do remember that researchers almost always are struggling with at least some limitation on the length of their report. In writing, they economize as much as possible to stay within the page- or word-count restrictions established by journal policy (and enforced by sharp-eyed editors). And because they often can assume that much of their readership will consist of other scholars who are quite familiar with the detail of common methodologies, they are more likely to cut corners in the "Method" section than, for example, in their presentation and discussion of findings. As a result, you must study and not merely read the account of methods.

As suggested (and illustrated) in Chapter 4, an effective way to achieve an understanding of a report is to list concepts and relationships, draw flowcharts to map sequential steps in data collection, or create diagrams of the study's overall design. In short, do everything possible to grasp the broad outline—and, when you reasonably can do so, forgive the absence of missing details. If they truly are important to your use of the report, a polite e-mail note often will retrieve them from the author, most often promptly and with appreciation for your interest.

Next, we discuss each of the five primary topics in the typical "Method" section (subjects, design, instrumentation, procedures, and analysis) in sequence. The appropriate critical questions for those topics will be placed at the end of each subsection. Please do remember that in actual practice, investigators might not use headings for each of the topics within the "Method" section, or they might identify the topics with labels that are different from the ones used here.

The Subjects

In most reports, the first description encountered in the "Method" section is of the subjects used in the study (for the purpose of this chapter, we will ignore the fact that some studies are of constructs, such as institutions or other human artifacts). The topics of sampling (Chapter 3) and randomized selection (Chapter 6) constitute the essential conceptual background for any discussion of how a study's subject population is formed. Here, however, we will focus primarily on the subjects themselves: their protection, nature, number, and source.

The targets of investigation might be human or animal, because both types provide useful information. Such living subjects are selected for particular reasons (and usually very carefully) because their nature must be exactly appropriate to the study's purpose. Selection of subjects, however, brings with it more than just technical problems. The use of humans (or even animals) brings with it important ethical considerations.

When humans are studied, what the researcher can do in the process of inquiry is limited by custom, ethics, law, and regulation. At the heart of the matter is the fact that no investigator has the right to use a human subject unless the individual agrees to it after being properly informed about the nature and purpose of the study. The tension between that human right and the procedural demands of research methodology produces a host of complex issues. We have discussed many of these problems in a previous text that you might find useful as an introduction to the topic (Locke, Spirduso, & Silverman, 2000). For the present purpose, we point out that even the language used to describe subjects is regarded as an important aspect of their protection.

The 2001 edition of the *Publication Manual of the American Psychological Association* (one of the most widely used guides for preparation of research reports) recommends that individuals be described not as generic "subjects" but as particular people—adults, males, children, athletes, social workers, and so on. The intention is to encourage awareness that people are not objects to be "used" but individual humans endowed with inalienable rights that must be respected. When such terminology is impossible or awkward, the manual suggests using the term *participant* instead of *subject*, thereby underscoring the volitional (and collaborative) status of people selected for inclusion in a study. The latter is a convention long in use for writing reports of qualitative studies— where you can judge for yourself whether such language seems to correlate with a respectful attitude on the part of investigators.

The exact nature of subjects selected for a study is usually carefully specified in the report—not only to show the logic of the choices made, but also to allow readers to estimate how closely the subjects resemble the people in whom they are interested (and to whom findings thus might or might not be applicable). For that latter purpose, authors should provide information about all of the important demographic characteristics (age, gender, race, marital status, education, socioeconomic level, health status, physical characteristics, and so on) that might reasonably be thought relevant to the research problem. No author can predict the subject-related concerns brought by all possible readers, but you have good reason to expect them to describe their subjects on a wide range of potentially important characteristics.

There are several other ways for you to exercise your critical faculties with regard to what reports tell you about subjects. If you are reviewing a number of studies on a single topic, it is useful to group the reports by the nature of the subjects and then to examine the findings. For example, if three studies involve men, five use women, and nine combine measurements from both men and women, you might find results that suggest a relationship between gender and the variable(s) under examination.

If the investigator provides descriptions of particular individuals within a sample, there is another way to look at the study with a critical eye. Ask yourself, "Does the description of the individual subject actually match the specifications given for the subject group as a whole?" In a sense, that match is a rough measure of the quality control exercised over selection of subjects. The presence of individuals who do not exactly meet one or several of the critical standards for selection suggests an ominous looseness in methodology.

The nature of subjects is not the only concern in reading the account of who was studied—how many were examined also is a vital part of method. Here, too, there is an inherent tension between the theoretical ideal and practical reality in research, which is well displayed by our own experiences over many years as research advisors. Hundreds of graduate students have come to us with the question, "How many subjects do I have to include in my study?" The phrase "have to include" in that query betrays a great deal, particularly when there is good reason to believe the students already know perfectly well how to determine the answer.

Our students are (perennially) responding to a simple human dilemma. On one hand, more subjects mean more work, more time, and more expense (all of them perceived by students as aversive variables). On the other hand, there is an implacable general rule about subject numbers. In general, the more that are used in the sample for a study, the greater the likelihood that what is observed in the subjects approximates what could be observed in the total population. Conversely, the fewer there are in the sample, the less likely it is that findings from the study will characterize the wider population that the subject sample was intended to represent. (As you will see in Chapter 8, in qualitative research, the more serious trade-off is between sample size and depth. The more participants or sites you have, the better their diversity and representativeness can be assessed, but the less you can learn about each one.) Fortunately, in quantitative studies, there are some conceptual and technical tools for extricating the researcher from the horns of the sample-size dilemma.

Statistical operations called *power tests* can sometimes be used to yield a rational basis for sample size (and, when their use is reported in the "Method" section, that is evidence of careful attention to the "How many?" problem). Beyond such technical tools, there are also a variety of rules of thumb that give some guidance in the matter. For example, the accuracy of measures is a consideration; if the measures are particularly accurate, that allows for smaller sample sizes. Also, guidelines exist for some kind of statistical analyses that, although subject to continuing debate by specialists, have wide use in research. For example, the rule that analysis of associations requires a minimum of 30 subjects is offered as a general guide in some research training programs (but is dismissed as archaic and simplistic in others). For our own part, we think the 30-subject rule can serve at least as a starting point when thinking about the problem of sample size in a particular study, even if it must be used with a reasonable degree of flexibility. When combined with the general proposition that the greater the number of variables being correlated, the larger the number of subjects ought to be, the rule seems to be reasonable. We suggest the same kind of commonsense analysis when you encounter other guidelines for how statistics should be done.

Our suggestion is that you look not only for the number of subjects employed in the study, but also for a clear explanation of exactly how (by logic, practical consideration, established convention, or technical manipulation) that number was determined. Furthermore, if the number of subjects imposes some limitation on the study, the author ought to be frank and explicit about that problem. Within rather broad limits, the matter of how carefully the number of subjects has been considered is of greater importance than its precise size.

If the "Method" section provides a satisfactory description of the nature and number of subjects, there still remains the question of how their service was acquired. It is no exaggeration to say that how subjects are recruited poses one of the most serious (and common) threats to validity and generalizability in any form of research. As you learned from Chapters 3 and 6, recruitment and selection of subjects is closely related to the type of research (e.g., true experiments require random selection). We will not repeat any of that information here but will attend instead to broader and less technical issues—the tangle of problems that pertain to recruitment and volunteerism.

In almost any quantitative research design, all other things being equal, the ideal procedure for deciding who is to be studied would be to take a truly random sample of the population. Because of the great logistic difficulty in doing so, including contacting those who are nominated by the random procedure and convincing them to participate, most researchers forgo the benefits afforded by randomization. It is costly, time consuming, and can still contain hidden forms of bias because, in the end, only those who wish to participate will do so.

Instead, most investigators recruit volunteers, perhaps then using stratification procedures (e.g., randomly selecting equal numbers of participants from volunteer groups of men and women). To obtain volunteers, researchers might simply make direct appeals, encouraging people in groups or communities such as school classes, hospitals, church congregations, clubs, businesses, or housing developments to be participants in a study. They also might advertise more widely by posting signs or placing radio, television, or Internet appeals, all designed to solicit volunteer subjects with certain needed characteristics (a certain gender, age, and so on).

Generally, researchers must offer an inducement that rewards volunteers, either in the form of money or the promise of some other benefit. Health-related studies, for example, often provide free feedback from testing (blood pressure, fitness status, visual acuity, and so on). Psychological studies sometimes promise access to interesting personal insights based on test results. Whatever means of attracting subjects is offered, and however the appeal is made, if you suspect that volunteers might differ from nonvolunteers in ways that are substantial and not always easy to detect, you are absolutely right!

Table 7.2   Characteristics of Volunteers

Relative to nonvolunteers:

- Subjects who volunteer tend to be

  Female

- If a study is of learning or personality, or if a study is relatively standard and nonthreatening, subjects who volunteer tend to be

  Younger

- If a study involves performance testing, subjects who volunteer tend to be

  More social
  Better adjusted psychologically
  In greater need of approval
  More intelligent (score higher on intelligence tests)
  More persistent on novel laboratory tests
  Better performers on physical tests of power and speed
  Higher in socioeconomic status
  Higher in level of education

Researchers have extensively studied this problem. With a striking degree of agreement, they have found a number of potentially important biases in volunteer samples. A list of some of the differences between volunteers and nonvolunteers is shown in Table 7.2. We have drawn your attention to this topic because we believe that for many studies, the subtle biases produced by recruitment methods involving volunteers is not a trivial issue, even if the final selection of subjects is done by random drawings from pools of volunteer candidates. How could you have confidence in the general applicability of findings from a study that used a volunteer sample to examine personality and the willingness to take career risks when there is ample evidence that volunteer subjects tend to be younger, better adjusted, more intelligent, more well off financially, and better educated than the population as a whole?

There are ways to confront (if not perfectly resolve) such problems, and that is exactly our point. Evidence should be provided in the "Method" section to demonstrate that the researcher proceeded with great care in determining not just the nature and number of subjects, but how they were recruited as well. If the author clarifies these issues and discusses any limitations produced by the process, you can proceed with reasonable confidence in that aspect of the study's methodology.

Critical evaluation: The subjects. How well did the author explain how decisions were made about the nature, number, and selection of subjects? Here are questions you should ask about the portions of the "Method" section that deal with those problems. You might choose to modify them or add others that reflect your special interests, but these represent the core concerns about subjects.

- Is there evidence that the subjects were treated with due consideration for ethical standards?
- Is there a clear explanation for why these particular subjects were selected?
- Are the selection criteria clearly specified?
- Is the selection process thoroughly explained?
- Has the author explained why the number of subjects is adequate to the procedures and purposes of the study?
- Is the quality of the subject sample high (i.e., do most of them closely match the selection criteria)?
- Does the author address any limitations produced by selection procedures?

The Research Plan or Design

Perhaps as part of the introduction to the study, but more commonly as part of the methodology, the author will include a short subsection dealing with the research plan—in formal terms, the *design*—employed in the study. Here, the broad strategy is identified—that is, whether the study is descriptive, correlational, experimental, or quasi-experimental. If the study is to employ statistics, it is also common at this point for the author to give an overview of those operations. Finally, the primary variables will be named and placed in their respective positions (for example, in an experiment, the variables will be identified as dependent or independent).

After the design is identified, most authors present a rationale for why that particular plan constitutes the best choice from among alternatives. This is also the place for arguing that the design used has particular advantages over the designs that have been used in the past, which is another way of linking the study to existing literature. For example, in a study to examine the relationship of hormone replacement therapy (HRT) and health, the researcher might note that HRT has recently been associated with increased health risk and that any experimental study which requires women to take HRT might jeopardize the participants. Further, the researcher might note that post hoc follow-up designs (i.e., an epidemiological study) have provided valuable information on risk factors and that the study reported used these methods to obtain data. The researcher might then conclude that the research design selected permits descriptions and the examination of associations without any possible further danger to the participants.

The word *design* (or plan) might not appear in a topic heading, and the placement of its discussion within the report will vary. Nevertheless, the reader is given a helpful tool when the general plan of attack is outlined before the details must be considered. Researchers who do not provide an overview of their strategy and a justification for its selection (at the most helpful point in the report) have failed an important test of their ability to explain the study.

Critical evaluation: The research plan or design. How clearly did the author explain the research strategy employed in the study, and was it presented before you had to begin digesting details about such things as sampling, subjects, instruments, and procedures? Here are questions you should ask about the portion of the "Method" section dealing with that topic. You might find it appropriate to modify the questions to better fit the types of research that interest you, but these are the kinds of questions you should ask.

- Did the author name the design and introduce the primary variables and their relationships?
- Was the general design of the study explained in clear terms?
- Was a rationale given for the selection?
- Was the subsection dealing with design placed where it was helpful in understanding the remainder of the report?

The Instrumentation

Every report must introduce the *artifacts* (tests, measuring instruments, and protocols for obtaining data) that were used in the study. These might include instrumentation ranging from hardware such as skin calipers, blood glucose detectors, or accelerometers to paper documents such as psychometric tests, questionnaires, survey forms, interview guidelines, computer programs, and rating scales. This subsection that describes the instrumentation is analogous to the list of ingredients placed at the top of a cooking recipe. Each ingredient is described in terms of such qualities as kind, amount, color, and condition, but nothing is said in the listing about how or when the substances will be mixed together.

Similar detail is given in the "Method" section concerning the instruments used in the study. A standardized test will be named, and its source (often with a citation) will be given. Values for reliability and validity will be noted, as will other aspects, such as the age group for which the test is appropriate. Pilot tests of researcher-constructed instruments might be described here, and special hardware might be diagrammed and its specifications listed.

Careful researchers usually explain why each instrument was selected and why they have confidence that it is the most accurate means of data collection for the purposes of the study. Sometimes, it is just as important to indicate why other (perhaps more familiar) instruments were not used. Frequently, there are trade-offs between economy and precision of measurement such that the best choice for a given research purpose is not always obvious. Whatever the complexity of the decisions, the important point here is that the report must describe what was used and why it was the most appropriate choice.

Critical evaluation: The instrumentation. How thoroughly did the author describe and justify the instrumentation for the study? If you are new to a field of investigation, you might not understand some of the technical detail. Nevertheless, you should not have to encounter measurement tools at some later point in the report that have not been named, described in at least general terms, and justified in this subsection. Here are questions you should ask concerning the part of the "Method" section that deals with the study's instruments. You can add to or modify our suggestions, but be sure you know the answers.

- Are all of the instruments used in the study named and described?
- In each case for which it is appropriate, are validity and reliability values provided?
- Have researcher-constructed instruments been pilot tested?
- Has a rationale been given for selection when there were other available options?

The Procedures

In this portion of the "Method" section, the author explains how the instruments were used. The purpose of understanding methods is to allow you to not only judge their adequacy but to compare them with what was used in other studies. This, therefore, is the place for detail. It is not sufficient to know that a questionnaire was used, even if its validity and reliability are given and a full copy of the document provided in an appendix to the report. You need to know how it was used.

The details of administration not only affect some portion of the responses obtained, but their description will tell you much about how sophisticated (and careful) the investigator was in planning and executing the data collection. For example, in the case of a questionnaire, you should expect to be given information concerning any of the following that seem potentially relevant to the quality of data. Was the questionnaire administered

- to individuals or to groups?
- by the investigator or by someone else?
- with scripted verbal instructions?
- in a classroom, laboratory, lunchroom (and so on)?
- under conditions that allowed subjects to ask about the meaning of questions?
- in the morning or the afternoon?
- under conditions that were the same for all subjects?
- with or without time limits for completion?
- with instructions that required anonymity of the subject?
- all at once or in subsections?
- so that all forms were complete?
- so that all forms were returned, whether complete or not?

As you can see, there is a great deal to know about test administration, and let us assure you that each of the factors implied by these questions might have an influence on how people respond. Where there are differences in responses to the same questionnaire when used in different studies, a common interpretation is to argue that the subjects were different and thus gave different responses. An alternative explanation, however, is that the conditions under which the instrument was administered were sufficiently different to produce the observed variation in results, regardless of differences in the subjects.

The same importance can be assigned to any other procedures used within a study, such as steps that do not involve measurement but deal instead with the conditions under which interventions are applied. If, for example, in a study of medication for facial acne, a topical lotion was applied twice each day by the patient, and, in a second study, the same kind and amount of lotion was applied once a day by a trained research assistant, and the results were favorable only in the second study, what has been learned? If none (or only some) of the administrative details was made clear in the reports, we know very little—and what we think we know might be erroneous or even dangerous.

Once again, the inexperienced novice in research is at a disadvantage in evaluating the quality of decisions made about procedural matters. Thus, the most important thing to look for is evidence that the researcher has sufficient sophistication to consider the details of procedure important and has enough concern about good report writing to describe those vital details for you.

Critical evaluation: The procedures. How thoroughly did the author explain the procedures for using all of the instrumentation for the study? Here are some questions you should ask concerning the portion of the "Method" section that deals with procedures. Not all of them will apply to each study or to all types of designs. You should add to the list or modify items to accommodate the studies you actually encounter. If you do not know how instruments are used, you lack information that is vital to understanding the data they produce.

- Were you informed of the environmental conditions under which each instrument was used?
- Does the report indicate the exact protocol to use for each instrument?
- Are you told how data from each instrument were recorded?
- Did the author explain the exact manner in which each intervention was applied to each subject?

The Analysis

In this final part of the "Method" section, the researcher describes how the data were organized and then subjected to analysis. In quantitative studies, these steps most commonly assume the form of statistical operations. As we indicated in Chapter 6, we have provided a brief beginner's guide to some of the most commonly encountered statistics in Appendix C. You might or might not elect to study that material, although we believe the contents are not particularly difficult and their application to many of the reports you encounter will be quite helpful. If you have been planning to try our beginner's guide, this is the appropriate point to do so—as a prelude to the remainder of this section.

Whatever your decision, we repeat our earlier advice about the topic of statistics—do not panic! Somewhere, in every report, is a plain-language description of the important information. The unfamiliar symbols and numerics can be ignored without great risk to your basic understanding of the study. Thorough knowledge of statistics is essential only if you intend to critically evaluate the investigator's choice and use of tools—an impossible task for any beginner, and often a difficult one for experienced researchers.

Please also remember our comments in Chapter 3 concerning the trust you award to published research. In almost every case, an editor and several reviewers have inspected the statistics used in the study. If the report is from a strong research journal, at least one of the reviewers was assigned because he or she possessed particular knowledge of and interest in the form of analysis employed. Our advice here is to read through the account of analytic procedures offered in the "Method" section, derive what you can from it, and then move on. For most of you, it will not be helpful at this point to suggest critical questions to ask about the description of statistical procedures, so we too will move on to the next section.

What Was Found?

At last we come to the really exciting part of any report: finding out what was discovered. Although we have argued that many of the valuables people retrieve from research reports have nothing to do with the findings, it is nevertheless true that virtually every reader will be interested in the final installments of the researcher's story. For some readers, of course, the findings (and conclusions) are the primary (if not sole) target of their search.

In traditional quantitative studies, aside from purely verbal descriptions of the findings (which are particularly useful for the beginning reader), authors have two options for indicating the results: (a) the end products of statistical analysis expressed in numeric form (usually embedded in the text or displayed in tables) and (b) symbolic representations such as graphs, diagrams, and photographs.

Description of the Findings

Begin your inspection of the section headed "Results" (or, less frequently, "Findings") by noting the subheadings and the order in which findings are presented. This should provide a reflection of the problems, questions, or hypotheses laid out in the opening section on the purpose(s) of the study. Sometimes, the author presents findings by repeating each question or hypothesis in its full form and then inserting the particular statistical indicator that provides the answer. That value is often accompanied by other statistics that provide support for its integrity. In addition, you might be directed to graphic portrayals that represent an alternative format for presenting findings, or to tables that can display more complex sets of outcome numbers.

Figures

The cliché that a picture is worth a thousand words is just as true in research reports as in any other type of writing. To say that two groups were different from each other supplies basic information, but a real understanding of the magnitude of that difference can best be portrayed by a picture—a graphic that captures the relative size of the variable in a vivid (and memorable) manner. Indeed, graphics are so much more effective than word descriptions for portraying complex relationships between or among variables that they have become ubiquitous in newspapers and magazines, as well as scientific journals.

Word processing and graphics programs that allow easy creation of graphs and other figures, as well as their quick insertion into manuscript copy, have encouraged such illustration in all kinds of print reporting. For that reason alone, learning how to look at graphic displays of information with a critical eye is necessary equipment for any educated person, whether he or she intends to read research reports or not.

In research reports, graphs and line drawings are always called *figures*. That distinguishes them from *tables*, which usually contain exact values in numerical form, although lists of discrete items of information in verbal form sometimes are also designated as tables. Both are more expensive to reproduce in a journal than text, and figures are generally costlier to include than tables. Accordingly, authors tend to use presentational devices when they offer significant improvements over straight prose in clarity and economy (by allowing for substantial reductions in text). Because they display data with high precision, tables are well suited for primary findings (in the language of many quantitative designs, the *main effects*). Conversely, figures are used when it is important to draw readers' attention to general comparisons (which require less precision) and to interactions among variables.

In the early part of the 20th century, when few scientific journals existed and not many scholars published empirical research, authors had the luxury of long reports (50 pages was not uncommon) and ample space for figures and tables. In those halcyon days, appendices even contained long tables of raw data so readers could calculate their own analyses. Today, in a world with thousands of journals and research scholars, and with publication page limitations (usually about 25 to 30 pages, either excluding or including figures, tables, and references, depending on editorial policy), a truly "complete presentation" of a study and all its findings is no more than a theoretical ideal. Consequently, researchers must evaluate their findings with an eye to presenting the most important ones in compact formats—tables that consolidate detail and figures that grab attention and clearly delineate relationships.

As a category of symbolic representations, figures include line graphs, cumulative line graphs, cumulative frequency graphs, surface (area) graphs, bar graphs (histograms), double-axis graphs, pie charts, drawings, and photographs. Figures are always described by captions that present the number of the figure as cited in the main text and that identify all of the constructs and relationships that are shown. Although captions are not always written in complete sentence form, they must be complete in another respect. A caption must allow the figure to stand alone as an intelligible presentation. If you study a graph, for example, and still cannot understand what finding is represented by a particular line, or if you have to go back into the text to retrieve the names of the variables displayed, the caption is defective—and the fault rests with the author or the editor, not you.

Critical evaluation: Figures. All figures must meet two standards. As the reader works to understand the findings, the figures must provide assistance that is in some way superior to what could be accomplished through text or tables, and they must be absolutely clear in themselves. Their superiority can be in terms of economy, emphasis of primary findings, or providing the impact of a dramatic visual image. Their clarity must meet the "stand-alone" test—everything has to be immediately available on the figure, in the caption, the legends, and the layout. Figures that deal with nonessential findings waste the reader's time, no matter how elegant. Figures that require laborious backtracking to the text make understanding more difficult and put accurate interpretation at risk.

Here are the critical questions you should ask concerning the display of findings through figures. Poor figures are more than just a nuisance—they are a warning signal for the more general problems of inadequate reporting and weak conceptualization.

- Does the caption clearly identify the variables displayed?
- Do the legends on the figure clearly identify the scales assigned to each axis?
- Does the caption provide essential information about the source of data at each interval, as well as significant differences or interactions?
- Was everything you needed to understand the findings easily available, or did you have to retreat to the text to retrieve explanatory information?

Tables

Although figures are the ideal format for revealing trends, relationships, and relative proportions, tables serve other important functions, such as condensing large volumes of raw data into an economical space and preserving the precise characteristics of those data. Points plotted on a graph might be generally accurate portrayals of the raw data, but they can rarely be precise. Not only are the data rounded off, but, because the real number often falls between the units of measure shown on the axes, it is impossible to tell what the exact value is. Thus, whenever it is necessary to display a substantial volume of data, and when it is more important for the reader to know specific numeric values than, for example, to know how various values relate to each other or to the whole, results should be displayed in a table.

As with figures, the best approach to tables is to read all of the information (i.e., all the actual numbers in the rows and columns) before focusing on any of the specific pieces of data that the table contains. All tables are explicitly referenced in the text, and authors often direct the reader's attention to particular points within the table. That is perfectly appropriate as part of the presentation, but we urge you to make a habit of first surveying the entire table as a context for what the author wants you to see. Comparisons, for example, are more likely to be correctly understood and evaluated if you have a sense of the whole display. Again, tables, like figures, are to be studied, not just read.

Critical evaluation: Tables. Here are critical questions you should ask about tables. As is the case with figures, if tables are difficult to follow, that fact suggests more general problems about the report.

- Does the title clearly identify all of the variables or categories of variables displayed in the table?
- Do the row and column headings clearly identify the exact nature of the data the table contains?
- If appropriate, is information about sample or treatment group sizes provided?
- If appropriate, are statistically significant numbers clearly marked and referenced in explanatory footnotes?
- Is the degree of numeric precision no greater than necessary for sustaining the meaning of the findings?
- Was everything you needed to understand the table easily available, or did you have to retreat to the text to retrieve explanatory information?

What Do the Results Mean?

In Chapter 5, we emphasized the distinction between the findings (or results) of a study and the investigator's conclusions. The former are simply reported, often without comment. The latter, which are usually contained in a section titled either "Discussion" or "Conclusions," is the point at which the author of the report considers all that has happened, decides what has been learned, and communicates it to readers, often with extensive comment.

It is in this section that the researcher matches findings with the original research purpose, indicates which aspect of the results is the most important, which might have been unexpected (and why), and gives an answer to the ever-present (if implicit) question, "So what?" Taken together, these reflections should provide an unambiguous indication of what the researcher believes the results mean. That standard should be held just as firmly, by the way, when the meaning of the results is ambiguous as when their meaning is clear.

If your primary interest is specifically attached to the outcome rather than what might be learned from all of the procedural aspects of the study, discussion and conclusions are the mother lode. You probably skimmed this section in the preliminary survey by which you selected the study for a full review, and now is the time to mine it more thoroughly for the information you seek. As you dig into that task, we offer several suggestions that will help you retain a critical eye about the author's conclusions.

In addition to our previous injunction that researchers ought to make a clear statement of what the findings mean to them, there are three other points that characterize good-quality discussion and sound conclusions. First, if there were unanticipated difficulties in the conduct of the study (from the original conceptualization through the analysis of data), this is where those should be discussed and their implications made clear. In many cases, it is also appropriate to remind the reader of limitations that were anticipated (in subjects, instruments, or procedure) so that conclusions can be considered in light of the full context for the study. Such acknowledgments should add to rather than detract from the researcher's credibility, and the failure to make a clean accounting should be taken as a warning of serious danger.

The second element that should appear in the discussion is an effort to place findings into the wider frame of existing knowledge. When this is done well, it often involves a return to examine sources cited in the introduction to the study. When present conclusions reinforce previous work, the author should explain how the new information extends the ongoing evolution of knowledge. When the conclusions are contradictory to previous results, it is the author's responsibility to offer whatever explanations are available for that discrepancy. There usually are a host of possible causes, and it is not enough to simply list them. To the extent that there are reasonable grounds of any kind, a good report will identify the strongest candidates.

Third, and finally, conclusions must follow logically from the findings. The data not only serve as the basis for making any assertion about what was learned, they also mark the limits of what can be claimed. It is quite possible that you will encounter a report in which the author, perhaps in a fit of exuberant enthusiasm, stretches the link between findings and conclusions beyond what you think it can reasonably bear. You should be neither surprised nor unduly shocked. At the end of a long and difficult study, the temptation to make that stretch can be substantial. Furthermore, in at least some studies, the decision about what does and does not constitute a reasonable claim truly is a matter of judgment.

There is nothing improper in speculating about the meaning of findings, and certainly not in discussing why the data might have appeared as they did. Both of these can be part of writing a thorough discussion of the results. However, the author must not allow any confusion between assertions that are and are not supported by the data. When that happens, the critical distinction between a research report and more general forms of expositional writing has been lost.

To close our consideration of the author's discussion, we would like to nominate one additional contribution that, although infrequently encountered, should receive special recognition and appreciation from readers of every kind. We hope we have made it abundantly clear that researchers ought to put themselves on the line and firmly "own" their conclusions, even if that ownership has to be hedged by an account of the limitations inherent in the findings. You should not take our appeal for ownership, however, to mean that all discussion of alternative interpretations is prohibited. Our belief is quite to the contrary. Having clearly indicated what the author believes to be the most reasonable conclusion(s), a brisk review of any serious rivals to that understanding is an invaluable service for the reader.

Please recall a point we have made repeatedly in this book. All conclusions are tentative and held contingent on future inquiry. In that sense, all conclusions are hypotheses. They are to be held like fencing foils—never so loosely that they can be easily dislodged, and never so tightly that they are immobilized in the hand and made useless for the swift changes of thrust and parry. Researchers might not care for that analogy, but we believe that the best of them care passionately about the belief it portrays.

Critical evaluation: What do the results mean? To give conclusions their due is to give the author his or her due—the respect deserved for conducting a careful study. Critical inspection here often demands some shuffling back and forth between this final section and previous parts of the report. There are critical questions to ask, however, and you owe it to yourself, as well as to the author, to know the answers.

- Do the conclusions stay within the bounds of the findings, or do they range into unsupported speculation?
- Are the conclusions presented in such a manner that it is easy to connect them with the purposes of the study and the specific research problems that shaped it?
- Does the author help you understand how the results fit into the fund of existing knowledge?
- Is the author frank and thorough in presenting the limitations to which the conclusions are subject?
- In retrospect, is it your sense that the author has made an adequate response to the question, "So what?"

❖ SUMMARY

With the examination of critical questions to ask about the "Discussion" or "Conclusion" section of a quantitative research report, we have now completed our effort to equip you with some basic skills for being thoughtfully critical while you read. The quality of the judgments you make will improve with practice and can be made more sophisticated by further study of research methods. There is no reason not to begin right now, however, with the very next quantitative study report that comes your way. You now possess the tools to be an active rather than a passive reader—by raising the questions you learned about in this chapter.

If that report happens to concern a study informed by the qualitative paradigm, however, you are going to need the tools for reading with a critical eye that are found in Chapter 8. So don't stop here. Press on and prepare yourself to be a careful consumer across the full range of research that might hold potential relevance to your interests.

8

Reading Reports
of Qualitative
Research—Critically

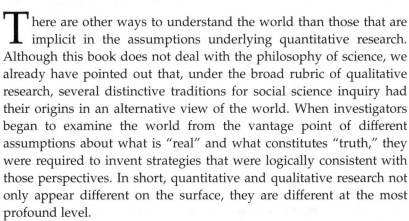

T here are other ways to understand the world than those that are
implicit in the assumptions underlying quantitative research.
Although this book does not deal with the philosophy of science, we
already have pointed out that, under the broad rubric of qualitative
research, several distinctive traditions for social science inquiry had
their origins in an alternative view of the world. When investigators
began to examine the world from the vantage point of different
assumptions about what is "real" and what constitutes "truth," they
were required to invent strategies that were logically consistent with
those perspectives. In short, quantitative and qualitative research not
only appear different on the surface, they are different at the most
profound level.

That having been said, this is an appropriate place for us to make
a distinction between paradigms and people. Just as there are differing
levels of explicit belief and ritual observance within any religion,
researchers have different levels of internalization for the assumptions
that undergird the kind of research they do. As an example, we know

qualitative researchers who seem to experience a world in which "truth" is always a wholly relative phenomenon, but we have other colleagues who find a relativistic vantage point necessary for the conduct of their research—but who appear to comfortably assume a far more standard "scientific" view in their personal lives.

The same is true in reverse for some of the quantitative researchers we know. In everyday life, many act as though social reality exists not "out there," but only in the minds of people and their individual interpretations. In their work, however, they assume that objective knowledge (fact) exists "out there," can be gained by direct experience or observations, and is the only true knowledge available to science. Yes, that indeed does lead us to expect researchers to be just as wonderfully inconsistent in their philosophies as the rest of us.

In addition to comprehending the reality of normal human variation, you must understand that a distinctive system of philosophic thought provided the influence that sculpted the outlines of qualitative inquiry. That, too, is a reality, although in this case it is one embedded in history rather than human nature. Thus, when qualitative researchers turn from conducting a study to authoring a report, what they produce will have discernable characteristics that are the product of the paradigm that lies behind their mode of study. Exactly the same thing is true for people doing quantitative studies. The two kinds of reports contain differences in appearance and content. And to that we can only say, "Vive la difference!"

Some aspects for sound reporting, of course, are fully shared between qualitative and quantitative studies. After all, clear, lively prose descriptions are appreciated in both genres. Other aspects of the two types of reports only appear to be similar when they actually are not. Writing about "generalizability" of findings in a quantitative report or about the "transferability" of findings in a qualitative report sound vaguely as though they represent the same task, but in some important ways they do not. Finally, yet other aspects of qualitative reporting have no equivalent at all in accounts of quantitative investigation. For example, explaining how the researcher's subjective responses were monitored and managed as part of data analysis is not likely to arise as an issue in describing the selection and operation of a statistical program for numeric data.

Not only will qualitative reports themselves look different to the reader, but what we have to suggest about reading them critically will have to assume a form that is different from our treatment of quantitative reports in Chapter 7. The reasons for that arise from several closely related sources.

The most obvious and distinctive characteristic of all qualitative research designs is that they are flexible. Regardless of the particular tradition at hand, qualitative studies are intended to be adjusted not only to the particular nature of the context for inquiry but to the surprises (opportunities and dead ends) exposed by direct and spontaneous interactions between researchers and participants. As with any unscripted human interaction, the process of gathering data rarely fails to turn up the unexpected. It follows, then, that when one speaks of a "design" for qualitative research, the referent often resembles an evolving set of questions and responsive tactics rather than the execution of a fixed plan.

That flexibility makes it impossible to devise a single and immutable list of characteristics for sound qualitative studies—even for those within a single tradition (such as ethnography, case study, or phenomenology). And, what is true of qualitative studies must then also be true of what we can expect from good reports of these studies. Their variability is high, and the utility of standardized textbook templates is low.

There are a number of permutations within the family of "experiments" in quantitative research. Further, adventitious adaptations that serve to get the job done are just as much a tradition among experimenters as among ethnographers. For these reasons, not all reports of quantitative research assume the same form. Nevertheless, there are templates for most of the commonly used quantitative designs, and investigators tend not to stray far beyond them without good reason to do so.

You will find that quantitative studies follow rules that are neither rigid nor mechanically prescriptive. You will also find, however, that the possibilities have been laid out with considerable formality and careful detail. For a true experiment (defined in Chapter 6), for example, it is not difficult even for a novice to tell whether the content of a report does or does not make perfectly clear that all the standards for a true experiment have been met.

Such templates for design and execution simply do not exist for qualitative studies. If they did, the list of criteria would be longer than you could read and, very likely, far longer than we would have the patience to write.

Beyond inherent flexibility and the absence of standard templates, several additional facts add complications to qualitative reports.

Modern forms of qualitative study are more diverse, less standardized, more vigorously disputed by scholars, and profoundly more complicated than comparable forms of inquiry that make use of quantitative data. In short, the domain of qualitative research is more difficult to describe and its content more elusive to grasp than what you will find in the well-established and relatively more stable domain of quantitative science.

At first, such an assertion about the relative complexities of qualitative and quantitative research might seem counterintuitive for many of our readers. In most cases, however, people are confusing statistics, with all of their highly technical and sometimes impenetrable mystery, with the underlying structure of quantitative designs. After statistics are set aside as no more than what they really are—mechanical tools for data analysis that are not at all integral to the internal logic of research—the majority of quantitative studies are easy to understand. The assumptions on which the research experiment is built, for example, are grounded in our everyday experience, and the logic for the basic design is wonderfully self-evident after it has been properly explained. (For a convincing example of such "obviousness" in quantitative designs, see Patten, 2002b.) In contrast, the assumptions made by qualitative researchers are not at all commonplace, and the logic of various designs has to be argued rather than simply revealed.

The end result of such complexity is that we have to be exceedingly careful in positing a list of critical questions to raise about qualitative studies and their contingent reports. If misused as though they were simple templates, our suggestions for evaluating what you find in qualitative research reports will be worse than merely a potential source of confusion or error. If taken as a list of what to expect in every report, our suggestions will endanger any chance you have of developing a useful degree of confidence in figuring out how much you trust what the author has written. Apply these standards gently, expect a great deal of variability in what the investigators do, and pay attention to your own common sense—as well as to our suggestions for what should be noticed with a critical eye.

A final reminder here is aimed at a common source of confusion. In your own thinking (and talking) about research, be sure to make a clear distinction between methods of data collection and the underlying paradigmatic assumptions that frame empirical studies. Methods are tools, but the use of a given tool does not posit (or require) any particular set of assumptions about the world. Thus, if interviews are used as part of a quantitative study, the investigation can remain firmly grounded on typical quantitative assumptions. In reverse, if it is useful to accumulate some numeric data as part of a qualitative design (and such occasionally is the case), the investigator will, nonetheless, continue to employ a set of assumptions that come from a qualitative perspective. In short, you should not be surprised to find quantitative studies in which the investigator records what subjects say, or qualitative studies in which quantities (and, not uncommonly, descriptive statistics) constitute a valuable part of the data set.

Another place where you might encounter such "crossing over" of methodologies is in reports from studies that utilize hybrid formats called *mixed methodology designs*. Research of this type was briefly introduced in Chapter 6, along with an illustrative specimen. These investigations purport to utilize both qualitative and quantitative perspectives for the analysis of data. We do not feel it appropriate (or necessary) to explain such sophisticated models in an introductory text. If you are curious about these increasingly common formats for inquiry, however, the texts by Tashakkori & Teddlie (1998, 2003) are a comprehensive source, but Creswell (2003) and Robson (2002) offer plain-language introductions that might be more appropriate.

❖ EXPECTATIONS FOR QUALITATIVE REPORTS: THE GENERIC AND GENERAL STANDARDS

Here are some things to watch for in qualitative reports. They are general in the sense that each pertains to what you should expect to learn from a large component part of the report, but they do not prescribe exactly how that should be accomplished. They are generic in the sense that all of them appear in student textbooks and reference sources that deal with qualitative research. In these sources, they are sometimes organized into lists (or even into tables), whereas in other places they are embedded in chapter-length text. Allowing for differences in length, order, format, wording, and degree of explicitness, however, they all pertain to the same set of broadly stated and widely shared concerns. All that we have contributed is the translation service required to make them readily accessible to our readers.

For examples of how introductory-level textbooks describe the form and content of basic qualitative reports, we suggest any (or several) of the following: Bogdan and Biklen (2003), Creswell (2003), Patton

(2001), Merriam (1998), Miles and Huberman (1994), Robson (2002), or Silverman (2000). If you would like to see actual reports that meet most (if not all) of these generic standards, an efficient tactic is to consult edited research collections in which the qualitative reports selected for inclusion have been carefully screened. For that purpose we suggest any (or several) of the collections noted in Chapter 4. Finally, in the pages of journals and reference collections, the continuing exchange among academics with regard to qualitative research has produced some useful implications for evaluating qualitative research reports. Many of these articles and chapters are not accessible for laypersons, but we can recommend several that would be both truly helpful and not unreasonably difficult: Ambert, Adler, Adler, & Detzner (1995); Anfara, Brown, and Mangione (2002); Creswell and Miller (2000); Johnson (1997); and Krefting (1991). These sources offer perspectives on what constitutes quality in qualitative research from a variety of professional areas, including occupational therapy, education, marriage and family services, and nursing.

In reading any published report of a qualitative study:

1. *You should find a description of the provenance of the study and what it is about.* Somewhere, and better early than late, the report should describe what the study is about. This description should include an account of what provided the impulse for the investigation, the origin of the researcher's interest or concern, what shaped the initial question(s), what facts might make the findings significant, and why a qualitative format for study was selected. The information might be offered in a single section or be scattered throughout a discursive introduction.

2. *You should find a description of the context in which the data were collected.* This might include social, economic, physical, and, when relevant, historical aspects of the locale. This description will answer the question "where?"—although much more than geography and physical circumstance are likely to be involved.

3. *You should find an account of what was done in that context.* Ordinarily, this should include answers to the standard questions: "Who?" "What?" "When?" "How?" and, particularly, "Why?" The topics circumscribed by these questions cover the unfolding story of design, method for data collection, and procedures for analysis of the data. Because many qualitative studies involve responses and adjustments to the data while it is being collected (and to the analysis that

often runs concurrently with data collection), the account might describe an evolving process rather than a series of fixed and predetermined steps.

For example, if a field study is under way, and it becomes apparent that interviews with informants that have one kind of role in an organization (such as a school or hospital) are not providing information about an event or process that seems vital to the purpose of the study, then informants with a different role and perspective will have to be recruited as participants. A description of why that was done and how it was accomplished must become a part of the report.

4. *You should find presentation of actual data.* The data are usually embedded in the description of what was done and how conclusions were drawn. For reasons of economy, data must be presented in compact and often abbreviated forms, such as selected quotations, short vignettes, diagrams of relationships, or even photographs. Such data displays should be (a) selected to highlight salient features of the data, (b) designed to give vivid color to the setting and participants, and (c) laid out in a manner that allows the reader to consider some of the same evidence that confronted the investigator. In that way, the reader gains insight into how the interpretations were developed and the subsequent conclusions formed—and how well supported by the data they all seem to be.

5. *You should find an explicit effort to summarize, as well as to articulate, one or several conclusions.* The summary might be formal and segregated under a single heading or be woven into the discussion in a closing section. It might include attention to data, analysis, or salient events encountered during the course of the study. The process of asserting conclusions involves a return to the purposes of the study and any explicit questions raised. That task requires two distinct activities: (a) explaining what has been learned from the study by stating what has been concluded from analysis of the data, and (b) describing how what has been learned can be fitted into the world of ideas—a world sometimes represented by existing (or proposed) research literature but in other instances by our common notions about how things work.

As is also the case with reports of quantitative research, some (although not all) qualitative researchers go on to include an additional component by noting how the study relates to the world of practice.

This might consist of something as explicit as a list of directions for policy or professional action, or it can be as oblique (and modest) as the noting of possible implications derived from the study. Although such a component is not a generally accepted requirement for a complete report, there is no doubt that many readers find it offers a satisfying kind of closure for the story of a study.

The structure of qualitative reports differs from that used for quantitative studies in several distinctive ways. The fixed elements of title and abstract at one end, and references at the other, are identical, as is an ubiquitous introductory section (most commonly without a heading). Also, as is recently the trend with quantitative investigators, qualitative researchers now are less inclined to employ an extensive and separate "review of the literature" section and more likely to distribute references to existing research throughout other sections (introduction, theoretical framework, research questions, findings, or even the closing discussion).

Distinctively, qualitative reports almost always combine data collection and data analysis in a section titled "Method"—for reasons discussed previously in this chapter. Typically, sections called "Findings" (or "Results") and then "Discussion" follow. A heading for "Conclusions" is not uncommon, but the distinctions we have made (in Chapter 5) between findings and conclusions are not always observed. In some reports, the author's discussion of the study might not be clearly demarcated from either the statement of findings or the drawing of conclusions. Finally, although many authors do make at least some allusion to the implications of their work (either for future research or for the improvement of practice), it now is relatively rare to find an entire section set aside with the heading "Implications."

Out of this discussion, one thing is clear. You should expect the format for reports to be as variable and unpredictable as the underlying flexibility of qualitative inquiry would suggest. General standards for qualitative reports can be useful in detecting serious omissions, but they must accommodate the diversity that is characteristic of real publications.

❖ EXPECTATIONS FOR QUALITATIVE REPORTS: THE SPECIFIC AND INDIVIDUAL STANDARDS

We turn now from expectations that are general to ones that are more specific to particular problems encountered in reading reports.

Although you can find discussions of each of the following points in almost any qualitative research textbook, these were selected by us (from among many possibilities) for more specific attention. The basis for that selection was our personal experience as readers of qualitative reports and our conclusion that (a) these problems reflect important threats to a reader's ability to evaluate the quality of a study, (b) these problems are among those most likely to be found in a typical qualitative report, and (c) these problems have characteristics that our readers would be able to both notice and comprehend as elements in good or poor reporting.

Before we begin, however, this is an appropriate place to remind you of several important points. First, remember that when you detect a flaw in a report, instead of halting and discarding the document, you should usually just make a careful note and then continue—adding this information to the calculus from which you later will extract a sense of how much trust to invest in the products of the study. Second, please do not fall into the trap of assuming that each of the points we raise will apply equally to all forms of qualitative research. The great diversity in approaches to qualitative study inevitably results in great diversity among reports. Our list of concerns was designed for typical reports that appear in mainline research journals. Some qualitative researchers use new writing practices that we have not even attempted to contemplate (see Richardson, 2000, for some vivid examples). We have not tried to invent here the one size that will fit all.

In reports of qualitative research for which the topic is relevant, you should notice:

1. How much do you learn about the investigator(s) as a person? If a researcher is the principal "instrument" for inquiry in a qualitative study, to assess the capabilities, dependability, and potential biases of that instrument, we believe that you need to know at least the essentials of its history with the topic, the context, the participants, and the methodology. It is essential here to remember that in qualitative research, objectivity can't be achieved by maintaining distance between researcher and participant. Although a degree of neutrality toward the data is what qualitative researchers struggle to sustain, they will be present as human entities throughout every step of the study. It is *absolutely essential* that they recognize their own subjectivity and monitor how that is functioning in the research context. It also is at least desirable that salient parts of that information be shared with the reader.

Under the pressure of space limitations, that desideratum is more violated than observed in what is published. We maintain, however, that you should notice when you are told little or nothing about the primary instrument used in the study—and wonder how that knowledge might have affected your trust.

2. How often does the report substitute a word or phrase label for an actual description of something done during the study? This question deals with the sin of *nominalism,* by which we refer to instances where the author of a qualitative report announces use of a procedure by naming (labeling) the procedure—and then gives no hint about what actually happened in its application. The implication is that if you are familiar with the procedure named, you will know (more or less) what was done and don't need to read about the messy details. In some cases, that is perfectly legitimate, either because the operation is simple and purely routine ("The list of volunteers was stratified by both gender and marital status."), or because the operation indeed was of such length and complexity that the author is forced to depend, in some measure, on the reader's prior knowledge ("The use of grounded theory determined both the strategy of the study and the primary mode of analysis.").

Those instances of "naming" and then (perhaps after citation of appropriate reference sources for the uninitiated) moving on with the report are unlikely to be problematic. The following list of procedures that we collected from recent reports, however, includes operations that we believe demand more than a label—but too often are identified only by name and, at most, a brief sentence or two of explication: triangulation, member-checking, purposeful sampling, peer debriefing, identification of emerging themes, search for (or analysis of) negative cases, thick description, prolonged engagement, and participant observation. We are sure you will soon find other examples of such rhetorical sin.

In such instances, we think you have a right to ask questions like, "But what happened?" "What did you do?" "What was found?" "How well did it work?" "Where did it come from?" "Could you give me an example?" "How did you define that?" and "Was it worth doing?" When these questions are not answered in the text of the report, you do not know with certainty that anything was done incorrectly in the study. All you do know with certainty is—that you do not know! You have been left unable to judge how much trust to invest in the story being told. How many times does that have to occur in a report for you to begin to wonder, "Why is so much detail missing?" The devils of quality in research almost always reside in the details of what was done and why. Nominalism should always make you uneasy—and, used too often or with topics that seem really important, it should make you downright distrustful.

3. *How carefully and openly does the author discuss alternatives to the decisions about design and method taken before and during the study, alternatives to his or her interpretations of the data, and alternatives to the conclusions derived from the findings?* It is an axiom among scholars that thoughtful discussion of *rival hypotheses* (a collective term covering alternative courses of action as well as other interpretations of data) is a sign of scientific maturity, self-confidence, and a strong sense of ethical responsibility. For us, that description might go a bit too far, but it is certain that when alternatives are entertained and discussed openly in a qualitative report—along with assertion of the argument(s) favoring the decision or interpretation selected—the reader is left with far more than an enhanced respect for the author's person. They have in hand information that allows them to audit the trail of process in the study, including not only accounts of what happened but answers to questions about "why?" as well. This form of detail is usually the most reassuring when reaching the conclusion that this is a careful study, likely to accurately represent the participants, and likely to deserve your trust.

4. *How vivid are the representations of the context, the participants, the researcher(s), and the events of the study?* Clear, forceful, uncomplicated writing produces the power of research reports—quantitative or qualitative. There are, however, some insufficiently appreciated differences between what constitutes effective writing for telling the study's story in the two types of research.

For quantitative reports, it is highly desirable to employ writing that is vivid in description and interesting in style, as well as just plain transparently clear. For qualitative reports, these characteristics are absolutely essential. Colorful descriptions, portrayals of intense affect, flashes of humor, and vivid sketches of context are at the heart of the investigator's purpose—to make the familiar seem strange and exotic, and the strange seem comfortably familiar. For that to be accomplished requires that the people seem alive, that the story of what is happening to them seem worth hearing, and that the insights gained into the human condition seem sharply defined and fully believable.

No, this is not an appeal for flashy writing to take the place of rigor, or for personal journalism to displace thorough description in qualitative reports. This is a judgment based upon how you respond to what you read. If you find the people and places of the study uninteresting and lifeless, if the study has no power over your thoughts and imagination (even if only for the time it takes to read the report), then we think the report has failed in one vital respect. And how will you make that evaluative judgment about a report? Read it, and you will know! The quick and the dead will always be with us, but nothing is so deadly as a boring research report.

❖ EXPECTATIONS FOR QUALITATIVE STUDIES: A CRITICAL LOOK BEHIND THE REPORT

Some of you will have noticed that we have tried (perhaps *struggled* would be a more accurate description) to keep this section focused on *reports* of qualitative research and how to read them with a critical eye for their adequacy. It is inevitable, however, that in thinking and writing about reports one slips easily into contemplation of the studies behind them—and how adequate they might be. The two foci are different but so intertwined that it is difficult to keep them separate.

The simple fact remains that, while writing this chapter, we often found ourselves considering how reports serve to reveal important (and sometimes ubiquitous) problems in the actual conduct of research. For that reason, we feel our task in this chapter would be incomplete if we did not share a few of the most insistent concerns that often draw our attention away from qualitative reports as documents—to the decisions and procedures of the studies themselves.

There is a wonderful cinematic moment near the end of *The Wizard of Oz* (Fleming, 1939) when Toto has knocked the screen aside to reveal the Wizard, frantically manipulating the machinery to produce what is visible. In a moment of panic at being revealed, he says: "Pay no attention to that man behind the curtain!" Contrary to the Wizard's injunction, we are inviting you to take a brief look at five pieces of the research machinery that always lurk behind the paper pages of qualitative research reports.

The Machinery of Time

We think that some qualitative researchers do not spend enough time in the contexts and with the participants that they purport to examine. There is no rule about this, not even a useful rule of thumb. In the end, however, the believability of a qualitative study depends upon our sense that the investigator got close enough to the data sources to be really familiar with what was going on. We want to be reassured that he or she was unlikely to be taken in by devious participants, was unlikely to distort descriptions because important aspects simply were overlooked, and was unlikely to have fastened onto the first interpretation that popped into mind, without listening and watching until something beyond the merely facile came into focus. All that takes time, repeated opportunities, and long contemplation of data.

There are, of course, compelling motives to be efficient in the use of valuable research time, but that is only an explanation for why data collection sometimes gets rushed—not a valid excuse for superficial work. We look in research reports for evidence that the investigator was able to "be there." This holds true even in studies for which interviews are a method of data collection, when "being there" consists of taking the time required to truly engage the participant, to listen closely, and to probe thoughtfully. In doing so, we always hope to come away with a sense that the pace of process within the study allowed the researcher to acquire enough intimacy to serve as a reliable guide. Too often we are disappointed, and our concern is that the problem lies not in the reporting, but in the doing. When you finish reading a qualitative report, ask yourself, "Am I convinced that the author stayed long enough to give me a really trustworthy account of what was going on?"

The Machinery of Subjectivity

Understandably, all researchers bring to the work of an investigation the freight of who they are, what they know, where they have lived, how they think, and why they are doing the study. What is less well understood is how important it is for them to (a) be aware of the content of that freight, (b) be watchful about how their unique subjectivity interacts with decisions about questions, data collection, analysis, and interpretation, (c) be firm and creative in devising ways to step back and allow the data to be what they are, (d) be diligent about keeping a careful record of subjective encounters within the study, and (e) be open and artful about sharing that record in the report.

After all, the researcher is the one who, with all of his or her humanity, serves as the primary instrument in all that transpires. How subjectivity is managed really matters (it can never be eliminated, nor should we wish it to be)—it must be dealt with by deliberate actions, not by confessional contrition, and it has consequences for both the quality of data and the believability of the story told in the report. We always look for evidence that researchers are concerned about their biases and that they have struggled to be aware of where those dispositions lie and how they might be at work. Too often, this topic is ignored, or it is briskly pushed aside with brief references to reliability procedures for coding and categorizing of data.

Such checks on consistency are nice, perhaps necessary, but certainly not sufficient to satisfy the need to detect and confront researcher bias—or to reassure nervous readers! We would rather read about answers to questions like: "What made me so interested in that?" "Why was I uneasy about this?" "Did my foreshadowed assumption really help in understanding that?" "What made that decision feel so inconsistent with my theoretical framework?" and "I wonder if the participants would share my interpretation?" That is the messy stuff of doing qualitative research and, untidy or not, it must be done with patience, skill, and honesty. When you finish reading a qualitative study, ask yourself, "Am I persuaded that the author was clearly conscious of who he or she was, and that, throughout the study, he or she was conscientiously watchful about the intrusion of personal bias into the research process?"

The Machinery of What Does Not Fit

The search for negative data, the analysis of outliers and extreme cases, the creation of explanations for the incongruent products of triangulation, and the disposition of divisive fallout from peer debriefing sessions (all of which are common requirements in a qualitative study) should involve *actually doing things*. It is here that the sins of nominalism run amok! The researcher should think about why exceptions in the data did occur and what they might mean, and then actually decide what to do about them. Simply ignoring what does not fit, or just taking cursory notice and moving on without response, represents dangerously inadequate use of qualitative methodology.

When something does not fit with the investigator's preferred understanding, the researcher has to take action, even if (in all honesty and after every effort has been made to find an alternative) that action is simply to recognize that, when people are studied, there are likely to be exceptions to any generally useful rule about their behavior. If the investigator does not respond to contrary data or to clearly visible alternative interpretations, those unexamined loose ends just hang around the study like uninvited ghosts—haunting the party and spoiling everyone's appetite.

To avoid that unhappy condition, we are more concerned about evidence that shows what happened in a study *after* a search for disconfirming cases was undertaken than we are impressed by mere assertions that it was done. When you finish reading a qualitative research report, ask yourself, "Am I persuaded that the author did not sweep anything under the rug (either data itself or alternative interpretations of the data) but gave everything encountered in the course of the study full and honest consideration?"

The Machinery of Relationships

Everyone knows that what people say to you and how they behave in your company is conditioned in large part by the nature of your relationship. Close friends and casual acquaintances do not exchange the same opinions, stories, jokes, or personal feelings. How you behave with clients or visitors in a professional setting is not how you behave with colleagues. And what happens between a researcher and a participant reflects how each presents himself or herself to the other and how the perception of mutual roles is progressively defined by subsequent interactions. We think it makes an important difference whether researchers elect to present themselves (and then act) as interested visitors, genuine friends, professional colleagues, needy supplicants (common with doctoral students), omniscient scholars (occasional with professorial types), political allies, dispassionate observers, the biological equivalents of a tape recorder, or warmly sympathetic listeners. The list of possibilities goes on, but, make no mistake, each relationship has an effect on what will be collected as data. That puts the interpersonal, and the nature of perceived relationship, at the heart of qualitative inquiry.

We have formed the impression that qualitative researchers and, most particularly, novices in the field are insufficiently attentive to this factor and, by that neglect, certainly appear to be naïve as to its power. We look for evidence that presentation of self is thoughtfully preplanned, carefully monitored, and watchfully shifted when required. Evidence that the researcher is aware of how various "researcher effects" can appear in data, and that he or she is concerned when participants seem to be trying too hard to offer information they think the researcher wants to hear, tells us that he or she recognizes the potential power of relationships to shape data. When you finish reading a qualitative research report, ask yourself, "Am I now completely clear about the relationships the author tried to establish with the participants, and did those social interactions seem to work for the purpose of completing a sound study?"

The Machinery of Context

Descriptions of context (physical, social, economic, historical) are given in the report and (among other functions) serve to allow the reader to decide about the appropriateness of transferring findings from the study to the reader's own environment. That process is made possible, however, by actions taken before and during the study. A sufficient body of facts and descriptive detail has to be collected if it is to support a thorough and vivid description of context. If there is any place that effort is well expended to develop what it is now trendy to call *thick description*, it is in the area of capturing the surroundings where the action takes place.

So much is explained about the participants by knowing their location—in culture, in social class, in economic strata, in regional geography, in their network of relationships, in the web of local customs, and in the very places where they live. All of this information can provide for the rich contextualization that (at the first level) helps the investigator interpret what is seen and heard, subsequently (at the second level) helps the reader more fully understand what is asserted in the findings and conclusions, and, finally (at the third level), allows assessment of the study's relevance to other contexts.

What we find in journal reports, however, too often looks like something clipped out of the real estate section of our hometown newspaper ("Well-maintained contemporary home in nice locality, near public transportation, and suitable for large family."). Charitably, we would like to assume that the researcher knew (and used) a great deal more information than is offered in that sketch—but how can we be sure?

We suspect that the paragraph or two devoted to contextualization in some reports might read like thin stuff because what the researcher actually had bothered to find out was itself thin stuff. We don't expect something of the order produced by Margaret Mead for the islands of the South Pacific, but we do think that some return to the respect awarded to the centrality of "place" in classical ethnography would not itself be out of place. When you finish reading a qualitative research report, ask yourself, "Did I learn enough from reading this report to have a picture in my mind of where the study took place, and does the picture have enough color and detail to let me sense how it might be both like and unlike other places that I know?"

❖ CONCLUDING REMARKS

With that brief examination of selected concerns about what is going on behind the screen of qualitative research reports, we close this two chapter-long effort to equip you with a confident sense of things to notice and questions to ask. You now should have acquired at least an introduction to the machinery of conducting and reporting both quantitative and qualitative research. Although there is obviously a good deal more to be known, you are already positioned to be reasonably prudent in deciding what to trust, in identifying sources of confusion, and in navigating through technical details to find what you seek.

We offer now a final caution that we hope you will recall when engaged with the task of actually reading and trying to understand reports. Hold your expectations lightly and apply our suggested standards gently. Away from the prescriptive pages of textbooks, real designs for investigation must, of necessity, assume a wide (perhaps even infinite) variety of forms. It is inevitable that some of those designs will be rather remote from the tidy diagrams of idealized plans you find in books. For that reason, researchers can be confronted with the challenge of explaining events or procedures that are well outside what readers have learned to anticipate. Investigators simply have to fit information into the report as well as they can, and that might require substantial departures from standard formats.

Finally, different authors can go about the writing of reports in quite different ways—and still produce perfectly sound documents. As long as the end result is a thorough, accurate, and clear accounting of the author's story, you should be content with such variation.

Adherence to a rigid format is not an appropriate standard for reporting qualitative research. Accuracy and thorough attention to essential detail, however, are the essential elements of rigor in all research, and clear, concise writing is what makes it possible to communicate those qualities to a reader. These characteristics are what you should expect to find in good research reports—irrespective of the paradigm.

This brings us to the end of the book and our effort to help you learn how to read and understand research reports. Our discussion on many topics has been short, and coverage always was constrained by our sense of how much your mind could encompass at a single sitting, as well as by how much we think you really need to get started. The brevity produced by these considerations led us to recommend a good set of supplemental references with which you could begin to fill the many thin or empty parts of this text.

That suggestion notwithstanding, although we do encourage you to go as far as time and inspiration allow, there is no reason to feel compulsive about learning more—or guilty about not doing so. If you have come this far, that is a great distance indeed. You already have the skills needed to read and use research, and, with practice, those skills will sharpen and expand. With that outcome, we will rest content. For our part, this book was worth revisiting and revising for a second edition. We hope that you, likewise, conclude that it was worth reading.

Appendix A

Annotated Bibliography
of Supplementary References

I n selecting the books below, we focused on those that might be
helpful to you when used either concurrently with some of the
chapters or as a "next step" after a first reading of the entire guide.
These are basic references that a novice can use to obtain information
quickly about a research-related topic, whether you really need it to
understand a report or simply find yourself interested in learning more.
Other books that provide much greater detail on specific topics (some of
which are noted in the main text) have been excluded here because they
require advanced knowledge beyond that needed to read and understand research reports. In making our selections, we gave particular
consideration to texts that our students have found helpful at the outset
of their journeys into the field of research methods and designs.

With each entry below, we provide comments that should help you
to decide whether or not a book will be valuable, either in resolving
specific problems you encounter while reading or in meeting a more
general need for further information. These books build on many of the
topics we have introduced, and, in most cases, you should find it relatively easy to make the transition from this guide to one of the supplemental references.

It is unlikely that you will need to do a complete reading of any
of these books (and certainly not in cover-to-cover sequence). In fact,
we encourage you to consult these or other resources primarily as a
way to locate the information you actually need to begin reading

reports—returning to them only as new questions are encountered. The ultimate goal is to become an effective reader of the kinds of research that interest (and concern) you. Toward that end, selective reading in the books annotated in this appendix should provide a foundation that is both eclectic in scope and economical in acquisition.

Benjafield, J. G. (1994). *Thinking critically about research methods.* Boston: Allyn & Bacon.

If you find it necessary to read research reports that deal with topics within the field of psychology (broadly defined), and particularly if you are confronted by experimental and quasi-experimental studies from that area of social science, this is an efficient and altogether pleasant way to lay the foundation for (as the title says) "thinking critically." An unpretentious paperback, this slim volume is as much intended for the use of people whose lives are influenced by findings from the discipline of psychology as it is for people who are, or are preparing to be, psychologists. Accordingly, this is not a standard textbook containing instructions for standard research methods in psychology. Instead, it is a broad outline of psychology as a research enterprise, with emphasis on how investigators must think about the task of inquiry and how they use careful logic and procedure to create the context for discovery.

After laying out the fundamentals of scientific thinking in psychology and the nature of the experimental process in the first half of the book, the author devotes the second half to a series of "experiments to think about." Each consists of a brief but artful annotation for a published study. In the course of that recounting, however, Benjafield interrupts at key points to ask readers to respond to provocative questions. The studies are so sequenced that by the time the book has been finished, the reader has accumulated a good sense of where critical questions should be asked and how to think carefully about what can be (and can't be) learned from experiments. If you find yourself a consumer of research involving psychological variables, this book offers a surprisingly painless way to begin acquiring some critical skills for reading and understanding.

Bogdan, R. C., & Biklen, S. K. (2003). *Qualitative research for education: An introduction to theories and methods* (4th ed.). Boston: Allyn & Bacon.

If your professional field lies in areas other than education, do not eliminate this text from your priority list just because that word appears in the title. Although some of the illustrative material does deal with educational settings, this is first and foremost a book for those who want to learn about qualitative research. A hallmark of its quality rests in the fact that authors of introductory-level research textbooks in a variety of fields often direct their readers to Bogdan and Biklen as the appropriate first step for any consideration of qualitative methods in research projects, theses, and dissertations.

Now passing its 20th year in print, the first edition once stood alone as the only resource for students in education. Although the book has been regularly updated to accommodate changes in the domain of qualitative research, the authors' primary objective of helping people actually plan and launch research projects remains unchanged—and very much at the center of the book. In our opinion, no single document can match the 48 pages of the opening chapter, "Foundations of Qualitative Research," as an economical, user-friendly, and eminently practical introduction to the paradigm and its several methodological traditions.

Those characteristics are best displayed in the sections containing brief guidelines (or homey advice) for what a beginning qualitative researcher must learn to do. Two of the most widely circulated among students in the social sciences appear in the first chapter: (a) eleven common questions asked about qualitative research (and how to answer them) and (b) guidelines for actually being ethical. Other examples scattered throughout the text include: (a) suggestions for the first day of observation, (b) common questions asked by participants (and the best way to respond), (c) how to do ongoing analysis while collecting data, and (d) ways to think about quantitative data as part of a qualitative study. Again, all of these involve questions that are likely to occur to you when reading qualitative reports—for which answers are rarely provided in other textbooks.

Campbell, D. T., & Stanley, J. C. (1963). *Experimental and quasi-experimental designs for research.* Chicago: Rand McNally.

As we noted in Chapter 6, this is a classic work on research design and one of the most lucid treatments of that topic ever produced for a broad readership. Although now more than 40 years old, this treatise has provided generations of readers with a broad overview of both the unique structures and the appropriate standards of quality for a wide range of quantitative designs. It remains a valuable resource for both beginning researchers and those wishing simply to access research reports. If you want to know how a quantitative study actually works, in many cases (although not all), the best way to find out is to consult this small monograph. The authors create a theoretical model for what constitutes validity in quantitative research and then apply that model to 16 designs. For each, they discuss the specific issues that bear upon validity within the unique situation of that particular research strategy. In doing so, Campbell and Stanley provide a framework for understanding what constitutes good research within the broad family of experimental and quasi-experimental approaches to inquiry.

Creswell, J. W. (2003). *Research design: Qualitative, quantitative, and mixed method approaches* (2nd ed.). Thousand Oaks, CA: Sage.

This paperback book was designed as an introduction to basic inquiry strategies (as distinct from specifics about methodology) for graduate students who intend to do research. Now in a second edition, the text includes a number of important additions. Most notable among these are a full chapter devoted to mixed method designs, substantial attention to issues concerning the ethics of research, and the inclusion of discussion and examples for advocacy, participatory, and emancipatory approaches to qualitative research.

Creswell provides an overview of the research process that ranges from finding an appropriate question to writing the final report. Although some of the text is directed to the needs of novice investigators, other parts attend to generic topics that will be of interest to research consumers. The latter sections will be particularly valuable to any reader who wishes to improve his or her ability to read different types of research.

Chapter 1, dealing with research paradigms, is a good place to begin if you would like to learn more about the differing assumptions that guide qualitative and quantitative research (as distinctive traditions for inquiry). Chapters 9, 10, and 11 provide brief overviews of both quantitative and qualitative designs, as well as mixed method strategies that combine elements of both. As a means of reinforcing the general discussion of broad strategies for inquiry, each chapter contains short examples and specific recommendations for planning and executing a sound study. Throughout the book, technical material is divided into sections of manageable size, making the text particularly suitable to the needs of a novice reader.

Dodge, L. G. (2003). *Dr. Laurie's introduction to statistical methods.* Los Angeles: Pyrczak.

This book was written "for students who need only a basic introduction so they will be prepared to use, comprehend, and feel comfortable with fundamental statistics" (p. ix). It is designed for an introductory statistics course but is very different from the typical text that serves students in that area. First, the page format replicates the open and informal style typical of workbooks rather than the forbiddingly dense structure of scientific texts. The print is large, and boldface is used throughout to highlight important terminology and to establish topical divisions. Second, the author is openly enthusiastic about the topic and clearly loves statistics— she even claims she and her college-aged children often discuss statistics at family gatherings. Third, each chapter includes directions for a group activity intended to help students reinforce material by discussing it with others.

The book begins with general principles and progresses to simple univariate inferential statistics and meta-analysis. Like us, Dr. Laurie emphasizes the importance of questions in guiding research, and she ties statistics to the particular kinds of research questions they can help to answer. The text has a conversational tone, and the examples and problems are engaging—sometimes because they unexpectedly veer from the beaten path. The equations used in the book are presented logically and are followed by a discussion that should not intimidate even the most tentative of readers. Each chapter ends with a review of newly introduced statistical terms—and a homework assignment. In coverage, this book goes further than the Pyrczak and Holcomb books annotated in this appendix. Accordingly, it is most appropriate for those who would like to learn more about statistics without having to venture into the sometimes less user-friendly territory of traditional textbooks.

Gall, M. D., Gall, J. P., & Borg, W. R. (2003). *Educational research: An introduction* (7th ed.). Boston: Allyn & Bacon.

This book, now in its seventh edition, provides in nearly 700 pages a survey of virtually all of the research designs and techniques used in education and the social sciences. Although the text is primarily addressed to an audience interested in topics related to education, its highly generic nature (in both coverage and explanations) makes it a fine resource for learning about research in any area of social and behavioral science.

This volume is primarily intended for those planning to do research, and, in consequence, it does address some topics that will be of less interest if you wish only to read reports. However, if your goal is to find more information about something encountered in a particular report, you are likely to find a helpful discussion here. Chapters on statistical techniques, sampling, and the most commonly used methods of data collection (field surveys, interviews, mail questionnaires, standardized tests, systematic observation, and so on) provide basic explanation of applications in a wide range of inquiry contexts. The chapters dealing with research design give attention to both qualitative and quantitative paradigms in sufficient detail to give the novice reader a sound foundation. The authors' also discuss evaluation research (strategies for determining the efficacy of treatments, policies, or programs); because that topic is not found in many introductory textbooks, this book might be of particular interest to some readers of this guide. Finally, each chapter ends with a list of recommendations that summarize what the reader should have learned about the proper conduct of an investigation.

Holcomb, Z. C. (2002). *Interpreting basic statistics: A guide and workbook based on excerpts from journal articles* (3rd ed.). Los Angeles: Pyrczak.

This is not a traditional college text. Using a workbook format, the guide contains an overview of 42 statistical techniques (from simple percentiles to complex inferential statistics). Each includes a short explanation of a technique followed by an excerpt from the results section of a research report in which the statistic was actually employed. In turn, the excerpt is accompanied by questions designed to test the reader's understanding of what was done and why.

Many readers will find Holcomb's approach helpful not only because of the illustrations of how statistics are used but because the structure of the workbook makes it possible to read about only the particular technique for which there is a question. Because the text does not provide answers to the exercise test items, you might need occasional assistance. In general, however, our students have found this book sufficiently clear and thorough to allow independent use.

Huck, S. W. (2004). *Reading statistics and research* (4th ed.). Boston: Pearson Education.

This not only is a big book (546 pages), it is both unusual in content and exceptionally detailed in coverage. The first characteristic, substantial size for a textbook, is mitigated by two factors: (a) it is available in a modestly priced paperbound edition, and (b) it can be used as a reference resource for help with particular questions and need not be consumed in a single gulp.

The unusual content is revealed by the following excerpt from the dedication. "This book is dedicated to ... those consumers of research reports who work at developing the skills needed to critically evaluate (and sometimes reject) the claims made by researchers. ..." (p. v). The result of that commitment is a layperson's book about statistics that avoids formulae and computations to focus instead on the concepts involved.

The third and final characteristic, however, is the book's ultimate hallmark—comprehensive and thorough coverage. Eighteen chapters provide a detailed, step-by-step exposition of what a consumer needs to know to recognize and then distinguish between correct and incorrect (misleading) uses of the statistical tools commonly encountered in research reports. Because there is less than perfect agreement among statisticians concerning the precise definition of what is acceptable and unacceptable in some of these matters, the author had to stick close to the fundamentals where such debates are unlikely. Put simply, if you find a statistic in a published study, there will be a section in this book to help you decipher its meaning (purpose) and recognize any substantial departure from generally accepted use.

More than 500 excerpts from recently published reports, selected to demonstrate correct and incorrect use of each statistic, richly illustrate the twin operations of smart consuming—deciphering and evaluating. If you refuse to allow yourself to be cowed by numbers, this book will give you both courage and practical support.

Locke, L. F., Spirduso, W. W., & Silverman, S. J. (2000). *Proposals that work: A guide for planning dissertations and grant proposals* (4th ed.). Thousand Oaks, CA: Sage.

Our first impulse here was to tell you that if you enjoyed the present text, you should rush out to purchase a copy of the guide listed here. On more sober reflection, however, we note only that it has been included because it provides a thorough explanation of how research is planned.

What you find in a report is a direct reflection of the author's initial map for investigation. Knowing something of how that map is drawn can provide a reader with a strong sense of what to look for at the other end of a study—in the report. *Research proposals* (formal written plans) must deal with issues that lurk in the gray area between adequate and less-than-adequate inquiry. As such, our descriptions of the various trade-offs that researchers must make between the ideal and the possible constitute an important lesson in the realities of struggling to do good scholarship.

Chapter 2, on the ethics of research, provides information you are unlikely to find in many introductory textbooks. As you become an informed consumer of research, questions related to the propriety of research procedures will present themselves with increasing clarity and urgency. This book is a good place to begin thinking about how you believe those important questions should be answered.

Written in a style similar to the book you are now reading, *Proposals That Work* covers the full gamut of inquiry problems, from developing a research question to presenting (either in oral or written form) the final report. Chapters are devoted to proposals for studies informed by both the qualitative and quantitative paradigms. For those who find examples particularly helpful, the guide contains four research proposals (experimental, quasi-experimental, qualitative, and a grant proposal) with our comments interspersed throughout as a means of helping the reader focus on the most important aspects of the plan for investigation.

Maxwell, J. A. (1996). *Qualitative research design: An interactive approach.* Thousand Oaks, CA: Sage.

This guidebook is intended to provide both an introduction to qualitative research and a brief discussion of the major steps in designing such a study. It is, in short, the perfect reference for the beginning reader of qualitative reports. Because it is a paperback of modest size (and cost), the author gets right to the main point at each step of thinking through a study. In doing so, he offers the novice a brisk but authoritative tour of the language, theoretical constructs, and procedural considerations that make investigations based on the qualitative paradigm (what we refer to as *interpretive research* in this text) a distinctive form of inquiry. A full chapter is devoted to the question of "Validity: How might you be wrong?" This book is an absolute necessity for the beginning reader who wishes to bring a cautious eye to the reading of qualitative reports.

This text is not a compendium of methods for data collection and analysis. Nor is it a thorough explication of the philosophical and theoretical underpinnings of the paradigm. It is a brisk overview of what qualitative researchers really do. Accordingly, examples are placed throughout the text as illustrations of each major point. This is in keeping with the author's intention of providing a generic introduction that is clear, explicit, and unapologetically reflective of his own opinion as to what beginners ought to know.

Merriam, S. B. (1998). *Qualitative research and case study applications in education* (2nd ed.). San Francisco: Jossey-Bass.

The subtitle for this text reveals its lineage: "Revised and expanded from *Case Study Research in Education*." The appearance of a second edition reflects both the considerable success of the earlier book and the ways in which use in the marketplace sometimes shapes form in the publishing industry. In the first edition, the author's announced intention was to introduce qualitative case study designs to students preparing to do research in educational settings. In actual use, however, the text came to serve a quite different purpose.

The concise writing style, powerful how-to-do-it format, and treatment of generic problems within the qualitative approach made the book ideal for use as a basic text in introductory research courses. The initial focus on case study was welcome but regarded as a secondary benefit. Thus, the emphasis in this revision has shifted to providing background appropriate to all forms of qualitative research—of which case studies are but one format among many.

Fortunately, all of the qualities that made the first edition so popular with students and professors are retained here. In our judgment, this is one of the best places to begin reading if you want an answer to the question "What is qualitative research?" Clarity and simplicity are the hallmarks of Merriam's writing style. Accordingly, it also is easy to recommend the book as a fine introduction to methods of data collection in the field or in interview settings.

Pyrczak, F. (1999). *Statistics with a sense of humor: A humorous workbook and guide to study skills* (2nd ed.). Los Angeles: Pyrczak.

As the title suggests, this workbook uses humor to present statistical concepts. It assumes very little about the academic preparation of the reader, providing a basic math review for those who might feel tentative about their grasp on eighth-grade arithmetic. The author presents 60 work sheets for practice in using statistical concepts. Each sheet starts with a riddle that can be answered only by completing the rest of the form (answers to odd-numbered questions are provided in the back of the book). Interspersed between work tasks are helpful hints for understanding and remembering important concepts and procedures in statistics.

Whereas some readers can work through this text and acquire a good overview of many of the statistical techniques encountered when reading reports, others will find it more useful as a review and reinforcement for concepts previously learned from other sources. Finally, our students would wish us to remind you that although humor certainly can enliven the presentation of any topic, not everyone finds the same things to be uproariously funny!

Robson, C. (2002). *Real world research: A resource for social scientists and practi-tioner-researchers* (2nd ed.). Malden, MA: Blackwell.

Although its publisher is headquartered in the United Kingdom, this book is readily available in North America (and in the United States, specifically, through Blackwell's office in Malden, MA). Despite its substantial size (600 pages), the book has been pro-duced in a relatively inexpensive paperbound format. At $44.95, this is a resource you can afford to own. Certainly, the cost of pur-chase will bring you what might be the most unusual approach to research among all of those annotated in this appendix.

The book's topic is how to do social science research out in the real world, using whatever tools for disciplined inquiry best fit the nature of your question. The target audience is not researchers or academics in higher education, but people who have questions that need answers and problems that need resolution—in hospi-tals, businesses, schools, and social agencies. Accordingly, the pri-mary characteristics of the research model laid out in this book are: (a) small scale, (b) in the field, (c) oriented to problem solving rather than knowledge acquisition, (d) sensitive to large effects rather than small statistical differences, and (e) having strict time and cost constraints. As you might guess, this highly pragmatic approach to research brings the reader down to basics with little waste of time, making it a valuable resource for those who are just starting out, whether they be consumers or potential investigators.

At every turn, the author takes the route of common sense. For example, instead of dividing the world of social research into quantitative and qualitative dominions, he uses a far more functional framework. Research strategies are characterized as relatively fixed and rule-bound (e.g., surveys and experiments), relatively flexible and open-ended (e.g., case studies and ethnographies), a combination of both fixed and flexible methods (e.g., mixed methods), or special purpose (e.g., evaluations, action research studies). Readers will be surprised by what this simple adjustment accomplishes by way of clarity.

Finally, the author won our hearts by his pervasive insistence that at the heart of things must be a good question, one that is answerable within the constraints imposed by the availability of time and resources. That is research reduced to the gritty bottom line. The book covers everything from a listing of questions to avoid when conducting interviews to instructions for selecting and using computer programs that save time when analyzing data. That a plain-language glossary of research terminology is included is consistent with the approach taken throughout—be realistic about how research actually gets done, and be practical about what nonspecialists truly need to know if they are to do it (or, we add, if they are to read about it with an appreciative and critical eye).

Shadish, W. R., Cook, T. D., & Campbell, D. T. (2002). *Experimental and quasi-experimental designs for general causal inference.* Boston: Houghton Mifflin.

A follow-up to Campbell and Stanley's 1963 work (noted previously in this appendix) and Cook and Campbell's (1979) *Quasi-experimentation: Design and analysis issues from field settings* (Chicago: Rand McNally), this book is a comprehensive discussion of validity in research design for everything from true experiments to all forms of quasi-experiments, including studies conducted in field settings such as schools, community centers, hospitals, and other field sites where it is difficult to control some of the variables. By discussing real-world settings where a great deal of social and behavioral research occurs, the authors address many topics that range beyond the comfortable confines of laboratory experiments. The authors provide in-depth discussion of a number of designs commonly used in field research, focusing on issues of validity for each.

Thomas, J. (1993). *Doing critical ethnography.* Newbury Park, CA: Sage.

In this easy-to-read paperback, Thomas offers an overview of critical research with a particular emphasis on the use of ethnographic techniques for data collection (field observation, interviews, and examination of documents). The book begins with a comparison of conventional and critical ethnography. The author then proceeds to introduce the main tenets of critical thought and method, with attention to the problems of reliability and validity within that context.

For beginners, Chapter 4, titled "Empirical Application," is particularly helpful. There, the author provides overviews of three critical studies that serve to illustrate the scope of concerns to which critical researchers attend. The final chapter deals with problems in writing reports of critical research. Although obviously intended for researchers, this discussion will be of interest to those reading critical study reports because the line between polemical discourse and data-grounded description (and analysis) can be less than clear. In a field where much of the background reading is difficult, if not impenetrable, for beginners, this book offers an introduction that is clear, thorough, and straightforward.

Appendix B

Examples of Completed 12-Step Forms and Flowcharts

The three 12-step examples provided here were prepared by the authors in the course of reading two actual (published) studies and a research review. You might find it difficult to completely understand all aspects of the studies on the basis of reading the forms—nor should you expect to do so. The 12-step forms are not intended, of course, to capture in abstracted form all of the detail contained in a report. As we explained in Chapters 4 and 5, they are tools designed to help the beginner stay organized. Not only should the forms omit a great deal of technical detail, they are highly *personal* documents. You have in this appendix what we found necessary or helpful to record on the forms. Your 12-step record might contain very different notes.

In that regard, you will find it to be an interesting (and possibly useful) exercise to retrieve and read the three items, and then to compare your own completed 12-step forms with ours. Finally, the flowcharts (Figures B.1 and B.3) and expanded flowcharts (Figures B.2 and B.4) appended to the 12-step quantitative and qualitative forms in this appendix can be used if you are baffled by our entry for any particular step on one of the forms.

12 Steps to Understanding a Quantitative Research Report

Directions: Record notes in only enough detail to support recall in the absence of the original document. Except for Step 1, use abbreviations, diagrams, shorthand, and a careful selection of no more than what is absolutely essential to the study. Work on this sheet alone (except for Step 6), and do not be tempted to run onto additional pages.

1. **CITATION.** What study report is this? Record a complete reference citation.
   Smith, J. K., Gerber, A. S., & Orlish, A. (2003). Self-prophecy effects and voter turnout: An experimental replication. *Political Psychology, 24,* 593–604.

2. **PURPOSE AND GENERAL RATIONALE.** In broad terms, what was the purpose of the study, and how did the author(s) make a case for its general importance?
   The purpose was to examine whether prediction (of whether he or she will vote) influenced voting behavior, and to test self-prophecy effects (if predicting you will do something makes you more likely to do it) in voting. Understanding voting turnout does not require creation of an artificial context because voting behavior can be determined through public records. The study is important because of the possible political implications if the self-prophecy effect impacts turnout.

3. **FIT AND SPECIFIC RATIONALE.** How does the topic of the study fit into the existing research literature, and how is that provenance used to make a specific case for the investigation?
   Discusses previous studies by Greenwald et al. that support self-prophecy effects in voting. Also notes research confirmation of same effect on other behaviors. Notes that Greenwald et al. (1987) should be replicated with a larger sample of registered voters who are more representative of the population of U.S. voters.

4. **PARTICIPANTS.** Describe who was studied (give number and characteristics) and how they were selected.
   Participants ($N = 1,160$) were randomly sampled from the voter list and randomly assigned to interview conditions (control, 288; asked to give prediction only, 300; asked to give reason why he or she might vote, 301; asked to give both prediction and reason, 271). They were from homes with 1 or 2 voters, and participant had to be registered in the Democratic or Republican party (and be eligible to vote).

5. **CONTEXT.** Where did the study take place? (Describe important characteristics.)
   The study took place in a southern New England town with approximately 50,000 residents in the days preceding the 2000 Super Tuesday primary.

6. **STEPS IN SEQUENCE.** In the order performed, what were the main procedural steps in the study? Describe or diagram in a flowchart, showing order and any important relationships among the steps.

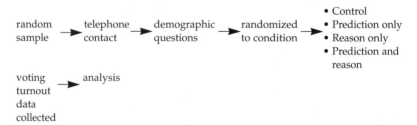

7. **DATA.** What constituted data (e.g., test scores, questionnaire responses, frequency counts), how was it collected, and what was the role of the investigator(s) in that process?

Data on prediction were collected during a telephone interview. Whether participants then voted in the election (and in the previous five elections) was ascertained from municipal voting records. Graduate students completed interviews from script.

8. **ANALYSIS.** What form of data analysis was used, and what specific questions was it designed to answer? What (if any) statistical operations and computer programs were employed?

Used chi-square analysis and *t* tests to determine whether voting rates for members of the three interview conditions differed when they actually voted (or failed to vote) in the current election, and chi-square was used to determine whether there were differences (by treatment group) in how often they had voted in previous elections.

9. **RESULTS.** What did the author(s) identify as the primary results (products or findings produced by the analysis of data)?

There were no statistically significant differences among the three interview conditions in voter turnout (43.4% for control, 43.3% for prediction, 39.2% for reason only, and 43.5% for both prediction and reason). This was true even when examined in terms of previous voting behavior. In other words, how many times they had voted in the previous five elections did not mediate the overall results.

10. **CONCLUSIONS.** What did the author(s) assert about how the results in Step 9 responded to the purpose(s) established in Step 2, and how did the events and experiences of the entire study contribute to that conclusion?

This replication yielded no evidence that the self-prophecy effect impacted voter turnout. The authors believe these results cast doubt on the political implications suggested by previous studies.

11. **CAUTIONS.** What cautions does the author(s) raise about the study itself, or about interpreting the results? Add here any of your own reservations.

The authors suggest that differences between these results and those found in previous studies might be the result of differences in samples and type of election. The authors suggested that if those participants who predicted they would or would not vote in the primary had been pooled together in the analysis, it might have provided a better indication of whether results were influenced by prediction.

12. **DISCUSSION.** What interesting facts or ideas did you learn from reading the report? Include here anything that was of value, including: results, research designs and methods, references, instruments, history, useful arguments, or personal inspiration.

It was interesting that the self-prophecy effect was not mediated by turnout in previous elections. The authors were able to determine voting for the previous five elections for 1,152 of 1,160 participants, and I found it surprising that such a high percentage of people remained continuously in the same community. The impact of telephone solicitation to get people to vote (or to get them to vote for a particular candidate) is important both for theory testing (in a real setting) and for the potential to influence voter turnout.

Figure B.1 Flowchart (Smith et al.—"Self-prophecy effects and voter turnout: An experimental replication")

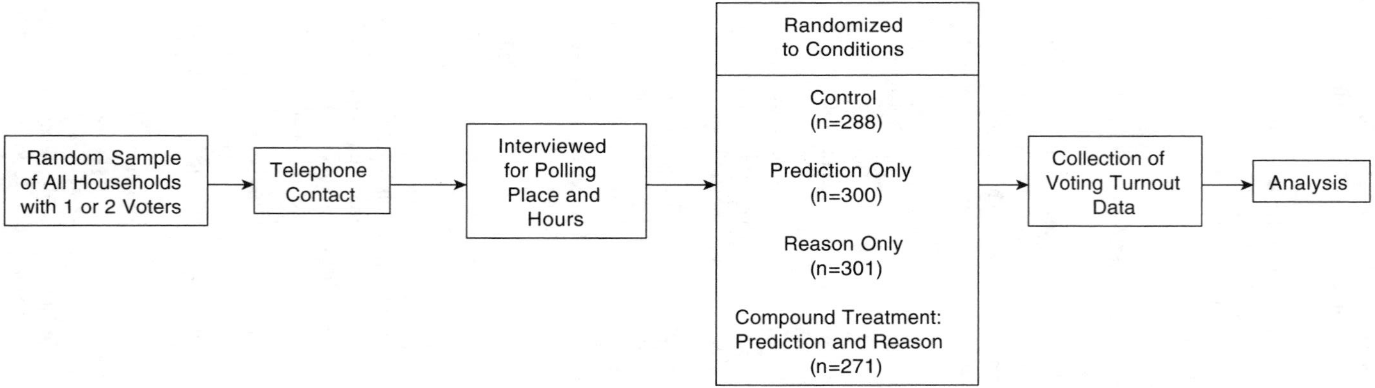

Figure B.2 Expanded Flowchart (Smith et al.—"Self-prophecy effects and voter turnout: An experimental replication")

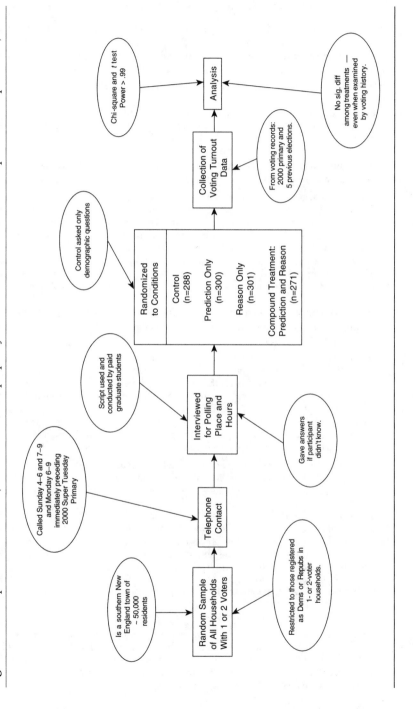

12 Steps to Understanding a Qualitative Research Report

Directions: Record notes in only enough detail to support recall in the absence of the original document. Except for Step 1, use abbreviations, diagrams, shorthand, and a careful selection of no more than what is absolutely essential to the study. Work on this sheet alone (except for Step 6), and do not be tempted to run onto additional pages.

1. **CITATION.** What study report is this? Record a complete reference citation.
   Hendrix, K. G. (1998). Student perception of the influence of race on professor credibility. *Journal of Black Studies, 28,* 738–763.

2. **PURPOSE AND GENERAL RATIONALE.** In broad terms, what was the purpose of the study, and how did the author(s) make a case for its general importance?

   The purpose was to determine what professors and students believe are the cues that lead to professorial credibility in the classroom, when the race of professor and students is the same, and when it is different. This was deemed important because (a) credibility is a vital factor in the ability of an instructor to promote student learning, (b) the research literature suggests that a classroom of white students might present a black professor with special and difficult challenges not faced by their white counterparts, and (c) despite this, black professors are held to the same standards of academic and pedagogical performance as their white colleagues.

3. **FIT AND SPECIFIC RATIONALE.** How does the topic of the study fit into the existing research literature, and how is that provenance used to make a specific case for doing the investigation?

   Despite the argument advanced in Step # 2, the author could locate no research on this particular topic [aside from the general background provided for items (a) and (b)]—thus, the particular provenance for the present study rests in the fact that there is a gap in the knowledge structure with regard to the proposed topic of investigation.

4. **PARTICIPANTS.** Who was the author(s) (important characteristics only), and how was he or she related to the purpose, participants, and study site? Describe who was studied (give number and characteristics) and how they were selected.

   The investigator indicated that she was a black female professor conducting the study in a predominantly white institution (her own). She discusses in detail how she managed her role relative to the student interviewees and the role she believes her race played in obtaining volunteers and collecting data. We are told nothing of her own background or experiences within the institution. She characterizes her professorial experience as "an outsider within." The participants were selected purposefully so as to obtain three male dyads ($N = 6$ professors), each consisting of professors of comparable teaching experience, subject matter, age, and gender, but different race (one white and one black). Also participating were 28 students purposefully selected (to represent gender, race, and year in school) from six undergraduate classes taught by the participating professors.

5. **CONTEXT.** Where did the study take place? (Describe important characteristics.)

   All data were collected at a large, 4-year research university in the Northwest. The institution had predominantly white student enrollment (76%). Out of 34,000 students, only 1,088 were black, and out of 3,986 professors, only 60 were black. All observations were made in the classrooms normally used for each course, and all interviews were held in the investigator's office.

6. **STEPS IN SEQUENCE.** In the order performed, what were the main procedural steps in the study? Describe or diagram in a flowchart, showing order, time required, and any important relationships among the steps.

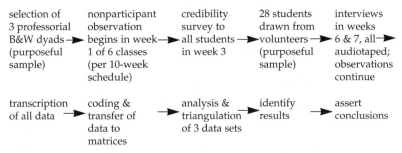

selection of 3 professorial B&W dyads (purposeful sample) → nonparticipant observation begins in week 1 of 6 classes (per 10-week schedule) → credibility survey to all students in week 3 → 28 students drawn from volunteers (purposeful sample) → interviews in weeks 6 & 7, all audiotaped; observations continue

transcription of all data → coding & transfer of data to matrices → analysis & triangulation of 3 data sets → identify results → assert conclusions

7. **DATA.** What constituted data (e.g., field notes, interview transcripts, photographs, diaries), how was it collected, and what was the role of the investigator(s) in that process?

    Data consisted of student responses to credibility survey forms in 6 classes, field notes from a 10-week schedule of nonparticipant observations, transcripts from audiotaped interviews with 28 volunteer students, and investigator notes taken during interviews. The investigator personally explained the study and distributed the survey in all classes, conducted all interviews, and, in first week, observed classes in a role identified as a visiting researcher collecting information about patterns of communication. For subsequent weeks, the role was described in an identical fashion except that the researcher's identity was expanded to encompass also being an investigator associated with the credibility survey.

8. **ANALYSIS.** What form of data analysis was used, and what was it designed to reveal? What computer program was used (if any)?

    Coded data segments (words, phrases, sentences) were hand coded and physically placed onto large matrix sheets that allowed cross-comparisons by class, professor, subject matter, and race. From this, regularities were identified and then illustrated by quotations (or paraphrases) drawn from the data.

9. **RESULTS.** What did the author(s) identify as the primary results (products or findings produced by the analysis of data)? In general, "What was going on there?"

    *   Students and professors reported that perceived credibility was a function of (a) apparent knowledge of subject matter, (b) ability to explain subject matter clearly (good pedagogy), and (c) work experience in a related applied field.
    *   For students, (a) without (b) was insufficient to yield credibility.
    *   Black professors were awarded high credibility when teaching subject matter related to race.
    *   At an explicit level, students asserted that perceived credibility was strictly a matter of competence in subject matter and teaching. Simultaneously, at a tacit level, they indicated that "others" would hold black professors to more stringent judgments about competence—and cited overheard conversations among "other" students as evidence.
    *   Negative stereotypes by students were displayed in data regarding intelligence and academic preparation of black professors, but this coexisted with opinion that

their black professors must be good because they would have had to work so much harder than white professors to obtain their university positions. After (and if) credibility was established, black professors were favorably regarded by all students (white and black).

10. **CONCLUSIONS.** What did the author(s) assert about how the results in Step 9 responded to the purpose(s) established in Step 2, and how did the events and experiences of the entire study contribute to that conclusion?

The results at Step 9 became the conclusions and, when rephrased, led to the more general assertion that social institutions can (as the literature had suggested) reflect the social ills of the culture within which they are created. More to the point of purposes indicated in Step 2, the author wrote (paraphrase from p. 762) [Students in my study were more likely to question the competence of black professors, except in courses with race as subject matter]. Thus, the experience of black professors in teaching is different in a fundamental way from the experience of white professors.

11. **CAUTIONS.** What cautions does the author(s) raise about the study itself, or about interpreting the results? Add here any of your own reservations, particularly those related to methods used to enhance credibility (trustworthiness and believability).

Data were collected on a one-shot basis (the survey and interviews), so there was no way to assess change in perceptions over time. Racial demographics were unusual in the context—in a city in which 10% of the population was black, the black student population at the university was only 3%—other distributions might have produced different results. The use of volunteers for interviews left open the question of a selection bias in those data—what would the silent nonvolunteers have said, and would there have been any important regularities in their dispositions regarding race and credibility? Triangulation among interview, observation, and survey data was used throughout and contributed to credibility of the study, but the procedures for developing analytic matrices was so complex that it would be impossible for most readers to follow or critique.

12. **DISCUSSION.** What interesting facts or ideas did you learn from reading the report? Include here anything that was of value, including: results, research designs and methods, references, instruments, history, useful arguments, or personal inspiration.

The notion of awarding high credibility to black professors in courses related to race and ethnicity had never occurred to me. Likewise, the whole idea of an uneven playing field for tenure and promotion—created by the fact that students (probably both black and white) offer challenges to the teaching tasks of black professors that are not confronted by white professors—was new and somewhat unsettling. I also was unaware of the paucity of empirical research on this topic. Finally, although I award full marks to the investigator for recognizing the problems associated with using a volunteer sample for her interviews, this study provides an almost classic case of the limitations imposed by such a research procedure. What would the students in that silent majority have said that might be different from her volunteers? I truly was disappointed by the general absence of attention (in the report) to what the six professors had to say about how they thought students might develop their perceptions of professorial credibility.

Figure B.3   Flowchart (Hendrix—"Student perception of the influence of race on professor credibility")

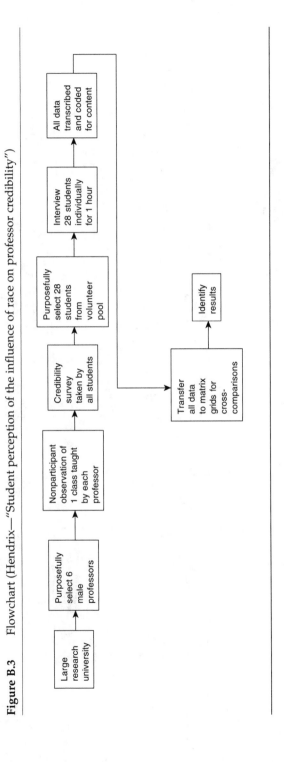

Figure B.4 Expanded Flowchart (Hendrix—"Student perception of the influence of race on professor credibility")

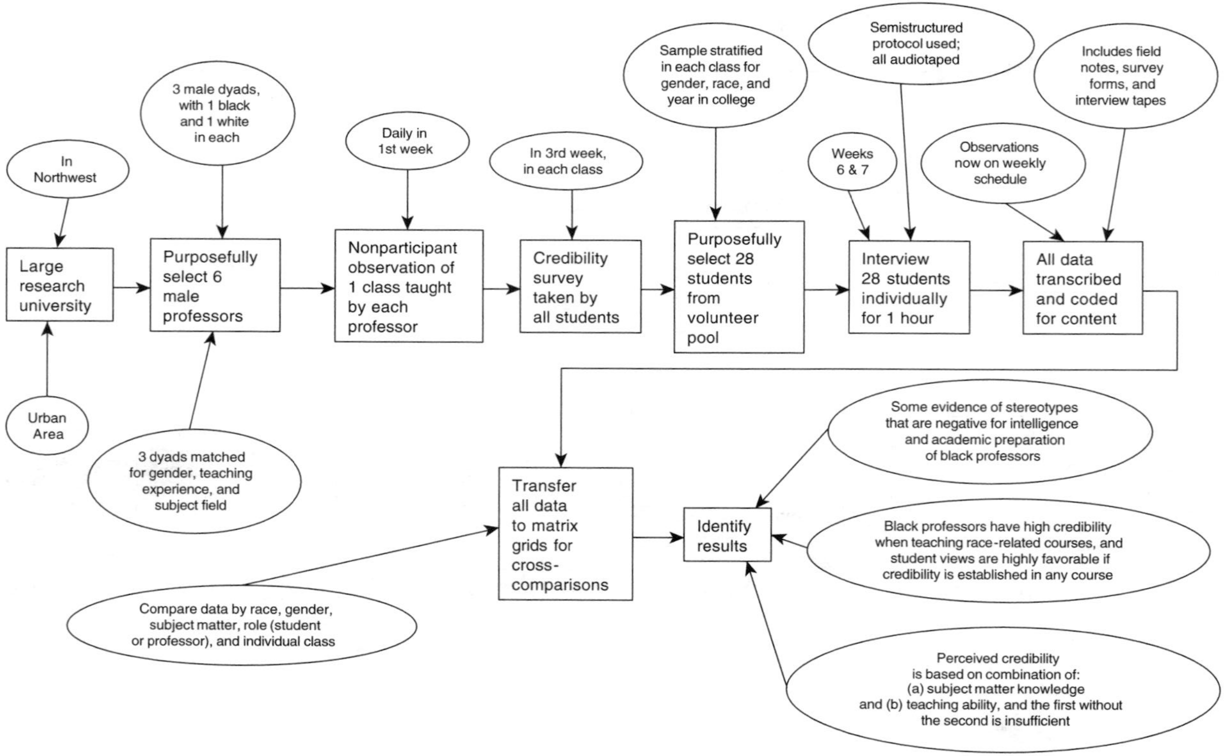

A 12-Step Map for Reading Research Reviews

Directions: Read through the 12 questions in the map below. Then, skim through the review, noting those portions that appear to be related to the questions. Finally, on your second and more thorough reading, record brief answers for each. Some of the items might not apply to the particular review at hand, and some important observations you can make about the review might not be covered by any one of the questions. Accordingly, *you must use this form as a guide to reading reviews, not as a comprehensive and invariant list of significant content.*

1. **CITATION.** What study report is this? Record a complete reference citation.

   Borsari, B., & Carey, K. B. (2001). Peer influences on college drinking: A review of the research. *Journal of Substance Abuse, 13,* 391–424.

2. **PURPOSE.** What was the purpose of the review, and how did the author(s) justify the importance of examining the topic?

   The authors note the great increase in alcohol use when students enter college and the need to understand what influences alcohol consumption. The purpose was to review why college drinking is so strongly influenced by peers and the multiple pathways of peer influence.

3. **SELECTION.** How were studies selected for the review (e.g., exhaustive, specified time period, type of design, population involved, methodology used, or some combination of factors)?

   The review was exhaustive, including all studies published after 1970 on American and Canadian college students.

4. **QUALITY.** How was the matter of quality handled in selecting studies for review? Was there a screening process, and, if so, what were the criteria?

   Studies were screened. They excluded presentations and unpublished manuscripts (for lack of peer review) and those with major flaws (e.g., design, definition of dependent variables, or inappropriate statistical analysis). The authors did not give examples beyond the general criteria for inclusion and exclusion.

5. **ORGANIZATION.** How did the author(s) sort or categorize studies for the review (e.g., a theoretical framework, date of publication, nature of results, sample size, type of design, or some combination of factors)?

   The paper is organized on the Kandel's (1985) framework using social learning theory. It is organized based on different influences on peers, with major sections on direct influence, indirect influence—modeling, and indirect influence—perceived norms. The paper concludes with a section on implications for future research and a short, general conclusion.

6. **DATA.** If actual data are cited, what kind(s) are provided? Give brief examples.

No data are actually reported. There are extensive tables listing each paper and its subjects, design, results, limitations, and whether the research was quantitative or qualitative.

7. **ANALYSIS.** Is there an attempt to identify (if so, give a brief example for each):

   a. problems related to the kind of question being asked in the reviewed studies?

   This was not addressed.

   b. technical difficulties (e.g., with designs, participant selection, or data analysis) in the reviewed studies?

   There is extensive discussion of technical difficulties with studies, including problems with: (a) self-report bias in retrospective studies, (b) external validity in studies using written scenarios and modeling, (c) definitions of norms, (d) order effects, (e) underrepresentation of minorities, and (f) the use of wine when beer is the preferred drink in this age group.

   c. need for additional research to resolve confusion or to confirm tentative results?

   Identifies many unresolved results, including the need: (a) to look at gender in norm interventions with socialization, (b) to look at differential parts of norm education programs, (c) for further study of direct peer influence, and (d) for replications of modeling studies from the1970s and 1980s.

8. **INTEGRATION.** How does the author(s) get from individual studies to the level of general assertions or conclusions about the status of research in the topical area (e.g., vote counting, meta-analysis, qualitative criteria)?

The authors use qualitative criteria throughout, but, at times, they note that different numbers of studies produced different or conflicting results.

9. **SUMMARY.** Where in the text, and in what detail, is the task of summarizing handled (after each organizational section, in a section at the end of the entire document, in the abstract only), and is the summary format brief or extended?

There are summaries throughout the manuscript.

10. **CONCLUSIONS.** What does the author(s) assert as the main conclusion(s) from the review?

- There are different types of peer influences—including many indirect peer influences.
- Offers to drink and peer influences are associated with alcohol use and problems.
- Perceived norms are associated only with alcohol use, not with other variables.
- Expectancies mediate the relationship between modeling and alcohol use and problems.
- There are different results for men and women, although women are not represented in many studies.
- Norm programs can help, but the mechanism is not known.

11. **APPLICATION.** If the conclusions at Step 10 are credible, what utility might they have (e.g., applications that are theoretical, practical, or personal)?

With the exception of future research, the researchers do not directly address applications. The results on expectations and norm training have the potential to help in developing interventions to help students use alcohol responsibly.

12. **EVALUATION.** What would you say if you were asked to review this review with regard to importance, clarity of writing, suitability of organization, and degree of credibility?

This review is very straightforward, easy to follow, and the writing is clear. The topic is important, and the authors communicate it in a way that does not sensationalize the issues. They note research problems and particularly are aware of how research design and the time period when the research was conducted might influence the results. Their presentation is credible in that they discuss limitations of the research throughout the paper.

Appendix C

Statistics: A Beginner's Guide

S tatistics are a collection of mathematical operations that can be used to find the answers to questions asked about numbers—particularly groups of numbers. Any one of those operations is called a *statistic*, and the field of inventing, refining, and investigating all such operations is itself called *statistics*. Not surprisingly, people who pursue academic and technical careers in that area are called *statisticians*. Functionally a branch of mathematics, statistics sometimes is referred to as a science in its own right. It finds most of its applications in research (notably, the natural and social sciences), as well as applied fields such as insurance, finance, public health, polling, and census taking.

In fact, any type of inquiry that records individual observations in the form of numbers is likely to produce large collections of them. In turn, the task of reporting a study creates the need to reduce and describe those accumulations in an economical shorthand. Writing the report also demands answers to questions about what the numbers mean. Those are the two functions that statistics perform in quantitative studies: (a) they allow description of dozens (or even thousands) of numbers in a report without taking up pages of space, and (b) they make use of the laws of probability to allow us to make decisions in the face of uncertainty by answering such important questions as, "What are the chances that this medicine is really helping patients to recover more rapidly?"

Thus, when the phrase "analysis of the data" appears in the report of a quantitative study, it always signals the use of statistics to describe or examine groups of numbers. The numbers were acquired through use of the investigation's methodology, and, collectively, they constitute what the report refers to as "the data." Statistical analyses, of course, are to be distinguished from operations performed on data that consist of words (and, more broadly, of text) in qualitative research. There, you might encounter "content analysis," "phenomenological analysis," or other nonstatistical ways of describing and inspecting the data.

In Chapter 6, as part of our discussion of quantitative research designs, we provided some general descriptions of statistical procedures that commonly appear in research reports (if you have not read that chapter, we urge you to do so now). The purpose of this appendix is to introduce you to some of those statistics in greater detail, explaining how they function, the service they provide in analyzing data, and how they are used to present the outcomes from such analysis in the "Results" section of the report.

Concerns about having to encounter statistics account for most of the apprehension people experience when they think about reading research reports. We do not want to dismiss that problem; the concerns are genuine, and the anxiety involved can become a serious impediment. The fact is, however, that at the basic level of statistical analysis (the level found in a great many reports), both the concepts and the operations themselves are astonishingly simple.

Indeed, we have speculated that it is the obvious use of simple mathematics that really bothers people. They just do not want to admit (or allow anyone to discover) that they actually did not completely understand such things as fractions, decimals, and long division back in the fourth grade! If you are one of those people, please be reassured. You are anything but alone. The majority of us have one or several such gaps in our education, and none of them need be fatal impediments to understanding basic statistics. The watchwords for getting started are, "Don't panic—you can do this!"

Statistics appear in research reports in two places. They can be inserted directly into the text, or they can be set aside in tables. An example of the former might be, "Subjects in the pool of volunteers $(N = 36)$ were weighed $(M = 165.4 \text{ lb})$ before random assignment to the four treatment groups." The letters, in this case, are shorthand for total number (N) of subjects and mean (M) of the measurement data. Translated, the sentence tells us that individuals in an initial group with 36 subjects in it weighed an average (*mean* is the term used in statistics for what is more commonly known as the arithmetic average) of 165.4 pounds before they were divided into four subgroups. The number of subjects in a subgroup is always noted with a lowercase letter, as in, "Members of the training group (n = 9) were weighed (M = 169.2 lb) before starting the program."

If there had been 10 such groups, however, reporting all the group numbers and means would have been cumbersome in text form, so the statistics would have been relegated to a small table. Then, the text would indicate simply, "Subjects in each of the four treatment groups were weighed before starting the program (see Table 1)." In the table, readers probably would find the 10 groups listed as rows and the corresponding figures for group size and mean subject weights entered in columns.

❖ DESCRIPTIVE STATISTICS

Whether they are located in the text or in a table, the most common type of statistics are those broadly categorized as *descriptive*. If you wanted to describe the cost of houses in your town, you probably would do so by citing the average price and the range from cheapest to most expensive. That is exactly what descriptive statistics do. The *mean* is the average of a set of scores (e.g., M = $156,000$), and the *range* is expressed simply by the lowest and highest scores in the group (e.g., range = $89,000–$224,000$).

The mean is not the only way to express what is "typical." You also will encounter statistics called the *median,* which is the value at the midpoint when a group of numbers are listed in order from high to low, and the *mode,* which is simply the number that occurs most frequently. Likewise, the range is not the only way to communicate how a group of numbers spread out (statisticians speak of that spread as the *distribution* or *dispersion* of a set of numbers). In fact, the range is very primitive because it tells you nothing about how the numbers are distributed between highest and lowest.

A group of test scores might, for example, be spread out evenly, be clustered near the low end, or—as happens when many naturally occurring phenomena are sampled randomly—be mostly within a few points above or below the middle (close to the mean). In the distribution for that latter case, only a few scores would be located at the extremes, near the highest and lowest values. The range statistic can convey none of that information.

Researchers, therefore, prefer a much more informative way to describe dispersion—the statistic called *standard deviation* (*sd*, or sometimes *SD*). Instead of telling you the highest and lowest number in a group, when used with the mean, *sd* allows you to visualize how the distribution would appear on a graph—most of the numbers clustered tightly around the middle, or most of them spread out on either side.

For example, if the home prices in the previous illustration were said to have an *sd* of $15,000, you would know that 68% of all the homes were priced within $30,000 of the mean price (or, substantially more than half of them were in the range from $15,000 below to $15,000 above the average price). Don't let the 68% bother you, it is just the way the standard deviation statistic works. If you want to know why, any introductory statistics text (e.g., Dodge, 2003) will provide a simple explanation.

The point to remember from this example is that relatively small standard deviations indicate that the numbers (in this case, price expressed in dollar units) are tightly clustered around the mean, with fewer spread out toward the high or low end. A larger *sd* would indicate the opposite—a more scattered distribution of prices. In other words, if you wanted a wide selection of inexpensive (or expensive) homes, you would do better in a community for which the housing cost *sd* was $50,000 than you would by shopping for a home in a community with the rather tightly clustered costs in our example. Remember, however, that the sizes of standard deviation values can be compared only when the units of measurement are the same (dollars with dollars, days on the market with days on the market, square feet with square feet, and so on).

To use a different illustration, if you were reading a report in which drug addiction programs were studied, and you saw that for the unsuccessful clients in one program, the number of days from program completion to relapse was described as (*M* = 50, *sd* = 15), and for another program (*M* = 30, *sd* = 7), you would have learned a great deal about the characteristic pattern of participant relapses in the two programs. In one, the impact of the program lasts longer, and the number of days to failure is highly variable, whereas in the other program, relapses come more quickly and are heavily clustered within several weeks of the mean at 30 days.

❖ STATISTICAL PROBABILITY

Sets of numbers that have been described with statistics such as mean and standard deviation (or other measures of typicality and dispersion) can then be subject to a variety of other statistical operations that function to answer useful questions. In research, the most common of those operations is to use a statistic to determine the probability of whether any two (or more) sets of numeric data are the same or different. As you would anticipate, that question usually has to do with the desire to contrast things: "Which is larger?" "Who has the least?" "Is it different this year?"

At this point, it is reasonable to ask the obvious question: "Why not just look at the data (or even at the descriptive statistics for the data) and see whether they are the same or different?" If numbers either are or are not the same, why is it necessary to use statistics? The answer is so simple that it is sometimes difficult to grasp. We are not really interested in the numbers but in what they represent. In the natural (as opposed to theoretical) world, if you measure two groups of anything, it is very unlikely that the numbers you obtain will be exactly identical. The world is full of variety, even in things that we normally regard as similar—telephone poles, muffins, adult males, and hot summer nights.

If we took the mean height of telephone poles in two adjacent towns, we would not expect the two numbers to be exactly the same— but they would be close, probably within a fraction of an inch. But what if the means were different by a full foot? What are the chances that a difference that large was just due to the accidents of natural variation in pole length? Could it be that the difference was not accidental at all, but a reflection of something that has systematically influenced the variable of pole height—such as a 10- or 20-year difference in the date of installation and a change in telephone company procedures during that interval?

If your common sense tells you that as the difference between means gets larger, the more one should suspect that the cause lies not just in the accidents of particular numbers, but in the actual nature of what is being measured—you already are thinking like a statistician! You probably know that chance can (in theory) produce large accidents. A coin can actually be flipped for 20 heads in a row. But you also know that the probability of such an occurrence is very small, exactly like the probability of a 1-foot difference in our two groups of poles.

Any time you flip 20 heads in a row, your first instinct should be to inspect the coin. Something is going on, and it probably is not the random 50/50 chance provided by a common coin. More likely, you have discovered a two-headed coin!

Statisticians make use of the theory of probability to estimate the likelihood that any two (or more) means (thus, any two or more groups of numbers) are different by accident—that is, by pure chance. If a research report says that there is a "significant" difference ($p = .05$) between the test scores for two groups (Group A, $M = 25$; Group B, $M = 32$), it means that 5 times in 100, a difference that large (7 points) will occur by chance among such comparisons.

We put the word *significant* in quotation marks above because it is used in a particular way in research reports. It always refers to statistical probability, and it is never used to simply denote "important," as it does in everyday speech. The lowercase *p* stands for the word *probability*, and the .05 assumes its decimal function of indicating five one-hundredths.

The *p* and its decimal are derived from a standard statistical table when the investigator enters the value produced by a test of significance (which is what all such formulae are called). One test of significance, for example, is called the *t* test. It produces a *t* value with which one can enter a table and find the appropriate probability value (*p*).

Please remember that with tests of significance, statistics produce only an estimate of the probabilities. As with coin flipping, the rare event that runs against the odds can occur. That is precisely what $p = .05$ means. If you gathered a sufficiently large number of test scores, then, over a long series of group comparisons, 5 out of every 100 differences between means would be as large as the one in our example above, just because of chance—and not because one group really was superior to the other in some kind of performance. In other words, in those five cases, the difference between groups would not reflect something true about the nature of the groups. It was just an accident.

The presence of such rare events might bar us from using statistical analysis to achieve certainty, but, by that very token—explicit knowledge about how probable the exception is likely to be—something valuable is achieved. We can improve the odds of making good decisions far beyond anything provided by guesswork, popular wisdom, or flipping a coin. As long as you remember the singular limitation of all calculations based on probability, statistics can be used as a practical and very powerful tool. Tests of the significance of difference deal with only the probability of things, not with actual events.

We have seen a T-shirt printed with a legend that tells it all: "Statistics means never having to say you're certain!"

❖ DIFFERENCES BETWEEN MEANS

There are various mathematical formulae for calculating the level of probability for chance differences between or among sets of numbers (the resultant is not always called p), but the simplest of them (such as the t test) require only the n, M, and a measure of dispersion (such as the sd) for each group. The three values are inserted in a standard formula, and the resultant is then used to locate the desired p in a special probability table. The calculation is simple, the process takes little time, and the results allow straightforward interpretation.

For complex reasons, most researchers further simplify matters by using either 1 in 100 ($p = .01$) or 5 in 100 ($p = .05$) as the probabilities they will accept for saying, "The difference between these groups is due to something in their nature and not to chance." In operational terms, if the value obtained from the statistical calculation leads to a p value (from the table) greater than the .01 or .05 level of probability (whichever the investigator has selected in advance), the report will not claim a significant result from the analysis of the data.

That way of making decisions might seem very arbitrary to you, and in some sense it is just that. A standard like .05 reflects the investigator's subjective sense of how willing she or he is to be wrong. As you probably have guessed, however, there are studies in which it is very dangerous to be wrong, so even the .01 level might not be a sufficiently rigorous hurdle. There are other studies (particularly those that are exploratory in nature) in which it is equally inappropriate to hold such a high standard that one misses (rejects as nonsignificant) a valuable clue to something subtle but important. In such cases, either looser standards are set (a requirement for reaching $p = .10$ might be appropriate) or else setting no standard at all might make the most sense. The p levels simply can be reported, leaving readers to decide on their own interpretation.

As you can see from this information, statistical analysis in quantitative research often catches the researcher between the horns of an elegant dilemma. Is it better (or worse) to say you believe something is there when it really is not? Or is it better (or worse) to say you believe it is not there when it really is?

Researchers are much concerned (properly, we believe) about both the risk management required by that dilemma and the related question of "At what point can statistical significance be regarded as an indication of practical significance?" Statisticians love to argue the fine points involved and have invented an array of tools to use in deciding these important issues. Nevertheless, we suggest that as a novice reader, you adopt our two much simpler and rather old-fashioned standards on all such matters.

First, where there is any question at all about what the statistical indicators really mean, look for reports of replication studies. The final test of an observed difference (or relationship) is whether or not it persists across studies or at least appears and disappears in predictable ways. Second, if the evidence provides good reason to believe that a true difference exists, but you want to know whether that difference has any practical value, ask the person who does the work to which you wish to apply a finding. Whether or not it is worth trying to take advantage of a bit of new knowledge requires a calculation based on experience in the field of application. Where such issues as cost-effectiveness, trade-offs, side effects, political consequences, and ethical considerations are concerned, researchers and statisticians do best when they stick to what they know best—statistical significance, not practical significance.

Another statistical tool that researchers employ to determine the magnitude of difference between means is to calculate the *effect size*. This statistic measures the difference as a function of the overall variability in the scores being compared. In other words, effect size allows us to determine the magnitude of the difference without examining the probability that such a difference could occur. In the simplest case, the effect size is reported in standard deviation units—so an effect size of 0 means that there is no difference between the means, and an effect size of 1 indicates that the means are one standard deviation apart. There are a variety of ways to calculate effect sizes (and different names for each). The important things to remember are that 0 represents no difference and that the larger the absolute value of the effect sizes, the larger the difference.

We should note that there is a lively discussion among scholars with regard to how to interpret differences between means. Some have suggested that *hypothesis testing*—determining the probability of the difference—should not be done, and only effect sizes should be reported. That discussion is well beyond the scope of this book. You will encounter tests of probability and effect sizes as you read reports. In fact, many journals (e.g., those that follow the style guidelines of the *Publication Manual of the American Psychological Association,* 2001) require the reporting of effect size whenever differences are being examined—and you will sometimes see both effect sizes and probability tests in the same report. Paying attention to both will provide you with a bit more information about what happened in the study.

There is one final detail that you will encounter in virtually every report involving statistical estimations of significant differences. Because the value produced by the calculation of statistical significance is almost never exactly at the predetermined level of .05 or .01, the accepted convention is simply to indicate that the actual probability is "better than" (or "beyond") the arbitrary standard. Thus, what you will find in reports is most likely to be $p < .05$, the backward-facing caret indicating that the probability of a chance difference being that large is "less than" 5 in 100.

Another technique for determining whether or not means are significantly different is analysis of variance (ANOVA) and its several permutations: analysis of covariance (ANCOVA) and multivariate analysis of variance (MANOVA). Analysis of variance produces an F value, from which the familiar p can be derived. We will not attempt to explain either the mathematical genesis of F or its correct interpretation (for general purposes, the larger the F value, the less likely the differences are due to chance). What we do want you to remember, however, is that the ANOVA statistic appears in reports for studies that require significance testing of more than two means at the same time.

One or several of the texts we recommend in Chapter 6 (see also the annotated references in Appendix A) will serve to introduce you to ANOVA and the powerful underlying concept of *variance* in groups of numbers. If you want to learn more about ANOVA, we suggest, however, that you not do so by just reading about it. Find several small groups of data (good sources include newspapers with league standings, batting averages, or even stock market reports) and list them in the form of what is called a *frequency distribution table* (most introductory texts will show you how to do that). From that listing, you can calculate your own simple statistics with pencil and paper (a calculator is helpful for roots and squares, but we urge you not to use a statistical program resident in either a computer or a calculator—you can quickly learn how to use those wonderful servants later, after you have acquired a sense of how the numbers behave in the basic ANOVA formula).

Watching how values such as variance, standard deviation, and correlation coefficients emerge from simple arithmetic operations, and how they are altered by changes in the data, provides a feel for how statistics really work that cannot be replicated by any other learning process. Also, no other experience can so thoroughly remove the mystery from statistics while at the same time revealing the wonderful beauty of their structures.

❖ ASSOCIATION STATISTICS AND CORRELATION

If Chapter 6 is still fresh in your memory, you will recall that association was introduced as an independent category of statistics. In its most basic sense, however, association statistics and correlation coefficients can be thought of as a descriptive statistic (in the same category with such constructs as mean and standard deviation). Instead of describing the average or distribution characteristics of a group of numbers, correlation describes the nature and degree of relationship between or among groups of numbers. Our earlier explanation (in Chapter 6) of the outcome of a correlation calculation (called a *coefficient*, and always expressed as a two-place decimal between the whole numbers of −1 and +1) will not be repeated here. There are several important things to add, however, that will help you understand association statistics when they appear in a report.

The most common form of correlation coefficient between two groups is called a *product-moment correlation* and yields a coefficient generally written as *r*. For example, "The correlation ($r = .68$) between height and weight for the individuals in the sample was significant ($p < .01$)." Although a coefficient of that size would be regarded as a strong association between two variables in any study, there are several limitations to remember with regard to both the *r* and the *p* values for a correlation statistic.

The first limitation deals with probability and, in doing so, brings us again to consider the problem of distinguishing between statistical significance and practical importance. The *p* value for a coefficient can be found simply by using a special probability table and locating the number that lies at the intersection of the appropriate *r* column and the row for *N* (*N* here being the total number of paired scores involved in the calculation). The *p* value, thus determined, expresses the probability (how many times out of 100) that a coefficient that large will be different from zero solely as a consequence of chance.

What that means, however, is that the N in the study has a powerful and direct influence over the p value (level of significance) found for any given correlation. If the N is large, it is more likely that a coefficient will be found significant at a predetermined level, such as .05. It is not uncommon for studies with a large number of subjects (e.g., 1,000) to find coefficients as small as $r = .05$ that are significant at and beyond the .01 level. Such findings indicate that something is shared between two groups (some factor that influences scores in the same way in both groups), but not something that is very large. If the study N had been smaller, perhaps 25 subjects, the same coefficient probably could not have reached even the .10 value of statistical significance.

Whether a significant coefficient has practical value for any purpose depends on the nature of the purpose and, as always, on how willing the investigator is to be wrong. In the studies that first revealed the relationship between cholesterol and heart attacks, the correlation coefficients were small ($r = .03$), but, because of the large numbers of subjects used in such epidemiological research, they were statistically significant. Those coefficients served as the clue that led to a revolution in health promotion policy.

On the other hand, if you wished to predict the grade point average of college students on the basis of its correlation with an academic aptitude test (the typical $r = .21$ for such correlations is much larger than that in the cholesterol studies), the coefficient would be useless—even though significant at .01! Your predictions of college success would be better than chance by only the slimmest of margins—certainly a poor basis for awarding scholarships. If you are not sure that you correctly followed the logic in these two examples, stay with us through the next paragraphs, and we think you will.

This discussion comes now to the second and related limitation to remember when contemplating correlation coefficients. People sometimes make the erroneous assumption that coefficients are like percentages—that they indicate the proportionate extent to which two (or more) variables share some factor in common. Thus, it might be believed that an r of .80 means that one set of scores could be predicted with 80% accuracy by knowing the other (correlated) set of scores. For complex reasons, that simply is not true. If you wish to know such a percentage of common connection between two correlated variables, it can be derived very simply. Just square the coefficient and convert the resultant to a percentage; this represents the percentage in common. When this percentage is subtracted from 100%, you obtain the percentage not shared in common.

Some quick calculation will reveal why we speak of this as an important understanding with which to temper your interpretation of coefficients. An $r = .20$ (significant or not) indicates that 96% of whatever is represented in one variable is unrelated to anything in the other variable. Even an $r = .50$ leaves 75% of the scores in one group completely unpredictable on the basis of scores in the other group. The squaring of a coefficient is called r-squared (r^2), and the resulting decimal is a most informative value for the wary reader of research reports. As we just indicated, when you encounter a correlation coefficient, do a quick mental calculation of r-squared and then reflect on the purpose to which you wish to put the results produced by the study.

How important is it to be right, in the decision you make, and how much of a problem is created should you sometimes be wrong? The fact that high cholesterol is found in many people who never have heart attacks is inconsequential. You can be wrong in that prediction without important risk, but the small increase in the number of right predictions is a matter of life and death. In medical decisions of that sort, a correlation coefficient of .03 might be a more-than-sufficient basis for action.

To determine financial support for college students, however, solely on the basis of an academic aptitude test score that leaves 96% (the r of .20 squared and subtracted from 100) of actual academic achievement unaccounted for would be both ineffective and unjust. To be wrong that often would be intolerable, and the small number of right predictions (a number that would be only marginally better than chance) would be nothing more than the equivalent of statistical junk food.

❖ CLOSING COMMENTS

This beginner's guide was intended to identify a small set of commonly employed statistics, describe how they function in the "Analysis and Results" section of a report, and identify some simple rules for their interpretation. As you doubtless now understand, what is here represents only a tiny fraction of what there is to know about statistics. On the other hand, it also should be clear that, at the basic level, statistics can be understood with reasonable clarity by the beginner. With some practice, and the help of an appropriate introductory text, your capacity for reading statistics with a critical eye can grow to an extent you might never have thought possible. So take heart! When necessary, you always can deal with statistics by skipping over them, but it is far more fun, and useful, to understand and appreciate them.

References

Ambert, A. M., Adler, P. A., Adler, P., & Detzner, D. F. (1995). Understanding and evaluating qualitative research. *Journal of Marriage and the Family, 57,* 879-893.

American Psychological Association. (2001). *Publication manual of the American Psychological Association* (5th ed.). Washington, DC: Author.

Anfara, V. A., Jr., Brown, K. M., & Mangione, T. L. (2002). Qualitative analysis on stage: Making the research process more public. *Educational Researcher, 31*(7), 28-38.

Bailey, K. D. (1994) *Methods of social research.* New York: Free Press.

Barber, J. G., & Gilbertson, R. (1996). An experimental study of brief unilateral intervention for the partners of heavy drinkers. *Research on Social Work Practice, 6,* 325-336.

Bogdan, R. C., & Biklen, S. K. (2003). *Qualitative research for education: An introduction to theories and methods* (4th ed.). Boston: Allyn & Bacon.

Borsari, B., & Carey, K. B. (2001). Peer influences on college drinking: A review of the research. *Journal of Substance Abuse, 13,* 391-424.

Brice, G. C., Gorey, K. M., Hall, R. M., & Angelino, S. (1996). The Staywell Program—Maximizing elders' capacity for independent living through health promotion and disease prevention activities: A quasi-experimental evaluation of its efficacy. *Research on Aging, 18,* 202-218.

Campbell, D. T., & Stanley, J. C. (1963). *Experimental and quasi-experimental designs for research.* Chicago: Rand McNally.

Carmines, E. G., & Zeller, R. A. (1979). *Reliability and validity assessment.* Beverly Hills, CA: Sage.

Cole, C. L., & Hribar, A. (1995). Celebrity feminism: Nike style—Post-Fordism, transcendence, and consumer power. *Sociology of Sport Journal, 12,* 347-369.

Cooper, H. (1996). Speaking power to truth: Reflections of an educational researcher after 4 years of school board service. *Educational Researcher, 25*(1), 29-34.

Coward, R. T., Duncan, R. P., & Uttaro, R. (1996). The rural nursing home industry: A national description. *Journal of Applied Gerontology, 15,* 153-171.

Creswell, J. W. (2003). *Research design: Qualitative, quantitative, and mixed method approaches* (2nd ed.). Thousand Oaks, CA: Sage.

Creswell, J. W., & Miller, D.L. (2000). Determining validity in qualitative inquiry. *Theory Into Practice, 39*(3), 124-130.

Denzin, N. K., & Lincoln, Y. S. (Eds.). (2000). *Handbook of qualitative research* (2nd ed.). Thousand Oaks, CA: Sage.

Dodge, L. G. (2003). *Dr. Laurie's introduction to statistical methods.* Los Angeles: Pyrczak.

Dowson, M., & McInerney, D. M. (2001). Psychological parameters of students' social and work avoidance goals: A qualitative investigation. *Journal of Educational Psychology, 93,* 35-42.

Etezadi-Amoli, J., & Farhoomand, A. F. (1996). A structural model of end user computing satisfaction and user performance. *Information and Management, 30*(2), 65-73.

Fleming, V. (Director). (1939). *The Wizard of Oz* [motion picture]. United States: Metro-Goldwyn-Meyer.

Flick, U. (2002). *An introduction to qualitative research* (2nd ed.). Thousand Oaks, CA: Sage.

Francis, L. E. (2000). Conflicting bureaucracies, conflicted work: Dilemmas in case management for homeless people with mental illness. *Journal of Sociology and Social Welfare, 27,* 97-112.

Gall, M. D., Gall, J. P., & Borg, W. R. (2003). *Educational research: An introduction* (7th ed.). Boston: Allyn & Bacon.

Gibaldi, J. (2003). *MLA handbook for writers of research papers* (6th ed.). New York: Modern Language Association.

Glaser, B., & Strauss, A. (1967). *The discovery of grounded theory.* New York: Aldine.

Green, J. C., & Caracelli, V. J. (Eds.). (1997). *Advances in mixed-method evaluation: The challenges and benefits of integrating diverse paradigms.* San Francisco: Jossey-Bass.

Greenwald, A. G., Carnot, C. G., Beach, R., & Young, B. (1987). Increasing voting behavior by asking people if they expect to vote. *Journal of Applied Psychology, 2,* 315-318.

Hedges, L.V. (1998). *Statistical method for meta-analysis.* New York: Academic Press.

Hendrix, K.G. (1998). Student perception of the influence of race on professor credibility. *Journal of Black Studies, 28,* 738-763.

Holcomb, Z. C. (1998). *Fundamentals of descriptive statistics.* Los Angeles: Pyrczak.

Holcomb, Z. C. (2002). *Interpreting basic statistics: A guide and workbook based on excerpts from journal articles* (3rd ed.). Los Angeles: Pyrczak.

Hunter, J. E., & Schmidt, F. L. (1995). *Methods of meta-analysis: Correcting error and bias in research findings.* Thousand Oaks, CA: Sage.

Johnson, J. M., & Pennypacker, H. S. (1993). *Strategies and tactics of behavioral research* (2nd ed.). Hillsdale, NJ: Lawrence Erlbaum.

Johnson, R. B. (1997). Examining the validity structure of qualitative research. *Education, 118,* 282-292.

Kandel, D. B. (1985). On process of peer influences in adolescent drug use: A developmental perspective. *Advances in Alcohol & Substance Use, 4,* 139-163.

Keefe, K., & Berndt, T. J. (1996). Relations of friendship quality to self-esteem in early adolescence. *Journal of Early Adolescence, 16,* 110-129.

Kirk, R. E. (1995). *Experimental design: Procedures for the behavioral sciences* (3rd ed). Pacific Grove, CA: Brooks/Cole.

Krathwohl, D. R. (1998). *Methods of educational and social science research: An integrated approach* (2nd ed.). Boston: Allyn & Bacon.

Krefting, L. (1991). Rigor in qualitative research: The assessment of trustworthiness. *The American Journal of Occupational Therapy, 45,* 214-222.

Lewis, K. G., & Moon, S. (1997). Always single and single-again women: A qualitative study. *Journal of Marital and Family Therapy, 23,* 115-134.

Lipsey, M. W., & Wilson, D. B. (2000). *Practical meta-analysis.* Thousand Oaks, CA: Sage.

Locke, L. F., Spirduso, W. W., & Silverman, S. J. (2000). *Proposals that work: A guide for planning dissertations and grant proposals* (4th ed.). Thousand Oaks, CA: Sage.

Lomand, T. C. (Ed.). (2002). *Social science research: A cross section of journal articles for discussion and evaluation* (3rd ed.). Los Angeles: Pyrczak.

Lyne, L. S. (Ed.). (1999). *A cross section of educational research: Journal articles for discussion and evaluation.* Los Angeles: Pyrczak.

Maguire, K. B., Lange, B., Scherling, M., & Grow, R. (1996). The use of rehearsal and positive reinforcement in the dental treatment of uncooperative patients with mental retardation. *Journal of Developmental and Physical Disabilities, 8,* 167-177.

Maxwell, J. A. (1996). *Qualitative research design: An interactive approach.* Thousand Oaks, CA: Sage.

Merriam, S. B. (1998). *Qualitative research and case study applications in education* (2nd ed.). San Francisco: Jossey-Bass.

Michaelson, H. B. (1990). *How to write and publish engineering papers and reports* (3rd ed.). Phoenix, AZ: Oryx.

Miles, M. B., & Huberman, A. M. (1994). *Qualitative data analysis: An expanded sourcebook* (2nd ed.). Thousand Oaks, CA: Sage.

Milinki, A. K. (Ed.). (1999). *Cases in qualitative research.* Los Angeles: Pyrczak.

Morse, J. M., & Richards, L. (2002). *Read me first for a user's guide to qualitative methods.* Thousand Oaks, CA: Sage.

Nichol, G., Detsky, A. S., Stiell, I. G., O'Rourke, K., Wells, G., & Laupacis, A. (1996). Effectiveness of emergency medical services for victims of out-of-hospital cardiac arrest: A meta-analysis. *Annals of Emergency Medicine, 27,* 700-710.

Papineau, D., & Kiely, M. C. (1996). Participatory evaluation in a community organization: Fostering stakeholder empowerment and utilization. *Evaluation and Program Planning, 19,* 79-93.

Patten, M. L. (Ed.). (2002a). *Educational and psychological research: A cross section of journal articles for analysis and evaluation* (3rd ed.). Los Angeles: Pyrczak.

Patten, M. L. (2002b). *Understanding research methods: An overview of the essentials* (3rd ed.). Los Angeles: Pyrczak.

Patton, M. Q. (2001). *Qualitative research and evaluation methods* (3rd ed.). Thousand Oaks, CA: Sage.

Pedhazur, E. J. (1997). *Multiple regression in behavioral research: Explanation and prediction* (3rd ed.). Fort Worth, TX: Harcourt Brace.

Peteva, R. J. (Ed.). (2003). *A cross section of nursing research: Journal articles for discussion and evaluation* (2nd ed.). Los Angeles: Pyrczak.

Pyrczak, F. (1999). *Statistics with a sense of humor: A humorous workbook and guide to study skills* (2nd ed.). Los Angeles: Pyrczak.

Pyrczak, F. (2001). *Making sense of statistics: A conceptual overview* (2nd ed.). Los Angeles: Pyrczak.

Pyrczak, F. (2002). *Success at statistics* (2nd ed.). Los Angeles: Pyrczak.

Richardson, L. (2000). New writing practices in qualitative research. *Sociology of Sport Journal, 17,* 5-20.

Richardson, V. (Ed.). (2001). *Handbook of research on teaching* (4th ed.). Washington, DC: American Educational Research Association.

Robson, C. (2002). *Real world research: A resource for social scientists and practitioner-researchers* (2nd ed.). Malden, MA: Blackwell.

Rossman, G. B., & Rallis, S. F. (2003). *Learning in the field* (2nd ed.). Thousand Oaks, CA: Sage.

Schwandt, T. A. (2001). *Dictionary of qualitative inquiry* (2nd ed.) Thousand Oaks, CA: Sage.

Shilts, R. (1987). *And the band played on: Politics, people, and the AIDS epidemic.* New York: St. Martin's.

Sidman, M. (1960). *Tactics of scientific research: Evaluating experimental data in psychology.* New York: Basic Books.

Silverman, D. (2000). *Doing qualitative research: A practical handbook.* Thousand Oaks, CA: Sage.

Simon, B. (2001). Public science: Media configuration and closure in the cold fusion controversy. *Public Understanding of Science, 10,* 383-402.

Smith, J. K., Gerber, A. S., & Orlish, A. (2003). Self-prophecy effects and voter turnout: An experimental replication. *Political Psychology, 24,* 593-604.

Stake, R. E. (1995). *The art of case study research.* Thousand Oaks, CA: Sage.

Stevens, J. P. (2002). *Applied multivariate statistics for the social sciences* (4th ed.). Hillsdale, NJ: Lawrence Erlbaum.

Tashakkori, A., & Teddlie, C. (1998). *Mixed methodology.* Thousand Oaks, CA: Sage.

Tashakkori, A., & Teddlie, C. (2003). *Handbook of mixed methods in social and behavioral research*. Thousand Oaks, CA: Sage.

Thomas, J. (1993). *Doing critical ethnography*. Newbury Park, CA: Sage.

Thomas, J. R., & Nelson, J. K. (2001). *Research methods in physical activity* (4th ed.). Champaign, IL: Human Kinetics.

Ungar, M. T. (2000). The myth of peer pressure. *Adolescence, 35,* 167-180.

University of Chicago Press. (2003). *The Chicago manual of style: The essential guide for writers, editors, and publishers* (15th ed.). Chicago: Author.

Vitaro, F., Ladouceur, R., & Bujold, A. (1996). Predictive and concurrent correlates of gambling in early adolescent boys. *Journal of Early Adolescence, 16,* 211-228.

Walker, A. J. (1996). Couples watching television: Gender, power, and the remote control. *Journal of Marriage and the Family, 58,* 813-823.

Wergin, J. F., & Swingen, J. N. (2000). *Departmental assessment: How some campuses are effectively evaluating the collective work of faculty* (Working Paper series # FR0003). Washington, DC: American Association for Higher Education.

Will, G. F. (1990). *Men at work*. New York: Macmillan.

Winer, B. J., Brown, D. R., & Michels, K. M. (1991). *Statistical principles in experimental design* (3rd ed.). New York: McGraw-Hill.